Theoretical Foundations for Digital Libraries

The 5S (Societies, Scenarios, Spaces, Structures, Streams) Approach

Synthesis Lectures on Information Concepts, Retrieval, and Services

Editor
Gary Marchionini, *University of North Carolina, Chapel Hill*

Synthesis Lectures on Information Concepts, Retrieval, and Services is edited by Gary Marchionini of the University of North Carolina. The series will publish 50- to 100-page publications on topics pertaining to information science and applications of technology to information discovery, production, distribution, and management. The scope will largely follow the purview of premier information and computer science conferences, such as ASIST, ACM SIGIR, ACM/IEEE JCDL, and ACM CIKM. Potential topics include, but are not limited to: data models, indexing theory and algorithms, classification, information architecture, information economics, privacy and identity, scholarly communication, bibliometrics and webometrics, personal information management, human information behavior, digital libraries, archives and preservation, cultural informatics, information retrieval evaluation, data fusion, relevance feedback, recommendation systems, question answering, natural language processing for retrieval, text summarization, multimedia retrieval, multilingual retrieval, and exploratory search.

Theoretical Foundations for Digital Libraries: The 5S (Societies, Scenarios, Spaces, Structures, Streams) Approach
Edward A. Fox, Marcos André Gonçalves, and Rao Shen
2012

The Future of Personal Information Management, Part I: Our Information, Always and Forever
William Jones
2012

Search User Interface Design
Max L. Wilson
2011

Information Retrieval Evaluation
Donna Harman
2011

Knowledge Management (KM) Processes in Organizations: Theoretical Foundations and Practice
Claire R. McInerney and Michael E. D. Koenig
2011

Search-Based Applications: At the Confluence of Search and Database Technologies
Gregory Grefenstette and Laura Wilber
2010

Information Concepts: From Books to Cyberspace Identities
Gary Marchionini
2010

Estimating the Query Difficulty for Information Retrieval
David Carmel and Elad Yom-Tov
2010

iRODS Primer: Integrated Rule-Oriented Data System
Arcot Rajasekar, Reagan Moore, Chien-Yi Hou, Christopher A. Lee, Richard Marciano, Antoine de Torcy, Michael Wan, Wayne Schroeder, Sheau-Yen Chen, Lucas Gilbert, Paul Tooby, and Bing Zhu
2010

Collaborative Web Search: Who, What, Where, When, and Why
Meredith Ringel Morris and Jaime Teevan
2009

Multimedia Information Retrieval
Stefan Rüger
2009

Online Multiplayer Games
William Sims Bainbridge
2009

Information Architecture: The Design and Integration of Information Spaces
Wei Ding and Xia Lin
2009

Reading and Writing the Electronic Book
Catherine C. Marshall
2009

Hypermedia Genes: An Evolutionary Perspective on Concepts, Models, and Architectures
Nuno M. Guimarães and Luís M. Carrico
2009

Understanding User-Web Interactions via Web Analytics
Bernard J. (Jim) Jansen
2009

XML Retrieval
Mounia Lalmas
2009

Faceted Search
Daniel Tunkelang
2009

Introduction to Webometrics: Quantitative Web Research for the Social Sciences
Michael Thelwall
2009

Exploratory Search: Beyond the Query-Response Paradigm
Ryen W. White and Resa A. Roth
2009

New Concepts in Digital Reference
R. David Lankes
2009

Automated Metadata in Multimedia Information Systems: Creation, Refinement, Use in Surrogates, and Evaluation
Michael G. Christel
2009

Theoretical Foundations for Digital Libraries: The 5S (Societies, Scenarios, Spaces, Structures, Streams) Approach

Edward A. Fox, Marcos André Gonçalves, and Rao Shen

ISBN: 978-3-031-01151-1   paperback
ISBN: 978-3-031-02279-1   ebook

DOI 10.1007/978-3-031-02279-1

A Publication in the Springer series
SYNTHESIS LECTURES ON INFORMATION CONCEPTS, RETRIEVAL, AND SERVICES

Lecture #22
Series Editor: Gary Marchionini, *University of North Carolina, Chapel Hill*
Series ISSN
Synthesis Lectures on Information Concepts, Retrieval, and Services
Print 1947-945X   Electronic 1947-9468

Theoretical Foundations for Digital Libraries

The 5S (Societies, Scenarios, Spaces, Structures, Streams) Approach

Edward A. Fox
Virginia Tech

Marcos André Gonçalves
Universidade Federal de Minas Gerais, Brazil

Rao Shen
Yahoo!

SYNTHESIS LECTURES ON INFORMATION CONCEPTS, RETRIEVAL, AND SERVICES #22

ABSTRACT

In 1991, a group of researchers chose the term *digital libraries* to describe an emerging field of research, development, and practice. Since then, Virginia Tech has had funded research in this area, largely through its Digital Library Research Laboratory. This book is the first in a four book series that reports our key findings and current research investigations.

Underlying this book series are six completed dissertations (Gonçalves, Kozievitch, Leidig, Murthy, Shen, Torres), eight dissertations underway, and many masters theses. These reflect our experience with a long string of prototype or production systems developed in the lab, such as CITIDEL, CODER, CTRnet, Ensemble, ETANA, ETD-db, MARIAN, and Open Digital Libraries. There are hundreds of related publications, presentations, tutorials, and reports. We have built upon that work so this book, and the others in the series, will address digital library related needs in many computer science, information science, and library science (e.g., LIS) courses, as well as the requirements of researchers, developers, and practitioners.

Much of the early work in the digital library field struck a balance between addressing real-world needs, integrating methods from related areas, and advancing an ever-expanding research agenda. Our work has fit in with these trends, but simultaneously has been driven by a desire to provide a firm conceptual and formal basis for the field. Our aim has been to move from engineering to science. We claim that our *5S* (Societies, Scenarios, Spaces, Structures, Streams) framework, discussed in publications dating back to at least 1998, provides a suitable basis. This book introduces 5S, and the key theoretical and formal aspects of the 5S framework.

While the 5S framework may be used to describe many types of information systems, and is likely to have even broader utility and appeal, we focus here on digital libraries. Our view of digital libraries is broad, so further generalization should be straightforward.

We have connected with related fields, including hypertext/hypermedia, information storage and retrieval, knowledge management, machine learning, multimedia, personal information management, and Web 2.0. Applications have included managing not only publications, but also archaeological information, educational resources, fish images, scientific datasets, and scientific experiments/simulations.

Supporting web site with appendices, guidelines and resources for teaching DL, and other resources, is here:

`https://sites.google.com/a/morganclaypool.com/dlibrary/`

KEYWORDS

5S framework, annotation, classification, complex objects, content based image retrieval (CBIR), digital libraries (DLs), digital objects, documents, e-science, education, electronic theses and dissertations (ETDs), evaluation, exploration, formalization, geospatial information, integration, LIS curriculum, metadata, ontologies, personalization, security, simulation, social networks

*This book is dedicated to all those
who have worked in, or collaborated with,
Virginia Tech's Digital Library Research Laboratory.*

Contents

Preface xiii

Acknowledgments xix

Figure Credits xxi

1 Introduction 1

   1.1   Context 1

   1.2   Background 3

        1.2.1 Definitions 3

        1.2.2 Perspectives 4

   1.3   Motivation 13

   1.4   Digital Library Curriculum 18

   1.5   High Level Constructs 20

   1.6   Digital Library Systems 22

   1.7   5S Intuition 23

        1.7.1 Streams 24

        1.7.2 Structures 25

        1.7.3 Spaces 27

        1.7.4 Scenarios 29

        1.7.5 Societies 32

   1.8   Digital Library Taxonomy 34

   1.9   Summary 40

   1.10 Exercises and Projects 41

2 Exploration 43

   2.1   Introduction 43

   2.2   Related Work 45

   2.3   Case Study: Exploring Services in ETANA-DL 46

        2.3.1 Multi-Dimensional Browsing 47

        2.3.2 Browsing and Searching Integration 48

        2.3.3 Browsing, Searching, and Visualization Integration 49

      2.3.4   ETANA-DL Exploring Services Formative Evaluation 54

2.4   Summary 57

2.5   Exercises and Projects 57

A   **Mathematical Preliminaries** **59**

B   **Minimal Digital Library** **63**

B.1   5S Formalization 63

B.2   Formalization of Minimal Digital Library 66

B.3   Formal Definitions for Digital Library 72

C   **Archaeological Digital Libraries** **77**

C.1   Background on the 5S Framework 77

C.2   Notation and Definitions 78

C.3   Architecture of an Integrated DL 84

D   **5S Results: Lemmas, Proofs, and 5SSuite** **87**

D.1   Exploring Service Formalization 87

D.2   Proofs 91

D.3   Integration Toolkit: 5SSuite 100

E   **Glossary** **103**

Bibliography **125**

Authors' Biographies **149**

Index **153**

Preface

At a workshop connected with ACM SIGIR 1991 in Chicago, Michael Lesk, Michael McGill, and I began to discuss how information retrieval could lead to broader practical impact. We led an effort to launch the field of digital libraries, that rapidly connected with parallel interests and activities of many other researchers. This also resonated with leaders at all levels, to help advance education, preserve and share cultural heritage, and move society forward into a new approach to creating, sharing, disseminating, discovering, and (re)using knowledge.

Now, decades later, the digital library field today is manifest in many ways. There is a LinkedIn group of over 5300, with many joining daily. Almost all publishers and scholarly societies now have their own digital library, or are part of one with suitable partners. Many nations, or national consortia like the European Union, or agencies thereof, run integrated digital libraries. Most universities, and in some cases multiple parts of those organizations, have an institutional repository. Content Management Systems are widely used in education, and in a variety of other contexts; in addition there are e-portfolio systems, e-print systems, and a variety of personal information management systems.

Thinking expansively, one might connect popular systems, used by billions of people, with the field of digital libraries. Consider, for example, offerings/services by companies such as Facebook, Flickr, Google, Microsoft, and Yahoo! There also are many specialized systems, like Drupal, DSpace, E-prints, Fedora Commons, Greenstone, and VITAL.

Because of the importance of digital libraries, we integrated, organized, and condensed our related findings and publications into a single volume version of this book series, ultimately over 600 pages in length, that was successfully used in a semester long class in 2011, as well as field tested at different universities. To make it easier for others to address their need for a digital library textbook, we have re-organized the original book into four parts, to cover: introduction and theoretical foundations, key issues, technologies/extensions, and applications. We are confident that this book, and the others in the series, will address digital library related needs in many computer science, information science, and library science (e.g., LIS) courses, as well as the requirements of researchers, developers, and practitioners.

The main reason is that our *5S* (Societies, Scenarios, Spaces, Structures, Streams) framework has broad descriptive power. This is proved in part by the recent expansion of interest related to each of the five Ss, e.g., Social networks, Scenario-based design, geoSpatial databases, Structure-based approaches (e.g., databases, metadata, ontologies, XML), and data Stream management systems.

This book, the essential opening to the four book series, has three main parts. Chapter 1 is the key to 5S, providing a theoretical foundation for the field of digital libraries in a gentle, intuitive, and easy-to-apply manner. Chapter 2 explains how 5S can be applied to digital libraries, in two ways.

First, it covers the most important services of digital libraries: browsing, searching, discovery, and visualization. Second, it demonstrates how 5S helps with the design, implementation, and evaluation of an integrated digital library (ETANA-DL, for archaeology). The third part of this book, made up by five appendices, demonstrates how 5S enables a formal treatment of digital libraries.

Appendix A gives a small set of definitions that cover the mathematical preliminaries underlying our work. Appendix B builds on that set to define each of the five Ss, and then uses them to define what we consider a minimal digital library. Thus, we allow people asking "Is X a digital library?" to answer that question definitively. Appendix C moves from a minimalist perspective to show how 5S can be used in a real, interesting, and complex application domain: archaeology. Appendix D builds upon all the definitions in Appendices A-C, to describe some key results of using 5S. This includes lemmas, proofs, and 5SSuite (software based on 5S). Finally, Appendix E, the Glossary, explains key terminology. Concluding the work is an extensive Bibliography, and a helpful Index. Supplementing all this, and providing updated versions of the Glossary and other Appendices, as well as lecture slides, videos, and other aids for teachers and learners, is an online Web site managed by the publisher[1].

In the following three books of this series are further elaborations of the 5S framework, as well as a comprehensive overview of related work on digital libraries. Book 2 discusses key issues in the digital library field: evaluation and integration. It covers the Information Life Cycle, metrics, and software to help evaluate digital libraries. It uses both archaeology, and electronic theses and dissertations, to provide additional context, since addressing quality in highly distributed digital libraries is particularly challenging.

Book 3 describes six case studies, of extensions beyond a minimal digital library. Its chapters cover: Complex Objects, Subdocuments, Ontologies, Classification, Text Extraction, and Security. *Regarding Complex Objects:* While many digital libraries focus on digital objects and/or metadata objects, with support for complex objects, they could easily be extended to handle aggregation and packaging. Fingerprint matching provides a useful context, since there are complex inter-relationships among crime scenes, latent fingerprints, individuals, hands, fingers, fingerprints, and images. *Regarding Subdocuments:* This builds upon work on superimposed information, closely related to hypertext, hypermedia, and annotation. Case studies cover fish images and Flickr. *Regarding Ontologies:* We address this key area of knowledge management, also integral to the Semantic Web. As a context, we consider our Crisis, Tragedy, and Recovery Network (CTRnet). That is quite broad, and involves interesting ontology development problems. *Regarding Classification:* We cover this core area of information retrieval and machine learning, as well as Library and Information Science (LIS). The context is electronic theses and dissertations (ETDs), since many of these works have no categories that can be found in their catalog or metadata records, and since none are categorized at the level of chapters. *Regarding Text Extraction:* Our coverage also is in the context of ETDs, where the high level structure should be identified, and where the valuable and voluminous sets of references can be isolated and shifted to canonical representations. *Regarding Security:* While many digital libraries

---

[1]https://sites.google.com/a/morganclaypool.com/dlibrary/

support open access, it has been clear since the early 1990s that industrial acceptance of digital library systems and technologies depends on their being trusted, requiring an integrated approach to security.

Book 4 completes the series, focusing on digital library applications, from a 5S perspective. Its chapters cover how to handle: Images, Education, Social Networks, e-Science (including bioinformatics and simulations), and Geospatial Information. *Regarding Images:* We move into the multimedia field, focusing on Content-based Image Retrieval (CBIR) – making use, for context, of the previously discussed work on fish images and CTRnet. *Regarding Education:* We describe systems for collecting, sharing, and providing access to educational resources, namely the AlgoViz and Ensemble systems. This is important since there has been considerable investment in digital libraries to help in education, all based on the fact that devising high quality educational resources is expensive, making sharing and reuse highly beneficial. *Regarding Social Networks:* We address very popular current issues, on the Societies side, namely Social Networks and Personalization. *Regarding e-Science:* There has only been a limited adaptation and extension of digital libraries to this important domain. Simulation helps many disciplines to test models and predictions on computers, addressing questions not feasible through other approaches to experimentation. More broadly, in keeping with progress toward e-Science, where data sets and shared information support much broader theories and investigations, we cover (using the SimDL and CINET projects as context) storing and archiving, as well as access and visualization, dealing not only with metadata, but also with specifications of experiments, experimental results, and derivative versions: summaries, findings, reports, and publications. *Regarding Geospatial Information:* Many GIS-related technologies are now readily available in cell phones, cameras, and GPS systems. Our coverage (that uses the CTRnet project as context) connects that with metadata, images, and maps.

How can computer scientists connect with all this? Though some of the early curricular guidelines advocated coverage of information, and current guidelines refer to the area of Information Management, generally courses in this area have focused instead either on data or knowledge. Fortunately, Virginia Tech has had graduate courses on information retrieval since the early 1970s and a senior course on "Multimedia, Hypertext, and Information Access" since the early 1990s. Now, there are offerings at many universities on multimedia, or with titles including keywords like "Web" or "search." Perhaps parts of this book series will provide a way for computing programs to address all areas of Information Management, building on a firm, formal, integrated approach. Further, computing professionals should feel comfortable with particular Ss, especially Structures (as in data structures) and Spaces (as in vector spaces), and to lesser extents Streams (related to multimedia) and Scenarios (related to human-computer interaction). Today, especially, there is growing interest in Societies (as in social networks).

How can information scientists connect with all this? Clearly, they are at home with "information" as a key construct. Streams (e.g., sequences of characters, or bitstreams) provide a first basis for all types of information. Coupled with Structures, they lead to all types of structured streams, as in documents and multimedia. Spaces may be less clear, but GIS systems are becoming ubiquitous, connecting with GPS, cell phone, Twitter, and other technologies. Scenarios, especially in the form of Services, are at the heart of most information systems. Societies, including users, groups, organizations, and a wide variety of social networks, are central, especially with human-centered design. Thus, information science can easily connect with 5S, and digital libraries are among the most important types of information systems. Accordingly, this book series may be fit nicely into capstone courses in information science or information systems. Further, our handling of "information" goes well beyond the narrow view associated with electrical engineering or even computer science; we connect content representations with context and application, across a range of human endeavors, and with semantics, pragmatics, and knowledge.

How can library scientists connect with all this? One might argue that many of the librarians of the future must be trained as digital librarians. Thus, this work should fit nicely into library science programs. While it could fit into theory or capstone courses, it also might serve well in introductory courses, if the more formal parts are skipped. Alternatively, this first book might work well early in a library school program, the second book could fit midway in the program, and the last two books might be covered in specialized courses that connect with technologies or applications. Further, those studying archival science might find the entire series to be of interest, though some topics like preservation are not covered in detail.

How can researchers connect with all this? We hope that those interested in formal approaches will help us expand the coverage of concepts reported herein. A wonderful goal would be to have an elegant formal basis, and useful framework, for all types of information systems. We also hope that the theses and dissertations related to this volume, all online (thanks to Virginia Tech's ETD initiative), will provide an even more in-depth coverage of the key topics covered herein. We hope you can build on this foundation to aid in your own research, as you advance the field further.

How can developers connect with all this? We hope that concepts, ideas, methods, techniques, systems, and approaches described herein will guide you to develop, implement, and deploy even better digital libraries. There should be less time "reinventing the wheel." Perhaps this will stimulate the emergence of a vibrant software and services industry as more and more digital libraries emerge. Further, if there is agreement on key concepts, then there should be improvements in: interoperability, integration, and understanding. Accordingly, we hope you can leverage this work to advance practices as well as provide better systems and services.

Even if you, the reader, do not fit clearly into the groups discussed above, we hope you nevertheless will find this book series interesting. Given the rich content, we trust that those interested in digital libraries, or in related systems, will find this book to be intellectually satisfying, illuminating, and helpful. It provides a solid foundation for the next three books in the series. We hope the full series will help move digital libraries forward into a science as well as a practice. We hope too that our four book series will broadly address the needs of the next generation of digital librarians. Please share with us and others what ways you found this work to be useful and helpful!

Edward A. Fox
Lead Author
Blacksburg, Virginia, July 2012

Acknowledgments

As lead author, my belief is that our greatest thanks go to our families. Accordingly, I thank my wife, Carol, and our sons, Jeffrey, Gregory, Michael, and Paul, along with their families, as well as my father and many other relatives. Similarly, on behalf of the co-authors, I thank all of their families.

Since this book is the first in a series of four books, and draws some definitions and other elements from content that will appear in the following three books, it is important to acknowledge the contributions of all of the other co-authors from the full series: Monika Akbar, Pranav Angara, Yinlin Chen, Lois M. Delcambre, Noha Elsherbiny, Eric Fouh, Nádia P. Kozievitch, Spencer Lee, Jonathan Leidig, Lin Tzy Li, Mohamed Magdy Gharib Farag, Uma Murthy, Sung Hee Park, Venkat Srinivasan, Ricardo da Silva Torres, and Seungwon Yang. Special thanks go to Uma Murthy for helping with the bibliography and to Monika Akbar, Pranav Angara, and Shashwat Dave for assistance with technical aspects of book production. Susan Marion helped prepare the Index, and Shashwat Dave assisted with the Glossary.

Teachers and mentors deserve a special note of thanks. My interest in research was stimulated and guided by J.C.R. Licklider, my undergraduate advisor, author of *Libraries of the Future*[2], who, when at ARPA, funded the start of the Internet. Michael Kessler, who introduced the concept of bibliographic coupling, was my BS thesis advisor; he also directed MIT's Project TIP (technical information project). Gerard Salton was my graduate advisor (1978–1983); he is sometimes called the "Father of Information Retrieval."

Likewise, we thank our many students, friends, collaborators, co-authors, and colleagues. In particular, we thank students who have collaborated in these matters, including: Pavel Calado, Yuxin Chen, Kiran Chitturi, Fernando Das Neves, Shahrooz Feizabadi, Robert France, Nithiwat Kampanya, Rohit Kelapure, S.H. Kim, Neill Kipp, Aaron Krowne, Sunshin Lee, Bing Liu, Ming Luo, Paul Mather, Unni. Ravindranathan, W. Ryan Richardson, Ohm Sornil, Hussein Suleman, Wensi Xi, Baoping Zhang, and Qinwei Zhu.

Further, we thank faculty and staff, at a variety of universities and other institutions, who have collaborated, including: Paul Bogen II, Lillian Cassel, Vinod Chachra, Hsinchun Chen, Debra Dudley, Roger Ehrich, Joanne Eustis, Weiguo Fan, James Flanagan, James French, Richard Furuta, Dan Garcia, C. Lee Giles, Martin Halbert, Eberhard Hilf, Gregory Hislop, John Impagliazzo, Filip Jagodzinski, Douglas Knight, Deborah Knox, Alberto Laender, Carl Lagoze, Gail McMillan, Claudia Medeiros, Manuel Perez Quinones, Naren Ramakrishnan, Frank Shipman, and Layne Watson.

---

[2]In this 1965 work, Licklider called for an integrative theory to support future automated libraries, one of the inspirations for this book.

Clearly, however, with regard to this volume, my special thanks go to my co-authors. Each has played a key role in the unfolding of the theory, practice, systems, and usability of what is described herein. Regarding 5S, Marcos André Gonçalves helped launch our formal framework[3], and has continued to exercise intellectual leadership in this regard. Rao Shen is largely responsible for Chapter 2 and Appendices C and D.1, and has worked hard to finalize this book[4].

At Virginia Tech, there are many in the Department of Computer Science and in Information Systems that have assisted, providing very nice facilities and a creative and supportive environment. The College of Engineering, and before that, of Arts and Sciences, provided an administrative home and intellectual context.

In addition, we acknowledge the support of the many sponsors of the research described in this volume. Our fingerprint work was supported by Award No. 2009-DN-BX-K229 from the National Institute of Justice, Office of Justice Programs, U.S. Department of Justice. The opinions, findings, and conclusions or recommendations expressed in this publication are those of the authors and do not necessarily reflect those of the Department of Justice.

Some of this material is based upon work supported by the National Science Foundation (NSF) under Grant Nos. CCF-0722259, DUE-9752190, DUE-9752408, DUE-0121679, DUE-0121741, DUE-0136690, DUE-0333531, DUE-0333601, DUE-0435059, DUE-0532825, DUE-0840719, IIS-9905026, IIS-9986089, IIS-0002935, IIS-0080748, IIS-0086227, IIS-0090153, IIS-0122201, IIS-0307867, IIS-0325579, IIS-0535057, IIS-0736055, IIS-0910183, IIS-0916733, ITR-0325579, OCI-0904844, OCI-1032677, and SES-0729441. Any opinions, findings, and conclusions or recommendations expressed in this material are those of the authors and do not necessarily reflect the views of the National Science Foundation.

This work has been partially supported by NIH MIDAS project 2U01GM070694-7, DTRA CNIMS Grant HDTRA1-07-C-0113, and R&D Grant HDTRA1-0901-0017.

We thank corporate and institutional sponsors, including Adobe, AOL, CNI, Google, IBM, Microsoft, NASA, NCR, OCLC, SOLINET, SUN, SURA, UNESCO, U.S. Dept. Ed. (FIPSE), and VTLS. A variety of institutions have supported tutorials or courses, including AUGM, CE-TREDE, CLEI, IFLA-LAC, and UFC.

Visitors and collaborators from Brazil, including from FUA, UFMG, and UNICAMP, have been supported by CAPES (4479-09-2), FAPESP, and CNPq. Our collaboration in Mexico had support from CONACyT, while that in Germany was supported by DFG. Students in our VT-MENA program in Egypt have been supported through that program.

Edward A. Fox, Marcos André Gonçalves, and Rao Shen
July 2012

---

[3]Various sections of this work are based on the Virginia Tech dissertation of Marcos Gonçalves [105], "Streams, Structures, Spaces, Scenarios, and Societies (5S): A Formal Digital Library Framework and Its Applications," © 2004. Used with permission.

[4]Various figures and sections of this work are based on the Virginia Tech dissertation of Rao Shen [212], "Applying the 5S Framework to Integrating Digital Libraries," © 2006. Used with permission.

Figure Credits

Figures 1.8, 1.29, 1.30   from Gonçalves, et al.: Streams, structures, spaces, scenarios, societies (5S): A formal model for digital libraries. *ACM Transactions on Information Systems*, 22(2):270-312, 2004. Copyright ©2004, Association for Computing Machinery, Inc. Reprinted by permission. `http://eprints.cs.vt.edu/archive/00000653/`

Figures 2.1, 2.2, 2.3, 2.4, 2.5, 2.6, 2.7, 2.8, 2.9, 2.10   based on Shen, et al.: Exploring digital libraries: integrating browsing, searching, and visualization. In *JCDL '06: Proceedings of the 6th ACM/IEEE-CS joint conference on Digital libraries*, pages 1-10, 2006. Copyright ©2006, Association for Computing Machinery, Inc. Reprinted by permission.

And based on Shen, *Applying the 5S Framework to Integrating Digital Libraries*. Ph.D. dissertation, Virginia Tech CS Department, Blacksburg, Virginia, 2006. `http://scholar.lib.vt.edu/theses/available/etd-04212006-135018/`. Used with permission.

Figures B.1, B.4, B.5, B.6   from Gonçalves, et al.: Streams, structures, spaces, scenarios, societies (5S): A formal model for digital libraries. *ACM Transactions on Information Systems*, 22(2):270-312, 2004. Copyright ©2004, Association for Computing Machinery, Inc. Reprinted by permission. `http://eprints.cs.vt.edu/archive/00000653/`

Figures D.5, D.7, D.8, D.13, D.14, D.15   from Shen, et al.: Exploring digital libraries: integrating browsing, searching, and visualization. In *JCDL '06: Proceedings of the 6th ACM/IEEE-CS joint conference on Digital libraries*, pages 1-10, 2006. Copyright ©2006, Association for Computing Machinery, Inc. Reprinted by permission.

And from Shen, *Applying the 5S Framework to Integrating Digital Libraries*. Ph.D. dissertation, Virginia Tech CS Department, Blacksburg, Virginia, 2006. `http://scholar.lib.vt.edu/theses/available/etd-04212006-135018/`. Used with permission.

Figure D.17   from Goncalves, *Streams, Structures, Spaces, Scenarios, and Societies (5S): A Formal Digital Library Framework and Its Applications*. Ph.D. dissertation, Virginia Tech, Blacksburg, VA, 2004. `http://scholar.lib.vt.edu/theses/available/etd-12052004-135923/`. Used with permission.

CHAPTER 1

Introduction

Abstract: Digital libraries (DLs) are researched, developed, implemented, deployed, and used by millions of people in a wide variety of domains. They include advanced information systems that address the full information life cycle, facilitating asynchronous communication, across time and space, and enabling new methods for scholarly communication in our flat world. Since there is strong motivation to build DLs, they are studied by many of those doing advanced work in computer, information, or library science. Though there are a variety of definitions related to DLs, and varied perspectives to consider, few have adopted a formal approach. The 5S framework provides a theoretical foundation to define key constructs, building upon: Societies, Scenarios, Spaces, Structures, and Streams. Using these 5Ss, definitions of important concepts are provided, leading ultimately to a definition of a minimal digital library. Further, 5S guides us to develop a taxonomy for the DL field.

1.1　CONTEXT

Information is a fundamental human need. This need is universal for individuals, leading to current interest in personal information management (PIM) [135], and is manifest for groups of people as well. Accordingly, institutions have arisen to help us with this need, including libraries, archives, museums, and a variety of information centers, such as for corporations or governments. Developing and operating these institutions involves information management, which requires planning, acquisition, and a variety of services. Special terms have developed for those who make use of these institutions, including: client, customer, patron, and user.

Today, (computerized) information systems help us meet that need. Digital libraries are perhaps the most advanced, integrated, and comprehensive information systems, supporting work with information, across its entire life cycle [26].

Fig. 1.1 makes clear that each phase of the information life cycle flows into the next. Thus, decisions made by an author, in a particular social context, effect how easy it will be to index, store, distribute, access, preserve, and reuse a document and its content. One labeling of parts of the cycle emphasizes level of activity, as shown on the outside of the circle. Key high level operations corresponding to that labeling include creation, searching, and utilization. On the other hand, focusing on more detailed operations, we find in the inside of the circle: authoring, organizing, retrieving, filtering, and modifying. Thus, digital libraries [8, 22, 28, 29, 61, 74, 150, 154, 253] build broadly upon advances in electronic publishing, information retrieval, networking, the World Wide Web, text mining, and other aspects of information management.

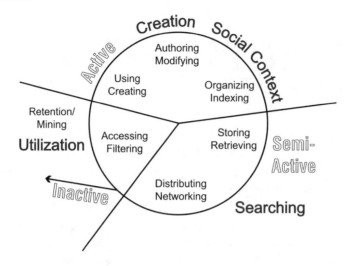

Figure 1.1: Information Life Cycle. Adapted from [26].

Three broad disciplines especially connect with digital libraries. From the first part of the name, there is a clear connection with computing, including computer science. Also from the name, there is a clear connection with libraries, including library science. Further, as is discussed above, information systems, information technology, and information science clearly connect.

These disciplines are closely related. Thus, as can be seen in Table 1.1, in the ACM/IEEE-CS Computing Curriculum from 2001 [42], fourteen sub-areas were specified for the area of information management. The last of those, digital libraries, may be thought of as a capstone for the set of sub-areas.

Table 1.1: CC2001 Information Management Areas (* Core components).	
IM1. Information models and systems*	IM8. Distributed DBs
IM2. Database systems*	IM9. Physical DB design
IM3. Data modeling*	IM10. Data mining
IM4. Relational DBs	IM11. Information storage and retrieval
IM5. Database query languages	IM12. Hypertext and hypermedia
IM6. Relational DB design	IM13. Multimedia information and systems
IM7. Transaction processing	IM14. Digital libraries

Table 1.1 can be thought of as one roadmap into this book and the following three in this series. Information models and data modeling are at the heart of our emphasis on the 5S framework (introduced later in this chapter). Databases are a key aspect of digital libraries, supporting abstractions like metadata record, catalog, and repository. Transactions undergird all of the digital

library services, in some cases related to developing secure digital libraries (see book 3 in this series). Security also can be considered in the context of cyberinfrastructure, which is simplified when open access is the goal. Distributed concerns are key to work on integration (see book 2). Data mining closely relates to text extraction work (see book 3). Information retrieval is discussed in a variety of contexts throughout the book series, but is covered especially in the next chapter. Hypertext and hypermedia also are discussed throughout, in part through their undergirding of the Web. Multimedia is considered particularly with regard to complex objects and image collections (see books 3 and 4). Digital libraries also connect with artificial intelligence, especially knowledge management, such as involving ontologies (see book 3). Linguistics, in particular computational linguistics, is at the heart of text extraction (see book 3), but also underlies indexing, which supports information retrieval, discussed above.

Digital libraries emerged at the same time as the global networking infrastructure was proliferating rapidly, including the spread of the commercial Internet and the rise of the World Wide Web. Hence, many standards that are followed in the digital library field come from Internet organizations, including the World Wide Web Consortium (W3C). Our coverage of e-science (see book 4) is closely connected with such infrastructure, and describes extending the cyberinfrastructure for science.

Thus, there is a broad context for the field of digital libraries (DLs), providing support for DL emergence and development. The next section provides additional background, from a variety of perspectives, including related definitions.

1.2 BACKGROUND

In the early days of the digital library field, many were concerned with names and definitions. For example, terms like *electronic library* and *virtual library* were considered, but ultimately, around 1991, *digital library* (DL) became the widely accepted term.

1.2.1 DEFINITIONS

Not as much agreement was achieved with definitions of *digital library*, however. Some of the competing visions cover the following alternative perspectives [27]:

- content, collections, and communities

- institutions or services

- databases

From a 1996 workshop, two complementary views emerged [25], arguing that digital libraries are:

1. "a set of electronic resources and associated technical capabilities for creating, searching and using information. In this sense they are an extension and enhancement of information storage and retrieval systems that manipulate digital data in any medium (text, images, sounds;

static or dynamic images) and exist in distributed networks. The content of digital libraries includes data, metadata that describe various aspects of the data (e.g., representation, creator, owner, reproduction rights) and metadata that consist of links or relationships to other data or metadata, whether internal or external to the digital library."

2. "constructed, collected and organized, by (and for) a community of users, and their functional capabilities support the information needs and uses of that community. They are a component of communities in which individuals and groups interact with each other, using data, information and knowledge resources and systems. In this sense they are an extension, enhancement and integration of a variety of information institutions as physical places where resources are selected, collected, organized, preserved and accessed in support of a user community. These information institutions include, among others, libraries, museums, archives and schools, but digital libraries also extend and serve other community settings, including classrooms, offices, laboratories, homes and public spaces."

Representative additional definitions include:

• "Digital libraries are organizations that provide the resources, including the specialized staff, to select, structure, offer intellectual access to, interpret, distribute, preserve the integrity of, and ensure the persistence over time of collections of digital works so that they are readily and economically available for use by a defined community or set of communities." [238]

• "A digital library is an organized and focused collection of digital objects, including text, images, video, and audio, along with methods of access and retrieval, and for selection, creation, organization, maintenance, and sharing of the collection." [250]

• "An organization, which might be virtual, that comprehensively collects, manages and preserves for the long term rich digital content, and offers to its user communities specialized functionality on that content, of measurable quality and according to codified policies." [35]

1.2.2   PERSPECTIVES

Though later in this chapter we give a very precise definition of *digital library*, perhaps the easiest characterization to remember is what is shown in Fig. 1.2.

Clearly, a comprehensive view of DLs must include people and content, as well as applications of technology. The labels on the sides of the triangle coincide nicely with phases of the information life cycle, discussed above. Fig. 1.3 flattens the circle or triangle, putting the DL system in the middle, connecting users and content. From such a systems perspective, many concerns arise, such as how the DL can be built. While the DL may be thought of as a monolithic single entity—convenient regarding naming, purchasing, and operation—in many cases, the DL software is composed of (distributed) components or modules that work together.

The variety of perspectives on digital libraries is a natural consequence of their many aspects or *facets*. Each of those covers a range of possibilities, reflecting the different uses that people desire.

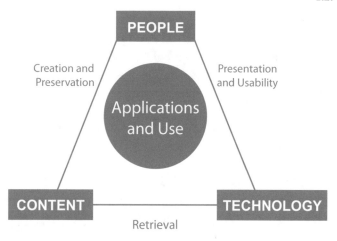

Figure 1.2: Chatham Workshop triangle. Adapted from [147].

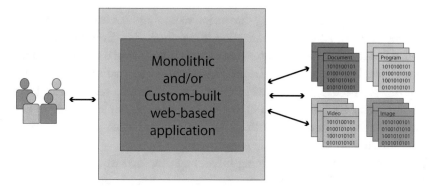

Figure 1.3: Digital library (in center) construction approaches.

For example, one dimension concerns Access vs. Preservation. This is so important as to be institutionalized; traditionally, libraries emphasize access while archives emphasize preservation[1]. Focusing on the issue of access, another controversy concerns Free vs. High Quality. While in actuality these reflect two different dimensions, namely cost and quality, many assume that what is free will have lower quality than what has a moderate to high cost. Fortunately, this assumption is not necessarily valid.

From a scientific perspective, it is more efficient to choose a set of independent dimensions to describe the range of options and choices related to DLs. The chapter on evaluation in book 2 illustrates this in detail, focusing on the quality dimension.

---

[1]This book series does not focus specifically on archivists, archives, or archival practices. There is little emphasis on preservation, or on selection of what should be added to an archive or culled from a collection. Nevertheless, much of the discussion (e.g., of content, services, technologies, and systems) should be of interest to archivists.

Another important dimension relates to organization. One dichotomy often posed about DLs is Managed vs. Comprehensive. Thus, a library is managed while the WWW is unmanaged (but closer to being comprehensive). Regarding degree of organization, in this book we generally use the term *structure*. Fig. 1.4 gives a high level categorization of structure, partially based on discussions at an early DL workshop in northern Italy, naming popular technologies (e.g., databases) and showing where they fit along that dimension. We argue that DLs must be organized, thus having a moderate degree of structure. Even in situations described as chaotic [101], from certain perspectives it is clear that there is (nonlinear) structure.

Figure 1.4: Degrees of structure for key technologies.

Focusing more on technology, a key dimension regarding DLs is Centralized vs. Distributed. For a personal or other small DL, centralization is common, though with the rapid proliferation of mobile and cloud technologies, even for those applications, centralization is diminishing. From a logical perspective, however, many DLs are centralized in an institution, even though, from a physical or device perspective, they are distributed. Thus, as can be seen in Fig. 1.5, the National Science Digital Library (NSDL), which is discussed in book 4, while sometimes considered as a single entity, in actuality has a distributed architecture, with multiple classes of content collections and services, connected through four different protocols.

Returning to the challenge of defining DLs, some ask what would be considered a DL, and what would not. Clearly, a DL can be a *digitized library*, but need not be; frequently, DLs go well beyond just being an electronic version of a paper-based library. More generally, while they *can* be a deconstruction of existing systems and institutions, which simply moves those systems to an electronic box in a library, DLs, at the least, usually add both value and functionality. Indeed, often they introduce a better solution to particular human needs. In the broadest sense, then, DLs give us new ways to deal with data, information, and knowledge.

To capture this breadth, and as a lead-in to the discussion later in this chapter, we give our simplified working definition as follows:

Digital libraries are complex systems that

1. help satisfy info needs of users (societies),

2. provide info services (scenarios),

3. organize info in usable ways (structures),

4. present info in usable ways (spaces), and

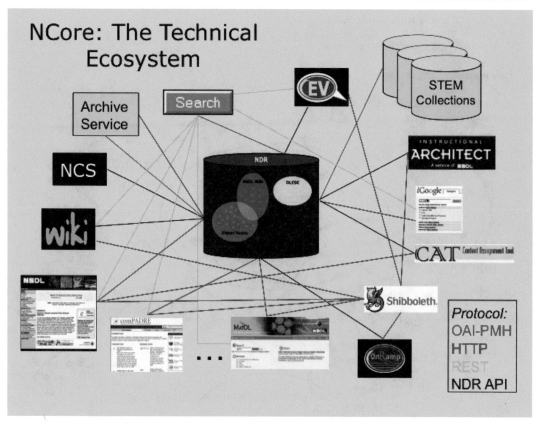

Figure 1.5: NSDL's technical architecture [141, 142].

5. communicate info with users (streams).

Further, as can be seen in Fig. 1.6, the five constructs identified (each starting with "S," hence 5S) can in turn be used to describe all of the key aspects of DLs, including their semantics and inter-relationships. For example, we can read off from Fig. 1.6 many important facts about DLs:

- Video contains images and audio.

- A metadata specification describes a digital object.

- Metadata specifications are included in a catalog.

- A catalog describes a collection.

- A repository stores a collection and a catalog.

- A service manager runs a service.

- A service is included in a scenario.

- An actor participates in a scenario.

- A scenario includes events.

- An event executes an operation.

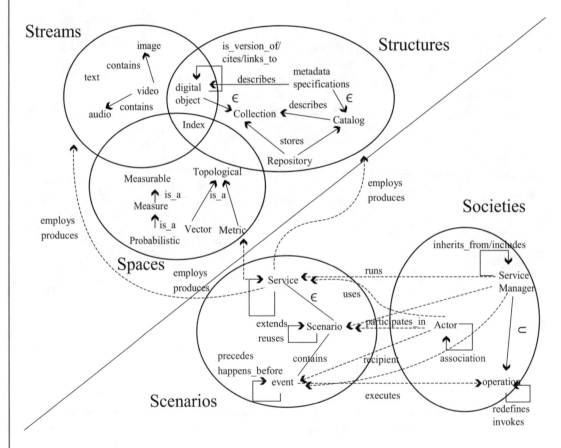

Figure 1.6: 5S-based semantics and relationships of DL elements. Adapted from [113].

Some additional observations are clear from Fig. 1.6. First, there is a natural split between the left and right parts. Three of the Ss are closely connected on the left, and relate especially to content. The other Ss, closely connected with people and services, also have strong cohesion. Second, some key elements of a DL, such as a *digital object*, are defined in terms of two or more of the Ss. Thus, while many DL elements can be defined solely or mostly using one of the Ss, others may have aspects drawn from multiple Ss; generally they are more complicated abstractions, e.g., an index. Third, the 5S approach, introduced superficially above, and discussed in depth below, is definitional, not programming-oriented. Thus, each concept and construct has a mathematical as well as an intuitive definition. While a particular digital library includes programs, and they are based on some approach, e.g., object-oriented, the 5S framework can lead to implementations using any programming paradigm.

While definitions are valuable, they become really meaningful when viewed from a variety of perspectives. One key perspective on DLs regards content. This is important; recall the left portion of Fig. 1.6, which addresses content representation. From the perspective of the information life cycle, content creation is of interest. Nowadays, with the widespread deployment of electronic publishing and other tools, much of the content in a DL is *born digital*. On the other hand, there are many other objects in the world that cannot be *in* DLs. Nevertheless, they can be described, using some metadata specification or format, leading to a metadata record. Sometimes, too, one or more surrogate representations of real-world objects also are created, typically through a digitization process[2]. Thus, one might have a number of digital image files from photographing or scanning an art object, at varying levels of detail, serving as surrogates for the real-world object. DLs that have both born digital and digitized content often are referred to as hybrid DLs.

These issues of entities and descriptions have led to the FRBR framework, developed by IFLA's Study Group on the Functional Requirements for Bibliographic Records [129]. They consider that

- Works

- are realized through

- Expressions

- which are embodied in

- Manifestations

- which are exemplified by

- Items.

This approach can help clarify thinking about digital objects and metadata, but also can be generalized through richer models connecting arbitrary entities with arbitrary relationships [45].

While the traditional view of a library is of books, in the digital age it is common to include many other types of content. Fig. 1.7 illustrates the broad range of content types that have been included in DLs. While some DLs cover just one type of content, others cover a variety of types. Accordingly, it is important that key DL services, like searching and browsing, operate across those types. Thus, book 4 discusses how information retrieval can be applied to digital images.

---

[2]Sometimes archives are distinguished since they often include globally unique objects, but more and more libraries are digitizing locally unique objects.

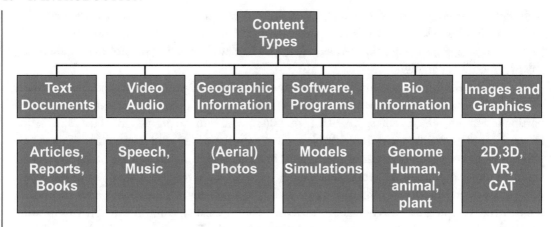

Figure 1.7: Digital library content.

As a result of such support for searching and browsing, people gain access to information. Accessibility has many aspects. Universal access refers to providing access for all people, in all places (i.e., ubiquitously), and at all times (i.e., 24/7/365). Accessibility also connotes accommodating special needs or disabilities, including regarding perception, e.g., visual (covering scale and color) and auditory. Further, accessibility refers to mobile use, relating to office, home, laptop, PDA, and a wide variety of other mobile devices. In addition to spatial coverage, there is access across time, often through an archive, which, if sustainable, aims toward permanence. Some archives result from a process of collection, but others are less costly, arising through donation or self-archiving [119]. Supporting such archives, the *Open Archives Initiative* [59, 175] arose in 1999, leading first to a protocol to support metadata harvesting (OAI-PMH) [174]. This allowed development of simple repositories; see Fig. 1.8. These repositories can harvest from other repositories, as can be seen in Fig. 1.9, making use of the protocol's support for selective and/or incremental gathering of metadata, thus supporting various approaches to aggregation (e.g., over space, organization, or topic).

The concept of being open, additionally, has a variety of aspects. Besides *open archives*, there are *open standards*, sometimes supported by *open source software*. While all three of these relate to digital libraries, open archives are most closely and specifically connected.

Though only recently made simple through OAI-PMH, the model of aggregation illustrated in Fig. 1.9 is not a new idea. Fig. 1.10 summarizes the similar, then almost prescient, vision of J.C.R. Licklider, from 1965.

Actually, from an historical perspective, there has been a rather continuous development of technologies leading toward modern digital libraries, beginning from the earliest days of computing [97, 164, 229]. Thus, in 1945, Vannevar Bush[3] conceived of *Memex* [33], often viewed as the clearest early vision leading to hypertext, hypermedia, and the World Wide Web.

---

[3]President Roosevelt's Science Advisor, Director of the Manhattan Project, and Founder of the US National Science Foundation

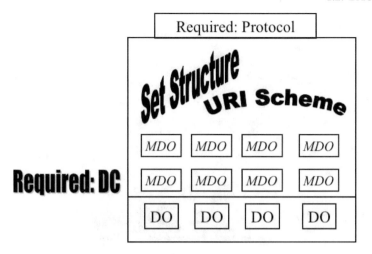

Figure 1.8: OAI – Repository perspective.

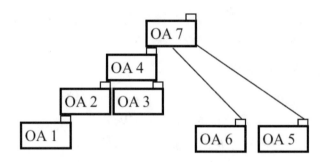

Figure 1.9: OAI – Black box perspective.

MIT, home to Drs. Bush and Licklider, also hosted key early automated information systems, including Project Intrex, as well as TIP, at the MIT Library, which more recently has been visible as the home for DSpace [62, 225, 226, 227].

Other parts of the history of digital libraries come from connection with funding initiatives. In the USA, in the early 1990s, support was provided for a number of workshops to launch the field [74]. These led to the (first) NSF-funded Digital Library Initiative [121], followed by a second program, DLI2 [71, 116, 149]. In Europe, too, there was governmental support, largely connected through a Network of Excellence, DELOS [3, 133, 191].

Partly encouraged by these initiatives and programs, focused digital library conferences emerged. Most notable among these are JCDL (usually in North America), ECDL (now TPDL, usually in Europe), and ICADL (usually in Australasia). Information on these, as well as federations and associations, magazines and journals, and research laboratories—all important for learning more

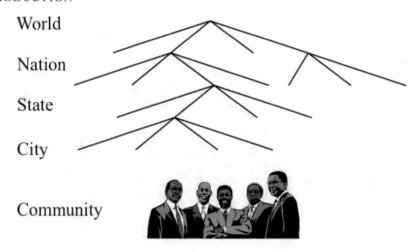

World

Nation

State

City

Community

Figure 1.10: An illustration summarizing "Libraries of the Future" [154].

about DLs—is summarized as follows [8, 22, 28, 29, 61, 74, 76, 150, 154, 253]. Some examples of sources of additional information about digital libraries include:

Magazine: `http://www.dlib.org`

Books: Source Book: `http://fox.cs.vt.edu/DLSB.html` (1993)

    MIT Press: Arms, plus by Borgman, Licklider (1965)

    Morgan Kaufmann: Witten (2nd ed.), Lesk (2nd ed.)

Conferences: ICADL: `http://www.icadl.org`

    JCDL: `http://www.jcdl.org`

    TPDL (formerly ECDL): `http://www.tpdl2012.org/`

Associations: ASIS&T SIG-DL: `http://www.asis.org/SIG/sigdl/`

    IEEE TCDL: `http://www.ieee-tcdl.org`

NSF DLI: • `http://www.dlib.org/dlib/july98/07griffin.html`

    • `http://web.archive.org/web/20090227060205/` `http://www.dli2.nsf.gov/`

    • Google (`http://www.nsf.gov/discoveries/disc_summ.jsp?cntn_id=100660`)

Labs: Cape Town: `www.cs.uct.ac.za/research/dll`

    Texas A&M: `www.csdl.tamu.edu`

    VT: `www.dlib.vt.edu`

1.3   MOTIVATION

In 1991, in connection with the Envision project [80, 82] we interviewed library and information scientists, as well as those interested in computing and computing education, to identify requirements in the new area of digital libraries. These are summarized as follows:

1. World Lit.: 24hr / 7day / from desktop

2. Integrated "super" information systems

3. Ubiquitous, Higher Quality, Lower Cost

4. Education, Knowledge Sharing, Discovery

5. Disintermediation — > Collaboration

6. Universities Reclaim Property

7. Interactive Courseware, Student Works

8. Scalable, Sustainable, Usable, Useful

The first entry summarizes long-held desires for access to all knowledge, at any time, from our desktops [243]. The second entry connects these wishes to the advance of information systems, and to a goal of this work: to develop a comprehensive theoretical foundation, 5S. The third entry extends from the desktop to other devices and settings, highlights concern for quality (see book 2), and points out the need for lowering barriers and decreasing the digital divide [173], as well as addressing the challenges of library budgets. The fourth entry ties in with the need for learning and for advancing scholarship, which builds upon prior knowledge. The fifth entry makes clear that there is a role for librarians, as partners not gatekeepers, since individuals should develop better skills for collecting and managing information, not delegating all responsibility to others. This fits well with the next entry, calling for universities to play more active roles; today we see them managing institutional repositories and many other information or knowledge management systems in addition to traditional library services. The seventh entry elaborates on this, which has led to handling of electronic theses and dissertations, e-portfolio systems, and courseware management systems. The final entry goes beyond basic quality concerns, to address system, user base, utility, and economic concerns.

Given such calls for digital libraries, one might ask regarding *why* people have been interested in digital libraries. Clearly, there is great interest, as is explained at the end of the prior section, but what are the deep reasons? As was discussed in Section 1.1, humans need information. As is clear from the rapidly growing interest in computer-supported communication (e.g., using Facebook), and is elucidated in book 4, humans also need to communicate.

For millenia, people have been communicating and sharing information synchronously, that is, at the same time, generally by being in the same place, as is illustrated in Fig. 1.11. With the advent of telecommunication devices, sychronous communication had been extended beyond the limitations of space, either directly, as with telephone, or in broadcast mode, as with radio and television.

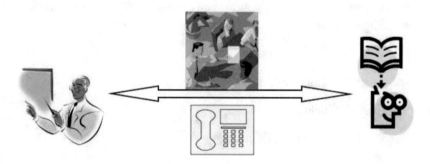

Figure 1.11: Synchronous scholarly communication: Same time; same or different place.

To futher extend communication and sharing of information across time, asynchronous methods are needed, as is illustrated in Fig. 1.12. These allow information to be recorded, so people can access it later, either in the same place or in different places, if something carrying that information is moved (sometimes by way of copies). Support for such asynchronous communication and access to information has been greatly enhanced for over 600 years through technologies related to paper and printing [28]. But with the emergence of digital libraries, such communication can be vastly extended and expanded.

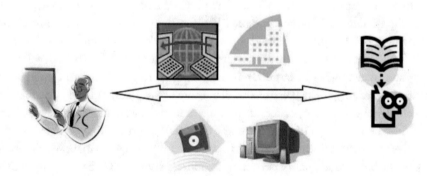

Figure 1.12: Asynchronous, digital library mediated scholarly communication: Different time and, possibly, place.

Asynchronous communication has been particularly important regarding scholarly communication, including journals that first arose about 350 years ago, supported by authors, editors, and reviewers. As can be seen in Fig. 1.13, there is a chain of steps, or workflow, aimed to add value and ensure quality. Institutions like publishers, abstracting and indexing (A&I) groups, and book consolidators (that aggregate shipments to libraries), support the process, but also lead to added costs.

Figure 1.13: The traditional publishing chain, which can be shortened.

Today, as can be seen in Fig. 1.14, the entire process can be flattened [90]. While the same process as has been carried out for centuries is possible, other scenarios can be supported as well. For example, an author can upload a work into a digital library, make it accessible to friends and colleagues, sometimes using a pre-print service or institutional repository. Over time, the work can be refined, and new versions added. Editors might notice that a work is having some impact, work with the author, typically with the aid of reviewers, and have a publisher's imprimatur added, whereupon the same work might be aggressively publicized. Since the same person may play different roles at different times, interacting with the digital library, less time may be needed to become familiar with its user interface. Additional savings in cost as well as time are possible, due to automation and flexible workflows. Further, new approaches to electronic publishing are possible, such as integration of conference and journal publishing activities.

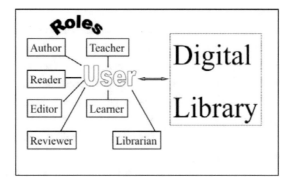

Figure 1.14: A flat digital library based alternative to traditional publishing.

Since digital libraries can serve such a wide variety of needs, they have been of interest to many world leaders. For example, during a workshop to explore collaboration between the USA and India regarding digital libraries [231], the president of India called to encourage our deliberations and to share a poem he had written on the topic. Some of the reasons that digital libraries are of global interest include:

- National projects can preserve antiquities and heritage: cultural, historical, linguistic, and scholarly.

- Knowledge and information are essential to economic and technological growth, and to education.

- Digital libraries serves as a domain for international collaboration:

  - wherein all can contribute and benefit,
  - which leverages investment in networking,
  - which provides useful content on Internet & WWW, and
  - which will tie nations and peoples together more strongly and through deeper understanding.

What is particularly exciting is that digital libraries may help expand the base of understanding among the peoples of the earth, as we appreciate our respective cultural heritages, and advance in education and growth.

The broad range of applicability of digital libraries is summarized in Table 1.2, which arose from a workshop exploring collaboration between the USA and South Korea [72]. The first column lists a broad set of application domains, in which digital libraries contribute, followed by an entry for a row so that cross-cutting issues can be considered. The second column lists representative institutions for each domain, while the third column gives examples of such institutions. Column 4 identifies technical challenges that should be addressed so digital libraries can serve better in a domain, leading to the benefits and positive impact summarized in the last column. For example, in the education domain, institutions served include schools, colleges, and universities; the NSDL (see book 4) is an example of a large digital library developed to help them. Regarding education, better knowledge management should help in part because of increased access to data, and reuse of educational materials also should increase access to resources that often are developed at great cost (see Fig. 1.15). Book 4 explores these matters in great depth, since education is so important in the modern Information Age, and since sharing can help us address ongoing economic woes connected with educational instutions, while at the same time allowing enhanced learning through use of interactive multimedia resources.

As can be seen from the row in Table 1.2 about art and culture, a key benefit would be increased global understanding. For that to result, we need technical advances to improve our ability to digitize a wide variety of types of objects, supplemented by cheaper and more accurate description schemes that

Table 1.2: Digital Library Challenges and Benefits. Based on report from 2002 Workshop [72].

Application Domain	Related Institutions	Examples	Technical Challenges	Benefit/Impact
Publishing	Publishers, Eprint archives	OAI	Quality control, openness	Aggregation, organization
Education	Schools, colleges, universities	NSDL, NCSTRL	Knowledge management, reusability	Access to data
Art, Culture	Museum	AMICO, PRDLA	Digitization, describing, cataloging	Global understanding
Science	Government, Academia, Commerce	NVO, PDG, SwissProt, UK e-Science, European Union Commission	Data models	Reproducibility, faster reuse, faster advance
(e) Government	Government Agencies (all levels)	Census	Intellectual property rights, privacy, multi-national	Accountability, homeland security
(e) Commerce, (e) Industry	Legal institutions	Court cases, patents	Developing standards	Standardization, economic development
History, Heritage	Foundations	American Memory	Content, context, interpretation	Long term view, perspective, documentation, recording, facilitating, interpretation, understanding
Cross-cutting	Library, Archive	Web, personal collections	Multi-language, preservation, scalability, interoperability, dynamic behavior, workflow, sustainability, ontologies, distributed data, infrastructure	Reduced cost, increased access, preservation, democratization, leveling, peace, competitiveness

can lead to comprehensive catalogs. Regarding the row on science, there is particular need to support e-science, as is discussed in book 4. For example, we must carefully describe scientific experiments, so they are reproducible, and must store data about those experiments for reuse, including parameters, raw data, results, and derived publications. This is of great importance as computing helps in the shift of emphasis in science toward a fourth paradigm [124], where data and computers are essential, as in simulation studies.

The last row mentions broad challenges, including preservation. Unless digital libraries will stand the test of time, and their content and services will be available ongoing, investment may be questioned, and those accustomed to other ways to access information may withhold trust. There are many works touching on this topic, and ongoing research [50, 60, 63, 127, 128, 151, 187, 197, 201, 237]. Fortunately, there already are practical [148] and promising approaches [155], if there is sufficient will, planning, and investment in this important problem.

These challenges reinforce and supplement what was articulated in 1991, summarized at the beginning of this section. In particular, we must continue to work toward scalability, sustainability, interoperability, and integration. These points are discussed repeatedly in subsequent chapters.

Figure 1.15: Resources for education, from the University of Colorado Digital Library [53].

1.4   DIGITAL LIBRARY CURRICULUM

Since digital libraries, and their many off-shoots (e.g., organizations like Google, and types of systems such as institutional repositories or content mangement systems), will be with us for the forseeable future, it is important that there be suitable training and education for digital librarians, as well as for those working in related areas, like information retrieval.

In the computing field, recommendations for curricular work achieved widespread popularity at least back to 1968 [9]. Current programs build upon the 2001 recommendations [41], updated in 2008, with a new revision planned for 2013. But for focused fields, like digital libraries, a more in-depth analysis is needed. This builds upon related work, for information retrieval [75] and multimedia [81, 83].

In 2005, a team at Virginia Tech and the University of North Carolina at Chapel Hill began work on a tailored curriculum for digital libraries. We reviewed the existing literature to identify topical coverage, and used computer analysis to help with our identification of sub-areas. Our work led to a website [86] and to a parallel representation in Wikiversity [85] so that the community could more easily work to improve the resources developed.

Covering a field can be carried out from a variety of perspectives. Some learners are interested in questions like: What? Why? How? Others prefer an historical approach, considering origins, evolution, current status, research problems, and future work. Those with an economic background have particular interest in costs, equity, and sustainability. Those with social concerns focus on users (sometimes called patrons), management, support of collaboration, and social networks. Those with a technical bent may have backgrounds in human-computer interaction, hypertext/hypermedia, information retrieval, information science, library science, or Web technologies. Accordingly, as we developed curricular resources [186], we focused on many different modules (i.e., detailed lesson plans), each to address a particular interest.

Thus, we aimed to support the needs of those in library or information science programs [185]. At the same time, we prepared modules for those in the computing field [184]. Ultimately, that led to the framework illustrated in Fig. 1.16.

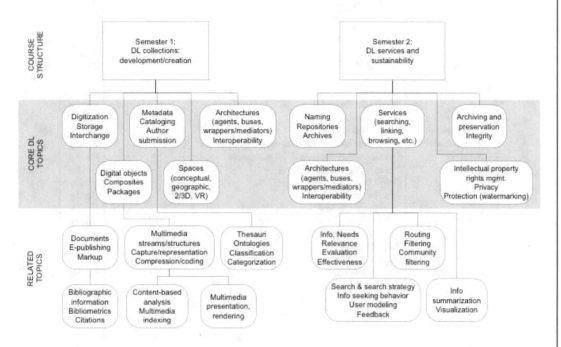

Figure 1.16: DL curriculum framework.

Clearly, at least two full semester long courses could be developed using this framework. The one on the left of Fig. 1.16 might fit best in a library school, while that on the right might fit in a computing program, but either type of academic program can make use of modules on any topics that are of interest. The middle portion of the figure identifies topics that are *core* for digital libraries, while the bottom portion covers related topics, that can be included in DL classes, or might be covered in other courses or studies.

Thanks to many faculty, researchers, and students, a diverse set of modules has been developed; see Table 1.3. Though almost all have been reviewed, some still need (more) field testing and refinement. Though most have been developed by instructors, some have been prepared by students, generally in graduate programs, but some undergraduate students have contributed through work on team term projects. In the lower part of the table, modules are associated with a software system, in which case the Core Topic is called Software. Development of new modules, and refinement of existing modules, are ongoing efforts—please see the online sites for additions and enhanced versions.

Table 1.3: List of curricular modules.

Core Topic	Module	Author
1. Overview	1-a (10-c): Conceptual frameworks, models, theories, definitions	Faculty
	1-b: History of DLs and library automation	Faculty
2. Digital Objects	2-c (8-d): File formats, transformation, migration	Faculty
3. Collection	3-b: Digitization	Faculty
Development	3-e (7-e): Web Publishing	Faculty
	3-f (7-f): Crawling	Faculty
4. Info/Knowledge	4-b: Metadata	Faculty
Organization		
5. Architecture	5-a: Architecture overview	Faculty
	5-b: Application software	Faculty
	5-d: Protocols	Faculty
6. User Behav-	6-a: Info needs, relevance	Faculty
ior/Interactions	6-b: Online info seeking behavior, search strategy	Faculty
	6-d: Interaction design, usability assessment	Faculty
7. Services	7-a: Indexing and searching	Faculty
	7-a(1): Image Retrieval	Faculty
	7-b: Reference services	Faculty
	7-c: Recommender systems	Faculty
	7-d: Routing	Faculty
	7-e (3-e): Web Publishing	Faculty
	7-f (3-f): Crawling	Faculty
	7-g: Personalization	Faculty
8: Preservation	8-a: Preservation	Faculty
	8-b: Web archiving	Faculty
	8-d (2-c): File formats, transformation, migration	Faculty
9: Management and	9-c: Evaluation and user studies	Faculty
Evaluation		
10: DL Education	10-c (1-a): Conceptual frameworks, models, theories, definitions	Faculty
and Research		
Software	7-h(1): Apache Solr (enterprise search platform)	Grad
	7-h(2): CLUTO (clustering high-dimensional datasets)	Grad
	7-h(3): Hadoop Map-Reduce (parallel processing of data)	Grad
	7-h(4): Lemur (language modeling and IR)	Grad
	7-h(5): NLTK (NLP and text analysis)	Grad
	7-h(6): R (language for statistical analysis)	Grad
	7-h(7): SEDNA XML Database (efficient XML retrieval)	Grad
	7-h(8): TREC Eval (for information retrieval systems)	Grad
	7-h(9): Weka (data mining in Java)	Grad
	7-h(10): WordNet (lexical database)	Grad
	7-i(1): PureData (sound manipulation)	Ugrad
	7-i(2): Media Computation (image manipulation)	Ugrad
	7-i(3): Fingerprint (NIST biometric images software)	Ugrad
	7-i(4): Audacity (recording and editing sounds)	Ugrad

1.5   HIGH LEVEL CONSTRUCTS

Digital libraries, viewed from a minimalist perspective [38], are characterized by a small set of essential constructs. Earlier in this chapter, some of those have been discussed, such as *digital object* and *metadata*. Also important are a number of higher level concepts, discussed in this sub-section.

First, there are *collections*. A library is not very interesting if it only has one object of content. When a digital library has a set of content objects, those digital objects constitute a collection. Accordingly, those who are responsible for building the collection are involved in the important work of collection development.

Second, to help manage the collection, there is a *catalog*. Catalogs contain metadata records, each describing a digital object in the collection. Likewise, every digital object in the collection should have a metadata record in the catalog. Often, then, there is a one-to-one relationship between entries in the collection and entries in the catalog. However, in some cases, when there are several metadata formats approved for the catalog, for example the Dublin Core [240, 241] and MARC [153], there can be a metadata record for a given digital object, in each of several metadata formats.

Third, there are *repositories*. There are multiple connotations to this term. One arose from a seminal article about digital object services [137]:

> "A repository is a network-accessible storage system in which digital objects may be stored for possible subsequent access or retrieval. The repository has mechanisms for adding new digital objects to its collection (depositing) and for making them available (accessing), using, at a minimum, the repository access protocol. The repository may contain other related information, services and management systems."

An important result of this perspective is the system to manage repositories called Fedora [56, 182, 218, 219], which today is quite popular with digital library developers. Thus, a repository is a key software component in a digital library, managing its collection of digital objects. *Repository* also refers to a digital library having some special type and/or collection of content. Thus, there are repositories for video [98], multimedia [44], mathematical software [23], and educational resources [94]. Another connotation of repository is as shorthand for *institutional repository* (IR) [134, 158]. An IR manages a range of digital objects for an institution, such as a department or university. Accordingly, particular digital library systems that are used to manage an institutional repository also are referred to as repository systems. Popular examples include EPrints [120], DSpace [227], and BEPress [19]. Finally, research in digital libraries that focuses on the repository portion sometimes leads to special phrases like *open repository* [39] or *secure repository* [145].

Fourth, there are *archives*. One connotation is as in Open Archives, illustrated earlier in Fig. 1.8. Another connotation is similar to repository, i.e., a digital library having some special type or collection of content, e.g., arXiv, supporting especially physics and computing [99]. Among the largest of these is the Internet Archive [131], aiming to preserve all Internet content. Also very large are national archives, as in the USA [232], hybrid in that they have both digital and non-digital content. These build upon a long tradition of archival science, practiced by archivists, similar to librarians, but with more emphasis on preservation and somewhat less on access [230]. In the digital age, new models are needed for archival information systems, e.g., OAIS [43]. Much research also is needed [198], as well as government policy [69].

Fifth, there are *services*. Often we hear of the service sector of the economy, as distinct from manufacturing, for example. Likewise, libraries are known for providing a variety of services, such as reference services [181]. In the Information Age, services are what computing systems provide. Thus, in client-server settings [163], servers perform services. In the context of the World Wide Web, there are web services [54], usually supporting distributed systems.

Finally, there is the concept of *federation*. For administrative, legal, political, or practical purposes, a set of services can be federated, so they act as a whole. For example, a client might want to search across a variety of online catalogs, using the Z39.50 standard [7, 157, 171] or its Web oriented successor, available as SRU and SRW [178]. Such federated search often involves mediators [65], allowing a heterogeneous set of remote services to be accessed from a single system [93, 110]. However, since some remote systems may not respond in a timely fashion, and since search ranking techniques vary widely, there may be effectiveness problems [89], especially if only some remote sites are selected for search [88]. Accordingly, many services shy away from federation, and, if there are not administrative or legal concerns, use harvesting, wherein a central system collects information, thus having greater control and higher performance [31, 32, 236].

1.6   DIGITAL LIBRARY SYSTEMS

The high level constructs described above lead to packaging into digital library systems. According to the Digital Library Manifesto [36] and the DELOS Reference Model [35], there are three levels at issue:

- DL: an organization providing content and services for a community;

- DLS: a software system that affords the functionality of the DL; and

- DLMS: a generic software system that can be instantiated on particular hardware and operated as a DLS.

There are many DLMSs available today [133, 207], some discussed briefly before. Here we consider three, arising in distant locations around the globe, though there are many others, including a growing number of commercial offerings, like CONTENTdm, DLXS, Virtua, VITAL, XTF, and others [242].

Greenstone was developed in New Zealand [249, 251, 252, 254, 256]. It evolved from the MG information retrieval system [257]. Thanks to a related textbook [250] and open source software [115] that has been enhanced for over a decade, there are many users, and numerous digital librarians have learned by way of this system. Since it runs on a variety of platforms, including small ones, and has been disseminated in connection with UNESCO efforts, it has wide use for small collections in disparate locations.

In 2005, a bridge was developed between Greenstone and DSpace [255]. DSpace also is open source software [62], but was developed, with support from HP, at MIT, in Cambridge, MA, USA [225, 226, 227]. DSpace has played a key role in the emergence of institutional repository systems, since it is relatively easy to install and operate, especially to help manage the digital library needs of a university. With a simple model connecting collections and communities, and with support for uploading both metadata and digital objects, many libraries have found it easy to deploy DSpace. For example, a number of universities installed DSpace to manage their electronic theses and dissertations [123]. Due to its popularity, Doug Gorton's Master's Thesis research targeted DSpace in his work with 5S-based generation of digital libraries from specifications (using 5SGen) [114]—so an install, build, and configuration could proceed in approximately 30 minutes. DSpace has engendered a wide variety of enhancement and complementary software. Recently, there has been a shift toward integration of DSpace with Fedora, through the DuraSpace initiative [64].

EPrints [228] evolved at the University of Southampton out of the CogPrints e-print archive [118], shortly after the Santa Fe Convention that launched the Open Archives Initiative [59]. It has matured greatly, and is now at version 3. Partly since JISC in the UK has given strong grant support for institutional repositories, and since EPrints is the local favorite, there is a substantial base of use in UK and Europe. More broadly, EPrints is deployed for many e-print and pre-print collections.

Building digital libraries often makes use of these popular digital library management systems, but there are many other supported products available as well. This is an improvement from the situation of ten to fifteen years ago, when many digital libraries were home-grown. At Virginia Tech, we have devised a series of such systems, including CODER [73], MARIAN [34, 87, 109, 110, 111, 260], Open Digital Libraries [220, 221, 222], CITIDEL [79, 84, 130, 138, 183], ETANA [192, 194, 213, 215], and Ensemble [5, 78]. While developing research software is important, often practitioners prefer toolkits [172] or generic systems, when running a production operation.

Given the above background, perspectives, and discussion of various constructs and systems, it is appropriate, to help ensure a deeper understanding of the field, to focus on a formal approach, starting with an intuitive explanation.

1.7   5S INTUITION

In traditional libraries, around the world, handling of books operates in a similar fashion, regardless of location, language, or culture. Access to information through such libraries thus is straightforward, and there is a high degree of interoperability. On the other hand, information systems in general, and digital libraries in particular, generally operate in different ways, and are accessible through a diverse set of different interfaces.

For applications to work together to support a range of activities (such as annotating, organizing, indexing, searching, browsing, and visualizing) in scholarly tasks, it is important for them to interoperate with each other. Precise theoretical definitions can help address interoperability problems that arise from ad hoc development and diverse implementation efforts. If applications have a foundation to build upon, there is a better chance of interoperability among similar functioning or complimentary applications.

A formal metamodel can help researchers to develop precise theoretical definitions that address this interoperability problem. A metamodel formally defines the key components that comprise a system. These components, in combination, can be used to define various instances of the system. A model is an abstraction of phenomena in the real world; a metamodel is yet another abstraction, highlighting properties of the model itself. A model conforms to its metamodel in the way that a computer program conforms to the grammar of the programming language in which it is written[4].

In the remainder of this chapter we introduce and explain the 5S framework, which integrates model and metamodel concepts. We provide an intuitive explanation; see Appendix B for formal definitions. The key constructs in all this begin with the letter "S," and since they number five, we use the abbreviation '5S'.

1.7.1   STREAMS

From an intuitive perspective (see Fig. 1.17), we think of streams in all walks of life: a river, the Gulf Stream, the Humboldt Current, rain, erosion, pollution from a plant/industry/smokestack, water from a tap, flow of blood or other organic fluids, oil in a pipeline, gasoline flowing into a car, stream of consciousness, the solar wind, sunshine on a solar cell, evolution, data from a sensor, a bit stream over a communication channel, data through a Unix pipe, audio over a telephone or from a radio, etc. (for a WordNet description, see Fig. 1.18). In a mathematical sense, streams are sequences of elements of an arbitrary type (e.g., bits, characters, images, etc.). In this sense, they can model both static and dynamic content. The first includes, for example, textual material, while the latter might be, for example, a presentation of a digital video, or a sequence of time and positional data (e.g., from a GPS) for a moving object.

A dynamic stream can represent an information flow—a sequence of messages encoded by the sender and communicated using a transmission channel possibly distorted with noise, to a receiver whose goal is to reconstruct the sender's messages and interpret message semantics [211]. Dynamic streams are thus important for representing whatever communications take place in the digital library. Examples of dynamic streams include video-on-demand delivered to a viewer, audio delivered to a listener, a timed sequence of news announcements sent to a client, a timed sequence of frames that allows the assembly of a virtual reality scenario, etc. Typically, a dynamic stream is understood through its temporal nature. A dynamic stream then can be interpreted as a finite sequence of clock times and associated values[5] that can be used to define a stream algebra, allowing operations on diverse kinds of multimedia streams [159]. The synchronization of streams can be specified with Petri Nets [177] or other approaches.

In the static interpretation, the temporal nature is generally ignored or is irrelevant, and a stream corresponds to some information content that is interpreted as a sequence of basic elements, often of the same type. A popular type of static stream according to this view is text (a sequence of characters). The type of the stream defines its semantics and area of application. For example, any text representation can be seen as a stream of characters, so that text documents, such as scientific articles and books, following a publishing house layout style, can be considered as structured streams.

---

[4]Source: http://en.wikipedia.org/wiki/Metamodeling.
[5]These values are undefined or a value of type T, e.g., boolean, integer, text, or image.

Figure 1.17: Photograph of the stream below the Cascades in southwest Virginia, taken by Edward A. Fox.

1.7.2 STRUCTURES

From an intuitive perspective (see Fig. 1.19), we relate structure to organization, an organization chart, geometric shapes, a maze, a grid, a bee hive, a cell, an organ, a biological system (e.g., circulation), cyberintrastructure, transportation infrastructure, form, architecture, a building (e.g, house, office tower, cathedral), etc. (for a WordNet description, see Fig. 1.20). From a mathematical perspective, a structure specifies the way in which parts of a whole are arranged or organized. In digital libraries, structures can represent hypertexts, taxonomies, system connections, user relationships, and containment—to cite a few. Books, for example, can be structured logically into chapters, sections, subsections, and paragraphs; or physically into cover, pages, line groups (paragraphs), and lines [96]. Structuring orients readers within a document's information.

Markup languages (e.g., SGML, XML, HTML) have been the primary form of exposing the internal structure of digital documents for retrieval and/or presentation purposes [6, 47, 103].

STREAM
Noun

> S: (n) stream, watercourse (a natural body of running water flowing on or under the earth)
>
> S: (n) stream, flow, current (dominant course (suggestive of running water) of successive events or ideas) "two streams of development run through American history"; "stream of consciousness"; "the flow of thought"; "the current of history"
>
> S: (n) flow, stream (the act of flowing or streaming; continuous progression)
>
> S: (n) stream, flow (something that resembles a flowing stream in moving continuously) "a stream of people emptied from the terminal"; "the museum had planned carefully for the flow of visitors"
>
> S: (n) current, stream (a steady flow of a fluid (usually from natural causes)) "the raft floated downstream on the current"; "he felt a stream of air"; "the hose ejected a stream of water" Verb

Verb

> S: (v) stream (to extend, wave or float outward, as if in the wind) "their manes streamed like stiff black pennants in the wind"
>
> S: (v) stream (exude profusely) "She was streaming with sweat"; "His nose streamed blood"
>
> S: (v) pour, swarm, stream, teem, pullulate (move in large numbers) "people were pouring out of the theater"; "beggars pullulated in the plaza"
>
> S: (v) pour, pelt, stream, rain cats and dogs, rain buckets (rain heavily) "Put on your rain coat-- it's pouring outside!"
>
> S: (v) stream, well out (flow freely and abundantly) "Tears streamed down her face"

Figure 1.18: Stream definitions, from WordNet Version 3.1 [259].

Relational and object-oriented databases impose strict structures on data, typically using tables or graphs as units of structuring [15], often specified using schema.

With the increase in heterogeneity of material continually being added to digital libraries, we find that much of this material is called "semistructured" or "unstructured." These terms refer to data that may have some structure, where the structure is not as rigid, regular, explicit, or complete as

Figure 1.19: Photograph of the hotel building (structure) at Mountain Lake in southwest Virginia, taken by Edward A. Fox.

the structure used by structured documents or traditional database management systems [1]. Query languages and algorithms can extract structure from these data [2, 144, 170]. Although most of those efforts have a "data-centric" view of semi-structured data, works with a more "document-centric view" have emerged [10, 91, 92]. In general, humans and natural language processing systems can expend considerable effort to unlock the interwoven structures found in texts at syntactic, semantic, pragmatic, and discourse levels.

1.7.3 SPACES

From an intuitive perspective (see Fig. 1.21), spaces relate to interstellar or interstitial regions, vertical or horizontal separations, a right of way, an open space, a Euclidean space, something represented by cartesian or polar coordinates, etc. (for a WordNet description, see Fig. 1.22). In a mathematical sense, a space is a set of objects together with operations on those objects that obey certain constraints.

STRUCTURE
Noun
```
    S: (n) structure, construction (a thing constructed; a complex
           entity constructed of many parts) "the structure consisted
           of a series of arches"; "she wore her hair in an amazing
           construction of whirls and ribbons"
    S: (n) structure (the manner of construction of something and the
           arrangement of its parts) "artists must study the structure
           of the human body"; "the structure of the benzene molecule"
    S: (n) structure (the complex composition of knowledge as elements
           and their combinations) "his lectures have no structure"
    S: (n) structure, anatomical structure, complex body part, bodily
           structure, body structure (a particular complex anatomical
           part of a living thing and its construction and arrangement)
           "he has good bone structure"
    S: (n) social organization, social organisation, social structure,
           social system, structure (the people in a society considered
           as a system organized by a characteristic pattern of
           relationships) "the social organization of England and
           America is very different"; "sociologists have studied the
           changing structure of the family" Verb
Verb
    S: (v) structure (give a structure to) "I need to structure my days"
```

Figure 1.20: Structure definitions, from WordNet Version 3.1 [259].

The combination of operations on objects in the set is what distinguishes spaces from streams and structures. Since this combination is such a powerful construct, when a part of a DL cannot be described well using another of the Ss, a space may well be applicable.

Because of the generality of their definition, spaces are extremely important mathematical constructs. The operations and constraints associated with a space define its properties. For example, in mathematics, affine, linear, metric, and topological spaces define the basis for algebra and analysis [102]. In the context of digital libraries, Licklider discusses spaces for information [154, p. 62]. In the information retrieval discipline, Salton and Lesk formulated an algebraic theory based on vector spaces and implemented it in the SMART system [204]. "Feature spaces" are sometimes used with image and document collections and are suitable for clustering or probabilistic retrieval [196], as well as broad areas of machine learning and pattern recognition. Spaces also can be defined by a regular language applied to a collection of documents. Document spaces are a key concept in many digital libraries.

Figure 1.21: Space image of CW Leo from NASA JPL, California Institute of Technology [167].

Human understanding can be described using conceptual spaces. Multimedia systems must represent real as well as synthetic spaces in one or several dimensions, limited by some metric or presentational space (windows, views, projections) and transformed to other spaces to facilitate processing (such as compression [58, 263]). Many of the synthetic spaces represented in virtual reality systems approximate interesting physical spaces. Digital libraries may model traditional libraries by using virtual reality spaces or environments [14, 55]. Also, spaces for computer-supported cooperative work provide a context for virtual meetings and collaborations [49, 188].

Again, spaces are distinguished by the operations on their elements. Digital libraries can use many types of spaces for indexing, visualizing, and other services they perform. The most prominent of these for digital libraries are measurable spaces, measure spaces, probability spaces, vector spaces, and topological spaces.

1.7.4   SCENARIOS

From a popular perspective (see Fig. 1.23), scenarios connect with stories, ballads, algorithms, processes (in computers or businesses), procedures, workflows, plans or options (in sports, homes, businesses, or governments), scenes or acts (in theatre, movie, radio, or TV), etc. (for a WordNet description, see Fig. 1.24). One important type of scenario is a story that describes possible ways to

```
SPACE
Noun
    S: (n) space, infinite (the unlimited expanse in which everything
           is located) "they tested his ability to locate objects in
           space"; "the boundless regions of the infinite"
    S: (n) space (an empty area (usually bounded in some way between
           things)) "the architect left space in front of the building";
           "they stopped at an open space in the jungle"; "the space
           between his teeth"
    S: (n) space (an area reserved for some particular purpose) "the
           laboratory's floor space"
    S: (n) outer space, space (any location outside the Earth's
           atmosphere) "the astronauts walked in outer space without a
           tether"; "the first major milestone in space exploration was
           in 1957, when the USSR's Sputnik 1 orbited the Earth"
    S: (n) space, blank (a blank character used to separate successive
           words in writing or printing) "he said the space is the most
           important character in the alphabet"
    S: (n) distance, space (the interval between two times) "the
           distance from birth to death"; "it all happened in the space
           of 10 minutes"
    S: (n) space, blank space, place (a blank area) "write your name in
           the space provided"
    S: (n) space (one of the areas between or below or above the lines
           of a musical staff) "the spaces are the notes F-A-C-E"
    S: (n) quad, space ((printing) a block of type without a raised
           letter; used for spacing between words or sentences) Verb
Verb
    S: (v) space (place at intervals) "Space the interviews so that you
           have some time between the different candidates"
```

Figure 1.22: Space definitions, from WordNet Version 3.1 [259].

use a system to accomplish some function that a user desires. Scenarios are useful as part of the process of designing information systems. Scenarios can be used to describe external system behavior from the user's point of view [143]; provide guidelines to build a cost-effective prototype [223]; or help to validate, infer, and support requirements specifications and provide acceptance criteria for testing [126, 146, 224]. Developers can quickly grasp the potentials and complexities of digital libraries through scenarios. Scenarios tell what happens to the streams, in the spaces, and through the structures. Taken together the scenarios describe services, activities, and tasks—and those ultimately specify the functionalities of a digital library.

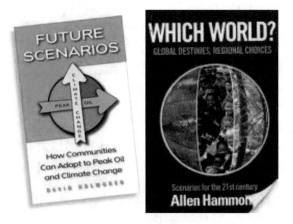

Figure 1.23: Book covers related to scenarios [117, 125].

```
SCENARIO - Noun
    S: (n) scenario (an outline or synopsis of a play (or, by extension,
           of a literary work))
    S: (n) scenario (a setting for a work of art or literature) "the
           scenario is France during the Reign of Terror"
    S: (n) scenario (a postulated sequence of possible events) "planners
           developed several scenarios in case of an attack"
```

Figure 1.24: Scenario definitions, from WordNet Version 3.1 [259].

For example, user scenarios describe one or more users engaged in some meaningful activity with an existing or envisioned system. This approach has been used as a design model for hypermedia applications [179]. Human information needs, and the processes of satisfying them in the context of digital libraries, are well suited to description with scenarios, including these key types: fact-finding, learning, gathering, and exploring [246]. Additionally, scenarios can aid understanding of how digital libraries affect organizations and societies, and how challenges to support social needs relate to underlying assumptions of digital libraries [152]. Scenarios also may help us understand the complexities of current publishing methods, as well as how they may be reshaped in the era of digital libraries, by considering publishing paths, associated participants, and publication functions [245].

The concepts of state and event are fundamental to understanding scenarios. Broadly speaking, a state is determined by what contents are in specified locations, as, for example, in a computer memory, disk storage, visualization, or the real world. The nature of the values and state locations related to contents in a system are granularity-dependent and their formal definitions and interpretations are out of the scope of this chapter; the reader is referred to [248] for a lengthy discussion. An event denotes a transition or change between states, for example, executing a command in a program. Scenarios specify sequences of events, which involve actions that modify states of a computation (including human information processing) and influence the occurrence and outcome of future events. Dataflows and workflows in digital libraries can be modeled using scenarios.

1.7.5   SOCIETIES

From a popular perspective (see Fig. 1.25), societies relate to empires, nations, cities, towns, villages, communities, families, religions, the military, ant colonies, those in ancient or prehistoric times, etc. (for a WordNet description, see Fig. 1.26). From a mathematical perspective, a society is a set of entities and the relationships between them. The entities include humans as well as hardware and software components, which either use or support digital library services. Societal relationships make connections between and among the entities and activities.

Figure 1.25: Society illustration, and cover of related book [122, 239].

Examples of specific human societies in digital libraries include patrons, authors, publishers, editors, maintainers, developers, and the library staff. There are also societies of learners and teachers. In a human society, people have roles, purposes, and relationships. In the DELOS Reference Model a key term used is "actors" (see Fig. 1.27). Societies follow certain rules and their members play different roles—participants, managers, leaders, contributors, or users. Members of societies have activities and relationships. During their activities, society members often create information artifacts—art, history, images, data—that can be managed by the library. Societies are holistic—substantially more than the sums of their constituents and the relationships between them. Electronic members of digital library societies, i.e., hardware and software components, are normally engaged in supporting and managing services used by humans.

```
SOCIETY - Noun
    S: (n) society (an extended social group having a distinctive
           cultural and economic organization)
    S: (n) club, social club, society, guild, gild, lodge, order (a
           formal association of people with similar interests) "he
           joined a golf club"; "they formed a small lunch society";
           "men from the fraternal order will staff the soup kitchen
           today"
    S: (n) company, companionship, fellowship, society (the state of
           being with someone) "he missed their company"; "he enjoyed
           the society of his friends"
    S: (n) society, high society, beau monde, smart set, bon ton (the
           fashionable elite)
```

Figure 1.26: Society definitions, from WordNet Version 3.1 [259].

A society is the highest-level component of a digital library, which exists to serve the information needs of its societies, in the contexts of its use. Digital libraries are used for collecting, preserving, and sharing information artifacts between society members. Cognitive models for information retrieval [18, 30, 68], for example, focus on user's information-seeking behavior (i.e., formation, nature, and properties of a user's information need) and on the ways in which information retrieval systems are used in operational environments.

Several societal issues arise when we consider them in the digital library context. These include policies for information use, reuse, privacy, ownership, intellectual property rights, access management, security, etc. [195]. Therefore, societal governance (law and its enforcement) is a fundamental concern in digital libraries. Language barriers are also an essential concern in information systems, and internationalization of online materials is an important issue in digital libraries, given their globally distributed nature [176].

Economics, a critical societal concern, is also key for digital libraries [136]. Collections that were "born electronic" are cheaper to house and maintain, while scanning paper documents to be used online can be relatively expensive. Internet access is widely available and in many settings is inexpensive. Online materials are seeing more use, including from distant locations. Since distribution costs of electronic materials are very low, digital delivery makes economic sense. However, it brings the problem of long-term storage and preservation, which must be adequately addressed, if the information being produced today is to be accessible to future generations [155, 156].

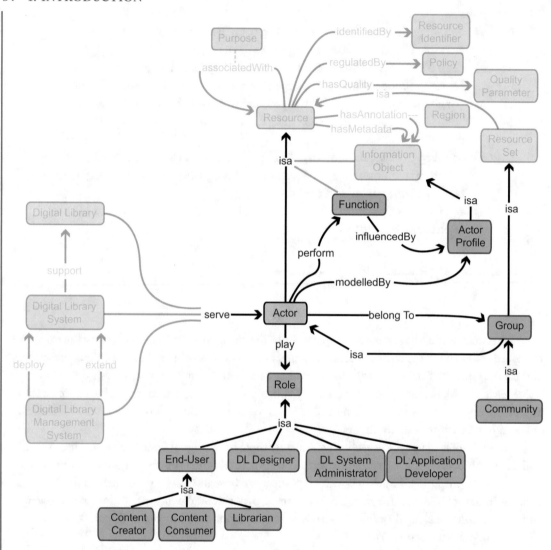

Figure 1.27: Society coverage, as actors. Adapted from the DELOS Reference Model [35].

1.8   DIGITAL LIBRARY TAXONOMY

A taxonomy is a classification system of empirical entities with the goal of classifying cases (i.e., for each case, identifying the correct category, among those that make up the classification system) according to their measured similarity on several variables [13]. Classifications are a premier descriptive tool and as such, they give a foundation toward an explanation for a phenomena. Classifications provide a terminology and vocabulary for a field and help to reduce complexity and achieve parsimony of description by logically arranging concepts through the identification of similarities and differences. We have built a taxonomy for digital libraries as a classification system of terms involved with the field. Our taxonomy describes the digital library field in conceptual terms and therefore its organization is amenable to be interpreted in the light of 5S. This interpretation aims toward a more informal conceptual understanding of the "Ss" and corresponding DL components.

In the process of building such a taxonomy, we have considered the principles of taxonomies in social sciences, notably cluster analysis, and faceted classification schemes [233]. In particular, we were guided by the idea that writing about a subject unequivocally reveals the appropriate facets for that subject [70], and that those facets are enough to describe the phenomenon [190]. We followed an agglomerative strategy using subjective relational concepts like association and correlation. During the construction of the taxonomy we tried to accommodate all the terms found in the literature and marginal fields, guarantee mutual exclusivity, and ensure consistency and clarity.

To collect the unstructured list of concepts, we went through the early literature to find all features, issues, and roles utilized, and identified specific terms [107]. As a starting point, we used an initial set of terms and phrases listed alphabetically in [77]. To this list we added other terms from various articles. When this was reasonably voluminous, we produced a grouping of terms of similar or related meaning into "notational families" known as facets. Each group was given a label that described the idea behind the homogeneity of the group or the main variable considered. From there, we grouped the clusters, and so on, until we achieved convergence into one unique facet called "digital library."

Once the initial taxonomy was complete, we noticed certain terms were missing or ambiguous, so we added terms and qualified them in each context. After several iterations of successive clustering, declustering, and reclustering, we released a more concrete and consistent working set for peer review and then improved the taxonomy based on comments received. The resulting taxonomy is shown in Figures 1.8, 1.29, and 1.30.

We must point out that, as with any classification system, our taxonomy must evolve to accommodate changes in the digital library field. However, two factors should contribute to the stability of the taxonomy, and therefore to its relative longevity. First the taxonomy was derived from a significant corpus of digital library literature; therefore it is more stable than personal opinions. Second, the higher-level groupings are significantly abstract so that they may be applied to many fields, with possible additions or changes necessary only at the level of specific categories. Clearly, such changes are likely due to the youth and rapid development of the field. In the following we describe the main facets and sub-facets of the taxonomy, making use of 5S as an analytical tool.

Actors: Who interacts with/within DLs?   In our context, actors are the users of a digital library. Actors interact with the DL through an interface design that is (or should be) affected by the actors" preferences and needs. Actors who have preferences and needs in common, display similar behavior in terms of services they use and interactions they practice. We say these actors form a

Actors

- **Distributed Computers**
  - Clients, Servers
  - Front/back ends
- **Electronic agents**
  - Collection agents
  - Crawlers
  - Knowbots
  - Mediator agents
  - User agents
- **Humans**
  - Administrators
  - Authors
  - Annotators
  - Designers
  - Editors
  - Evaluators
  - Funders
  - Implementers
  - Learners, Teachers
  - Librarians
  - Maintainers
  - Managers
  - Patrons
  - Publishers
  - Readers
  - Reviewers
  - Tool builders

Activities

- **Abstracting**
  - Cogitating (reflecting)
  - Comparing
  - Extracting
  - Relating
  - Summarizing
- **Collecting**
  - Acquiring
    * Digitizing/ OCRing
    * Purchasing/ Licensing
  - Focused Crawling
  - Submitting
- **Creating**
  - Authoring
  - Transforming
- **Disseminating**
  - Collaborating
  - Email/Listservs
  - Filtering
  - Providing access
  - Publicizing
    * Marketing/ Advertising
  - Translating
- **Evaluating/Assessing**
  - Action research
  - Analyzing logs
  - Certifying
  - Ethnographics/ sociological study
  - Focus groups
  - Measuring
  - Surveying
  - Reviewing (peer)
- **Modeling**
  - Describing
  - Linking
- **Organizing**
  - Analyzing
  - Annotating
    * Narrating
    * Rating
    * Tagging
  - Cataloguing
  - Classifying
    * Training (classifier)
  - Clustering
  - Indexing
  - Logging
- **Personalizing**
  - Customizing
  - Recommending
- **Preserving/Archiving**
  - Conserving
  - Converting
  - Copying/Replicating
  - Curating
  - Emulating
  - Renewing
  - Translating
- **Requesting**
- **Selecting**
  - Binding
  - Browsing
  - Expanding (query)
  - Federating
  - Harvesting
  - Navigating
  - Searching
  - Visualizing

Figure 1.28: Taxonomy of digital libraries terms, part 1. Adapted from [108].

Components

- **Documents**

  - Annotations
  - Articles
  - Books
  - Courseware
  - Databases
  - Diagrams
  - E-artifacts
  - Hyperbases
  - Hypermedia
  - Hypertext
  - Images
  - Maps
  - Multimedia
  - Music
  - Photographs
  - Semi-structured documents
  - Speech
  - Structured docs
  - Sub-documents
  - Versions
  - Video

- **Handles**

  - DOIs

  - URI/URLs, PURLs, URNs

- **Knowledge organization sources**

  - Catalogs
    * Attributes
    * Metadata records
  - Relationship groups
    * Ontologies
    * Schema
    * Semantic nets
    * Thesauri
  - Term lists
    * Authority files
    * Categorizations
    * Classifications
    * Dictionaries
    * Gazetteers
    * Glossaries
    * Subject headings
    * Taxonomies

- **Repositories**

  - Collections
    * Annotations
    * Data
    * Facts

    * Information
    * Knowledge
    * Logs
    * Relationships/ Hyperlinks
    * User profiles

- **Substrate**

  - Communications
    * Internet
    * Networks
    * Protocols
    * Web
  - Modules/Systems
    * Distributed
    * File
    * Information re-trieval
    * Multimedia
    * Object databases
    * Operating
    * Relational databases
    * Servers (e.g., audio, video)
    * User interfaces
    * Warehouses

Figure 1.29: Taxonomy of digital libraries terms, part 2. Adapted from [108].

Socio-economic/Legal Issues

- **Qualities**
  - Accessibility
  - Interoperability
  - Maintainability
  - Scalability
  - Sustainability
  - Usability

- **Policies**
  - Billing/Charging
    * Pay-per-view
    * Subscriptions
  - Copyright
  - Intellectual property (IP)
  - Multilingual access
  - Privacy
  - Rights management, licensing
  - Security
    * Authentication
    * Authorization
    * Trusting
  - Special-needs access

- **Standards**
  - Access
  - Archiving
  - Descriptions
  - Operation
  - Storage
  - Transmission

Environment

- **Academic disciplines**
  - Agriculture
  - Anthropology
  - Archaeology
  - Archival science
  - Business
    * Copyright law
    * Economics
    * Management
    * Marketing
    * Publishing
  - Computer science
    * Databases
    * Graphics
    * HCI
    * Hypertext
    * Information retrieval
    * Multimedia
    * Software engineering
  - Economics
  - Education
  - Engineering
  - Ethnography
  - Humanities
    * Museum sci.
  - Information sci.
  - Law
  - Library science
  - Life science
  - Psychology
  - Philosophy
  - Sociology

- **Purposes**
  - Commercial
  - Education
  - National archive
  - National library
  - Public services
  - Training

- **Scope**
  - Association
  - Company
  - Department
  - Discipline
  - Group
  - Nation
  - Personal
  - State
  - Worldwide

Figure 1.30: Taxonomy of digital libraries terms, part 3. Adapted from [108].

digital community, the building blocks of a digital library society[6]. Communities —e.g., of students, teachers, librarians—interact with digital libraries and use digital libraries to interact, following pre-specified scenarios. Communities can act as a query-generator service, from the point of view of the library, and as a teaching, learning, and support service, from the point of view of other humans and organizations. Communications between actors and among the same and different communities occur through the exchange of streams. Communities of autonomous agents and computers also play roles in digital libraries. They instantiate scenarios upon requests by the actors of a DL. To operate, they need structures of vocabulary and protocols. They act by sending (possibly structured) streams of queries and retrieving streams of results.

Activities: What happens in DLs?   Activities of digital libraries—e.g., abstracting, collecting, creating, disseminating, evaluating, modeling, organizing, personalizing, preserving, requesting, and selecting—all can be described and implemented using scenarios, and occur in the DL setting as a result of actors using services. Furthermore, these activities make and characterize relationships within and between societies, streams, and structures. Each activity happens in a setting, arena, or space. The relationships developed can be seen in the context of larger structures (e.g., social networks [139, 208]).

Components: What constitutes DLs?   Digital libraries can contain repositories of knowledge, information, data, metadata, relationships, logs, annotations, user profiles, and documents. They can be associated with higher-level structuring and organizational materials: term lists (e.g., authority files, dictionaries), classification tools (e.g., subject headings and taxonomies), thesauri, ontologies, and metadata catalogs. These knowledge organization sources are normally applied to collections of digital objects and support a number of services such as metadata-based resource discovery, query expansion with thesauri, hierarchical browsing with classification systems, and ontology-based cross-walks among disparate metadata formats and vocabularies. Finally, DLs are served by a substrate—a foundational complex amalgamation of different combinations of Ss that involves computers, network connections, file and operating systems, user interfaces, communication links, and protocols.

Socio-economic, Legal Aspects: What surrounds the DL?   This facet is mainly related to the societal aspects of the DL and their relationships and interactions, including regulations, measures, and derivatives. It abstracts aspects surrounding the other DL issues and involves policies, economic issues, standards, and qualities. For example, policies may dictate that only certain communities have the right to use specific portions of a collection. Some of these DL issues can be established regarding normative structured documents. Policies and quality control also can be enforced by specific services, for example, authentication, authorization [100], encryption, and specific practices (scenarios) or protocols, which can involve other communication services and serialized streams.

---

[6]Digital communities are formed by actors who interact with a DL, possibly through the same interface paradigm. The actors might belong to distinct social communities of the real world. For instance, a digital community might be instantiated by the adoption of a particular architecture and interface for a DL (e.g., a chat room or MOO). This instantiation is somewhat arbitrary and artificial. Social communities, on the other hand, appear much more naturally as a result of complex social interactions.

Environment: In what contexts are DLs embedded?   The environment involves a set of spaces (e.g., the physical space, or a concept space defined by the words of a natural language) that defines the use and the context of a DL. The environment also involves the society that sets up the DL and uses it. But the environment is also how the DL fits into the structure of community and its organization and dictates the scenarios by which its activities are performed. Those who pursue *Academic Disciplines* define a problem area "per se" and build a rational consensus of ideas and information about the problem that leads to a solution [206]. Thus, they carve out a space for their approaches (e.g., in terms of concepts in a domain language, etc.), and structure some subject knowledge jointly with specific scenarios that define the methods or activities used to solve their specific problems. *Purposes* and *Scope* define types of societies served by the DL and determine a specific library structure.

Extending this work on terms, to consider services, we have developed another taxonomy, perhaps of even greater interest [113]. Please see Table 1.4.

Table 1.4: Taxonomy of digital libraries services. Adapted from [113].

Infrastructure Services			Information Satisfaction Services
Repository-Building		Add Value	
Creational	Preservational		
Acquiring	Conserving	Annotating	Binding
Authoring	Converting	Classifying	Browsing
Cataloging	Copying/Replicating	Clustering	Collaborating
Crawling (focused)	Emulating	Evaluating	Customizing
Describing	Renewing	Extracting	Disseminating
Digitizing	Translating (format)	Indexing	Expanding (query)
Federating		Linking	Federating (search)
Harvesting		Logging	Filtering
Purchasing		Measuring	Personalizing
Submitting		Mining (data/text)	Providing access
Uploading		Publicizing	Recommending
		Rating	Requesting
		Reviewing (peer)	Searching
		Surveying	Visualizing
		Tagging	
		Training (classifier)	
		Translating (language)	

1.9   SUMMARY

Two important efforts in formally defining DLs are the 5S framework [105, 108] and the DELOS Reference Model [35]. The 5S framework uses the notions of streams, structures, spaces, scenarios, and societies to describe essential DL concepts, such as digital object, metadata, collection, and services. These, in turn, are used to define a *minimal* digital library. This definition has been extended to define, among others, an integrated DL (see book 2 in this series and [212]), exploring services in DLs (see Chapter 2 and [212, 214]), and a quality model for DLs (see book 2 and [112]). On the other hand, the DELOS Reference Model emphasizes being exhaustive and listing all possible DL concepts, relating them using concept maps, and then explaining them. In some cases, a deep analysis also has resulted; for example, a formal model of annotations by Agosti and Ferro [4] rigorously defines an annotation and its components.

Thus, this chapter provides both a broad introduction, and a foundation for the following chapters, where the 5S framework is explored at the basic, advanced, and applied levels.

1.10   EXERCISES AND PROJECTS

1. Pick your favorite digital library. Describe it at a high level using the 5S approach.

2. Pick your favorite digital library. Describe what services it provides, using as a partial checklist Table 1.4.

3. Pick your favorite digital library. Describe how it relates to the taxonomy of terms given in Figures 1.8, 1.29, and 1.30.

4. Consider your favorite digital library and Fig. 1.1. What parts of the Information Life Cycle are not supported by that digital library? What other support is provided, outside that digital library, for other parts of the Life Cycle?

5. Elaborate the simple 5S definition of "digital library" given in Section 1.2.1 to include some of the key ideas given in other definitions included.

6. Assume you are to develop a syllabus for a course on digital libraries. Considering Table 1.1, Fig. 1.16, and Table 1.3, make up a draft syllabus.

7. Fig. 1.4 suggests that the WWW is not a digital library. Do you agree? Why or why not? Hint: Consider the constructs discussed in Section 1.5 and the discussion of minimal digital library in Appendix B.

8. Among your areas of interest, pick one where there there is no well known digital library. Considering the discussion in Section 1.3, why might it be a good idea to build such a digital library?

9. Consider the various types of content, such as those given in Fig. 1.7. Pick one you find of greatest interest. If you know of a digital library that supports that type of content, describe what special features it has to support such content. If you know of no such digital library, give some scenarios of how it might operate to fit best with the special characteristics of such content.

10. Research the Open Archives Initiative, using the WWW. Describe, using 5S, at least two metadata repositories that work with OAI-PMH and that have bibliographic content you find of interest.

11. Consider the possibilities of digital libraries that provide a flat view of working with content, as shown in Fig. 1.14. Give two innovative scenarios that describe how people, in different roles, might collaborate on submission, quality enhancement, discovery, and use of information managed by such a digital library.

12. Assume you are to meet with your local government representative and want to give a short but convincing argument showing the importance of support for digital library research. Considering Table 1.2, prepare a short essay that you believe would be most effective.

CHAPTER 2

Exploration

Abstract: Exploring services for digital libraries (DLs) include two major paradigms, browsing and searching, as well as other services such as clustering and visualization. In this chapter, we explain how 5S can be applied to digital libraries, and demonstrate how 5S helps with the design, implementation, and evaluation of exploring services for an integrated archaeological digital library, ETANA-DL. Its integrated browsing and searching can support users in moving seamlessly between browsing and searching, minimizing context switching, and keeping users focused. It also integrates browsing and searching into a single visual interface for DL exploration. We conducted a user study to evaluate ETANA-DL's exploring services and to test our hypotheses.

2.1 INTRODUCTION

Browsing and searching are two major paradigms for exploring DLs. They are often provided by DLs as separate services. Developers commonly see these functions as having different underlying mechanisms, and they follow a functional, rather than a task-oriented approach to interaction design. While exhibiting complementary advantages, neither paradigm alone is adequate for complex information needs (e.g., that lend themselves partially to browsing and partially to searching [180]). Searching is popular because of its ability to identify information quickly. On the other hand, browsing is useful when appropriate search keywords are unavailable to users (e.g., a user may not be certain of what she is looking for until the available options are presented during browsing; certain criteria do not lend well to keyword search; the exact terminology used by the system may not be known). Browsing also is appropriate when a great deal of contextual information is obtained along the navigation path. Therefore, a synergy between searching and browsing is required to support users' information-seeking goals [16, 17, 95, 104, 161]. Accordingly, a panel at the World Wide Web Conference in 2005 brought together experts to discuss the trends in the integration of searching and browsing, and in 1995 there was a panel on "Browsing vs. Search: Can We Find a Synergy?" at the Conference on Human Factors in Computing Systems. More recently, faceted search has been supported by both open source and commercial retrieval systems, and provides a partial synthesis of searching and browsing.

Text mining and visualization techniques provide DLs additional powerful exploring services, with possible beneficial effects on browsing and searching. Our study of the CitiViz system [138], which combines browsing, searching, document clustering, and information visualization, showed its advantages, in user performance and preference, relative to traditional interfaces.

Though many research projects have developed different interaction strategies allowing smooth transition between browsing and searching, to the best of our knowledge, none of them generalize these two predominant exploring services in DLs. Reflecting upon the current state of the art and different types of exploring services for DLs has led us to the following research questions:

1. Are browsing and searching dualistic or can they be converted to each other when certain conditions are met?

2. Can we generalize these DL exploring services within a formal DL framework?

3. Can the formal generalization guide development of exploring services for domain focused DLs?

To address the above mentioned questions, we

1. Generalize DL exploring services such as browsing, searching, clustering, and visualization in the context of the 5S DL theory (see Chapter 1 and [105, 108]) and develop theorems and lemmas (see Appendix D) based on the formal generalization.

2. Prove that browsing and searching can be converted and mapped to each other under certain conditions based on the theorems and lemmas developed.

3. Use an integrated archaeological DL, ETANA-DL [192, 213], as a case study to illustrate the application of our theoretical approach. We conducted a user study to evaluate ETANA-DL's exploring services. We found that users significantly prefer to integrate browsing and searching.

To the best of our knowledge, we were the first to approach DL exploring services based on a DL theory. Studying DL exploring from this viewpoint has provided several insights. For instance, the formalisms bring a theoretical approach to the subject and the theorems we developed indicate browsing and searching can be converted and switched to each other under certain conditions. In addition, the theoretical approach provides a systematic and functional method to design and implement DL exploring services.

We believe our work has made contributions to aid both users and developers of DLs. For users, fluidity between browsing and searching supports them in achieving their information-seeking goals, thus helping bridge their mental model of an/the information space with the information systems representation. For DL developers, we suggest some new possibilities for blurring the dividing line between browsing and searching. If these two services are not considered to have different underlying mechanisms, they will not be provided as separate functions in DLs, and may be better integrated.

The remainder of this chapter is structured as follows. Section 2 discusses related work. Section 3 describes the exploring services for our archaeological DL, developed based on the theorems and lemmas in Appendix D. Summaries are outlined in Section 4.

2.2   RELATED WORK

The idea of integrating searching and browsing can be found in some early systems in the 1980s, such as I3R [52] and RABBIT [247]. Though I3R had that idea, it did not implement it. While affording compelling browsing experiences, the interface to a database provided by RABBIT is based on the paradigm of retrieval by reformulation.

About 10 years after RABBIT and I3R appeared, searching and browsing integration resurfaced in many efforts, such as PESTO [37] and DataWeb [162]. PESTO integrated browsing and querying via a "query-in-place" paradigm for exploring the contents of object databases. It allowed a user to issue a query relative to the point that her navigation had reached. However, PESTO was not equipped for browsing semi-structured data.

Navigation is the primary mode for DataWeb to interact with the database. DataWeb viewed navigation as a process of query rewriting and query refinement. One can browse or search to attain a different hierarchy at any point while interacting with the DataWeb system. While in this context queries induce hierarchies, there is also an initial set of pre-existing hierarchies available as exemplars for a user to browse prior to querying. Thus, a user may begin an information-seeking activity in the DataWeb system with a query, or browse an extant hierarchy.

Typically, XML data elements are nested, making XML documents conducive to browsing hierarchically. Thus, interactively blending browsing and querying of XML is quite natural. The MIX project [165] provided virtual (i.e., non-materialized) integrated views of distributed XML sources and facilitated the interleaved browsing and querying of the views at both the front-end level and the programmatic level. At the front-end level it provided the BBQ GUI [166], which adopted PESTO's feature of "query-in-place." At the programmatic level MIX provided an API called QDOM (Querible Document Object Model) supporting interleaved querying and browsing of virtual XML views, specified in an XQuery-like language. The navigation commands are a subset of the navigation commands of the standard DOM API. QDOM allowed an "in-place-query" to be issued from any node in the result of previous queries. The query generates a new "answer" object from which a new series of navigation commands may start.

Though searching and browsing integration were embraced in the database area as shown in some projects mentioned above, the combined paradigm is exhibited by Web users during their information-seeking, and presented in many research efforts such as AMIT [258], WebGlimpse [160], ScentTrails [180], and SenseMaker [12]. AMIT (Animated Multiscale Interactive TreeViewer) [258] is a Java applet that integrates fisheye tree browsing with search and filtering techniques. WebGlimpse [160] allowed the search to be limited to a neighborhood of the current document.

ScentTrails [180] annotated the hyperlinks of retrieved Web pages with search cues: indications that a link leads to content that matches the search query. The annotation was done by visually highlighting links to complement the browsing cues (textual or graphical indications of the content reachable via a link) already embedded in each page.

SenseMaker [12] increased the fluidity between browsing and searching DLs by introducing structured-based filtering and structured-based searching. In SenseMaker, a user issued a query and aggregated the retrieved results into bundles by a "bundling criterion" (e.g., "same author"). Structured-based filtering allowed users to focus on selected bundles and to employ structure to limit a collection of results quickly and at a high level of granularity. The structured-based searching involves growing selected bundles or adding related bundles. Searching by growing selected bundles involves formulating a query that describes the "template" bundles and then issuing that new query. Therefore, the "template" bundles can be viewed as surrogates of queries. Searching by adding related bundles involves identifying the key characteristics of the selected bundles, accessing an external source (e.g., a classification scheme) that records relationships among these characteristics, and issuing a query for items with newly defined characteristics.

Web browsing experience has been used to improve Web search application by Yahoo! and Google. Users' browsing history can be interpreted by the clickthrough logs, which are a large and important source of user behavior information. This feedback provides detailed and valuable information about users' interactions with the system as the issued query, the retrieved documents and their ranking.

Though many research projects have developed different interaction strategies allowing smooth transition between browsing and searching, to the best of our knowledge, none of them generalize these two predominant exploring services in DLs. In Appendix D, we show that related works like those above can be viewed as cases of our theoretical approach. We formalize the DL exploring services in the context of the 5S DL theory (see Chapter 1 and [105, 108]) in Appendix C; then in Appendix D, we prove that, when certain conditions are met, searching and browsing are duals; thus, mapping or conversions between them are readily supported.

2.3 CASE STUDY: EXPLORING SERVICES IN ETANA-DL

Our theory-based approach to describing DL exploring services allows us to understand browsing and searching in a new way. It guided us to design and implement exploring services for an archaeo-logical DL, ETANA-DL. ETANA-DL is an integrated archaeological DL supporting integration of a number of (ETANA) sites in the Near East. It integrates searching and browsing, allowing users to browse at will and shift between browsing and searching seamlessly. It also provides a visual interface applying data analysis and information visualization techniques to help archaeologists test hypothe-ses and extend the understanding of past (material) cultures and environments. In this section, we first introduce a multi-dimensional browsing service, which can actually be considered as a search-ing service according to Lemma 2 in Appendix D. We then illustrate how ETANA-DL combines browsing and searching in two ways. The first way extends and empowers the multi-dimensional browsing. It can be viewed as query refining and extension based on Lemma 3 in Appendix D. Organizing searching results hierarchically is the second way. Both ways allow seamless transition between browsing and searching, as suggested by Lemma 4 in Appendix D. We finally describe the visualization service, which integrates browsing and searching into a single visual interface, as suggested by Theorem 4 in Appendix D.

2.3.1   MULTI-DIMENSIONAL BROWSING

Multi-dimensional browsing allows users to move along any of the navigational dimensions, or a combination thereof. By navigational dimension we mean a hierarchical structure used to browse digital objects. Digital objects in ETANA-DL are various archaeological data, e.g., figurine images, bone records, locus sheets, and site plans. They are organized by different hierarchical structures (e.g., animal bone records are organized based on sites where they are excavated, temporal sequence, and animal names). These hierarchical structures contain one or more hierarchically arranged categories that are determined by the elements of the global schema of ETANA-DL. In addition to this, they can be refined based on taxonomies existing in botany and zoology, or from classification and description of artifacts by archaeologists.

You are in: Main >> SITE=Bab edh-Dhra >> PARTITION=A >> SUBPARTITION=056   Save this Navigation Path

Search within this context for [＿＿＿＿＿＿] Go

View Records for the Context Below

Browse by space:: SITE=Bab edh-Dhra::PARTITION=A::SUBPARTITION=056:: LOCUS
  Unclassified

Browse by object:: :: OBJECTTYPE
  Pottery

Browse by time:: :: Period
  EARLY BRONZE II   EARLY BRONZE III

Figure 2.1: Multi-dimensional browsing interface [212, 214].

Typical DLs provide a directory-style browsing interface (as in Open Directory), with levels in the hierarchy displayed as clickable category names and DL items in that category shown below them. Though some DLs (such as CITIDEL [79, 84, 130, 138, 183]) allow users to browse through several dimensions, they are limited in that users cannot navigate through all dimensions simultaneously, or across different dimensions.

In ETANA-DL, a user can browse through three dimensions: space, object, and time. She can start from any of these dimensions and move along by clicking. The scenario shown in Fig. 2.1 tells that she is interested in the artifact records from the tomb numbered 056 in area A of the Bab edh-Dhra site. The clickstream representing her navigation path is denoted '$Site = Babedh - Dhra \gg PARTITION = A \gg SUPARTITION = 056$'. While the navigation path is within the first dimension, it is associated with the other dimensions. The second dimension shows there is only one

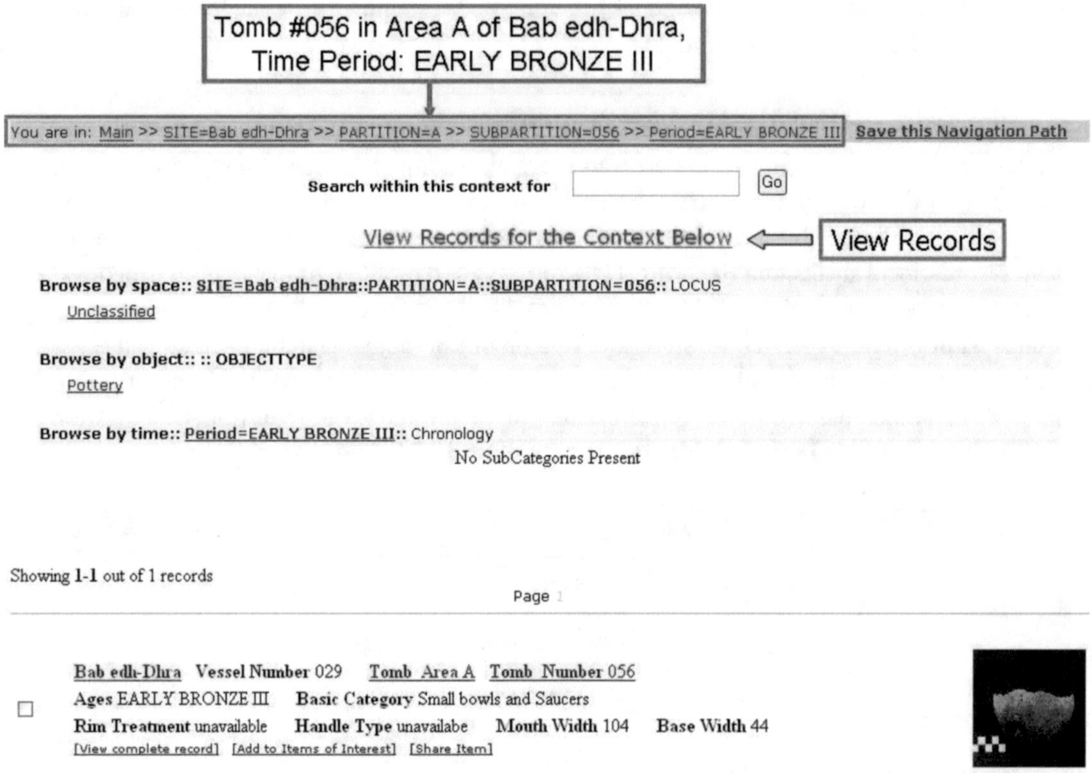

┌─────────────────────────────────────┐
│   Tomb #056 in Area A of Bab edh-Dhra, │
│   Time Period: EARLY BRONZE III   │
└─────────────────────────────────────┘

You are in: Main >> SITE=Bab edh-Dhra >> PARTITION=A >> SUBPARTITION=056 >> Period=EARLY BRONZE III | Save this Navigation Path

Search within this context for [   ] [Go]

View Records for the Context Below ⟸ [View Records]

Browse by space:: SITE=Bab edh-Dhra::PARTITION=A::SUBPARTITION=056:: LOCUS
  Unclassified

Browse by object:: :: OBJECTTYPE
  Pottery

Browse by time:: Period=EARLY BRONZE III:: Chronology
                        No SubCategories Present

Showing 1-1 out of 1 records
                          Page 1

☐   Bab edh-Dhra Vessel Number 029   Tomb Area A Tomb Number 056
    Ages EARLY BRONZE III   Basic Category Small bowls and Saucers
    Rim Treatment unavailable   Handle Type unavailabe   Mouth Width 104   Base Width 44
    [View complete record] [Add to Items of Interest] [Share Item]

Figure 2.2: Save current navigation path for later use and view records [212, 214].

type of objects, i.e., pottery, from that particular location. The third dimension presents the two time periods associated with those pottery records. Hence, the dynamic coverage and hierarchical structure of those dimensions yields a learning and exploration tool. The user can navigate across dimensions. By clicking "EARLY BRONZE II" in the third dimension, she can view all her interested artifact records from the EARLY BRONZE II period. Her current navigation path (see the top of Fig. 2.2) can be saved for later use. It can be considered as a surrogate for a query for the records in that particular location and time period. Therefore, according to Lemma 2 in Appendix D, the multi-dimensional browsing service can be viewed as searching, i.e., $browsing \Rightarrow searching$.

2.3.2   BROWSING AND SEARCHING INTEGRATION

1. Search within browsing context

Searching within a browsing context blends querying and browsing and is reminiscent of IBM's PESTO GUI for "in-place querying" [37]. The main idea is that browsing will present a useful starting point for active exploration of an answer space. Subsequent browsing and searching is employed to refine or enhance users' initial, possibly under-specified, information needs.

Browsing context is associated with a user's navigation path. "Browsing results" within a certain browsing context is defined as a set of records (Web pages), e.g., there are 35 pottery records within the browsing context represented by the navigation path '$Site = Babedh - Dhra \gg PARTITION = A \gg SUPARTITION = 056$'. Assume a user wants to find saucer records in the set of 35 pottery records. She types "saucer" in the search box as shown in Fig. 2.3. According to Lemma 3 in Appendix D, she switches from browsing to searching, and searching then is a natural extension of browsing. Since the navigation path is a surrogate of a query, searching within a browsing context can be viewed as query refining.

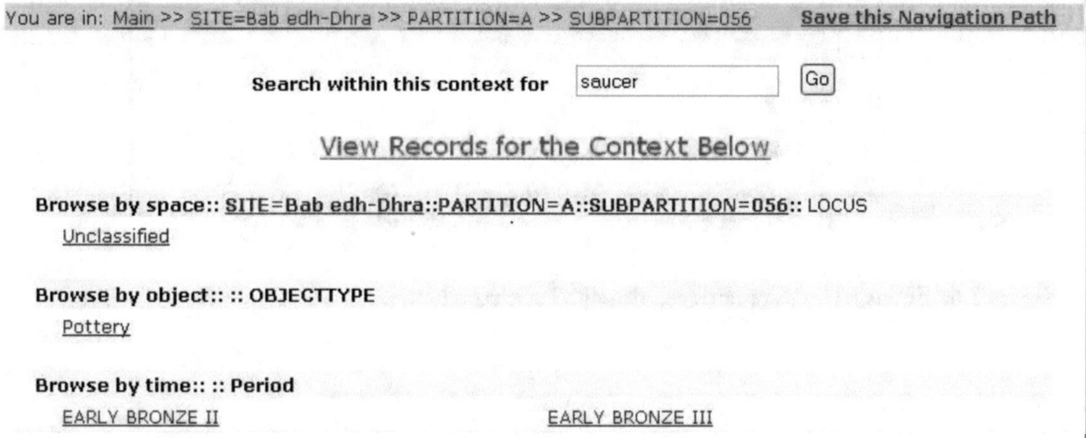

You are in: Main >> SITE=Bab edh-Dhra >> PARTITION=A >> SUBPARTITION=056   **Save this Navigation Path**

Search within this context for   saucer   Go

View Records for the Context Below

Browse by space:: SITE=Bab edh-Dhra::PARTITION=A::SUBPARTITION=056:: LOCUS
   Unclassified

Browse by object:: :: OBJECTTYPE
   Pottery

Browse by time:: :: Period
   EARLY BRONZE II   EARLY BRONZE III

Figure 2.3: Search saucer records [212, 214].

2. Organize searching results hierarchically

Eighty eight equus records are retrieved through the basic searching service (see a query named "equus" in Fig. 2.4). They are organized into three dimensions after the user clicks the button "View search results hierarchically" (see Fig. 2.5). The user starts browsing and then selects "Nimrin" in the first category to view the records. Thirty-six equus records are displayed as shown in Fig. 2.6. According to Lemma 4 in Appendix D, she switches from searching to browsing. During the next exploring stage of browsing, she can search as illustrated in the previous section. Therefore, she switches seamlessly between browsing and searching, to specify her information needs.

2.3.3   BROWSING, SEARCHING, AND VISUALIZATION INTEGRATION

While the searching and browsing services provided by ETANA-DL allow users to access primary archaeological data, their help with comprehending specific archaeological DL phenomena is limited

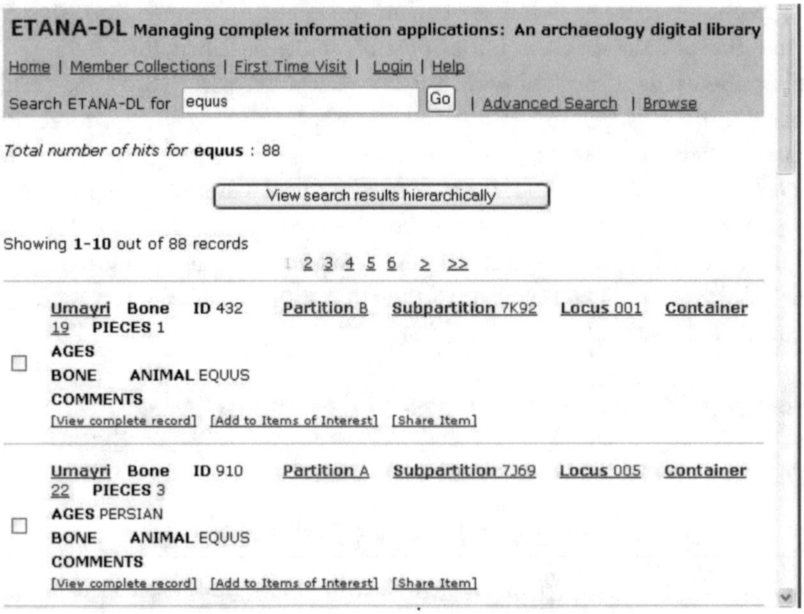

Figure 2.4: Equus records are retrieved through basic searching [212, 214].

when vast quantities of data are harvested into ETANA-DL. Fortunately, visual interfaces to DLs enable powerful data analysis and information visualization techniques to help archaeologists test hypotheses and extend the understanding of past (material) cultures and environments. Data generated from the sites interpretation then provides a basis for future work, including publication, museum displays, and, in due course, input into future project planning. Thus, we developed EtanaGIS and EtanaViz to support visually exploring archaeological DLs. EtanaGIS allows integration of Geographic Information System (GIS) data for related archaeological sites into ETANA-DL. It provides a Web-based GIS portal to allow users to spatially explore ETANA-DL.

In this section, we focus on EtanaViz. It integrates searching, browsing, clustering, and visualization into a single interface. Its initial interface is shown in Fig. 2.7. The top left of the screen is a query box. On the top right is a hyperbolic tree showing hierarchical relationships among excavation data based on spatial, temporal, and artifact-related taxonomies. A node name represents a category, and a bubble attached to a node represents a set of archaeological records. The size of a bubble attached to a node reflects the number of records belonging to that category. The hyperbolic tree supports "focus + context" navigation; it also provides an overview of records organized in ETANA-DL. It shows that the records are from seven archaeological sites (the Megiddo site has the most) and are of eight different types.

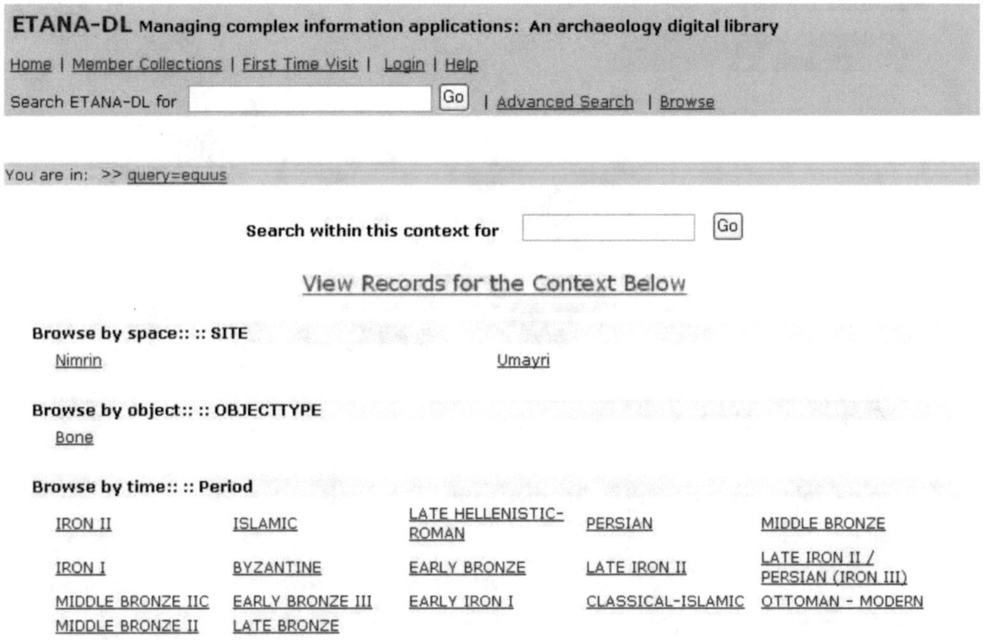

ETANA-DL Managing complex information applications: An archaeology digital library

Home | Member Collections | First Time Visit | Login | Help

Search ETANA-DL for [_____] [Go] | Advanced Search | Browse

You are in: >> query=equus

Search within this context for [_____] [Go]

View Records for the Context Below

Browse by space:: :: SITE

Nimrin   Umayri

Browse by object:: :: OBJECTTYPE

Bone

Browse by time:: :: Period

IRON II	ISLAMIC	LATE HELLENISTIC-ROMAN	PERSIAN	MIDDLE BRONZE
IRON I	BYZANTINE	EARLY BRONZE	LATE IRON II	LATE IRON II / PERSIAN (IRON III)
MIDDLE BRONZE IIC	EARLY BRONZE III	EARLY IRON I	CLASSICAL-ISLAMIC	OTTOMAN - MODERN
MIDDLE BRONZE II	LATE BRONZE			

Figure 2.5: Retrieved equus records are organized into 3 dimensions [212, 214].

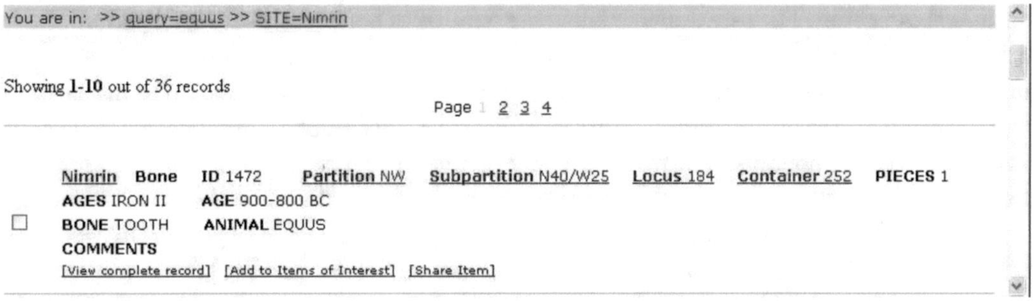

You are in: >> query=equus >> SITE=Nimrin

Showing **1-10** out of 36 records

Page 1 **2 3 4**

Nimrin Bone ID 1472 **Partition** NW **Subpartition** N40/W25 **Locus** 184 **Container** 252 **PIECES** 1
AGES IRON II **AGE** 900-800 BC
☐ **BONE** TOOTH **ANIMAL** EQUUS
COMMENTS
[View complete record] [Add to Items of Interest] [Share Item]

Figure 2.6: Browse the 36 equus records from the Nimrin site after searching [212, 214].

According to Def. AR.C.2 in Appendix C, a cluster (group) of records is associated with a vector of two elements, i.e., name and size of the cluster; a cluster is mapped to a visual mark: bubble (circle); the name and size of the cluster are mapped to two visual properties: label and size of the bubble, respectively. EtanaViz supports exploring to gain insights, as is illustrated in the following example scenarios.

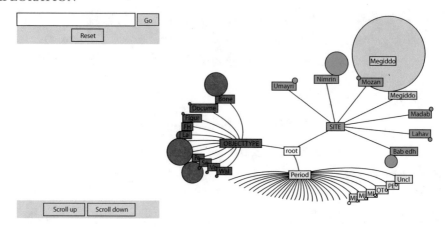

Figure 2.7: Initial interface of EtanaViz. Adapted from [212, 214].

A user is interested in excavated animal bones from site Nimrin, located in the Jordan Valley. She inputs query "SITE=Nimrin & OBJECTTYPE=Bone." The results are displayed as a hyperbolic tree, as illustrated in Fig. 2.8. All excavation bone records are grouped into cultural phases (time periods). They are Middle Bronze, Iron I, Iron II, Persian, Late Hellenistic/Roman, Byzantine, Islamic, and Ottoman-Modern. The records also are classified by archaeological site organization and animal categories. The user wants to know the number of bone records for each period. She left clicks a node labeled "MIDDLE BRONZE" in the hyperbolic tree and selects the "add to compare" option to view total bones throughout the Middle Bronze Age. This causes a bar to be displayed in a chart below the hyperbolic tree and an entry to be listed on the left. She continues to add more bars to view bones throughout the entire time sequence of Tell Nimrin occupation. When she moves the mouse over a bar, a tool tip shows the number of animal bones for the corresponding culture phase.

She continues navigating the hyperbolic tree. She left clicks a node labeled "SUS" and selects the "add to view distribution" option. She then left clicks the "BOS," "CAPRA," and "OVIS" nodes to show how those animal bones constitute the identified bones in each culture phrase. Eight stacked bars representing percentages of those bones are displayed, and four entries with different colors are included in the list on the left of the screen (see Fig. 2.9).

The color of the entry can be changed to help distinguish different categories. It is always synchronized with the color in the stacked bars. The red bars (at the bottom of the stacked bars), representing sus (pig) bones, show that sus constitute 4.71% of the Middle Bronze Age faunal assemblage, but less than 1% at the beginning of the Iron Age. The user is wondering why the percentage for pig bones drops dramatically over time at Tell Nimrin. She may hypothesize that the reasons are probably twofold: 1) the introduction of religious taboos against eating pork, and 2) increased demand for clean water sources as human populations grew at Nimrin [244].

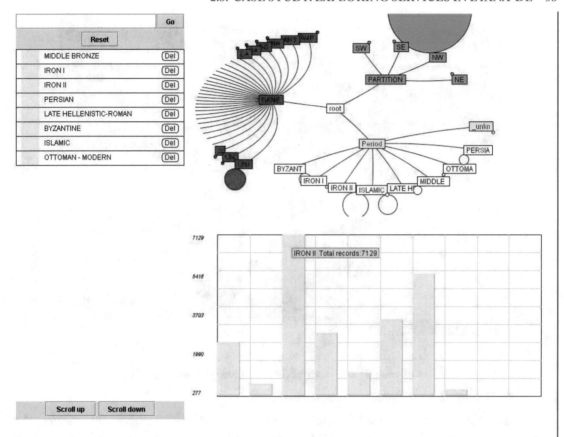

Figure 2.8: Total number of animal bones across Nimrin culture phrases [212, 214].

Light blue bars (on top of the red sus bars) represent bos (cattle) bones percentages. Two light blue bars are higher than the others. They are corresponding to the Iron II and Late Hellenistic/Roman culture phrases, respectively. The user, considering that cattle figure most prominently during these periods, may suggest improved grazing conditions in the Jordan Valley during that time.

Pink bars and blue bars (the top two of the stacked bars) represent ovis (sheep) bones and capra (goat) bones, respectively. Pink bars are slightly higher than blue bars. This means that ovis bones slightly outnumber capra bones across culture phrases of Tell Nimrin. This would suggest that past environmental conditions in the Jordan Valley provided enhanced forage for sheep while goats would have been employed as browsers on drier vegetation. Relatively stable percentages of slightly higher sheep populations versus those of goats may indicate that favorable environmental conditions and environmental or cultural desertification did not greatly impact the agrarian way of life at Tell Nimrin on the banks of the Jordan, over time [244].

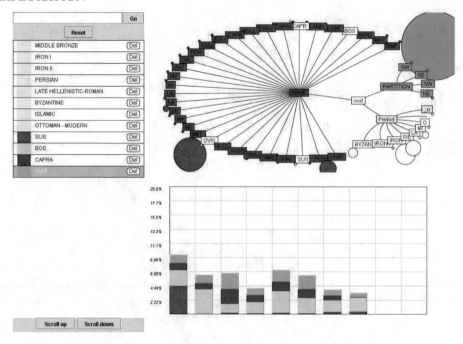

Figure 2.9:   Percentages of animal bones across Nimrin culture phrases [212, 214].

The user may be interested in animal bones excavated from other sites. By repeating the interaction with EtanaViz, as described before, she starts to analyze animal bones excavated from the Umayri site. She also can make inter-site comparisons.

2.3.4   ETANA-DL EXPLORING SERVICES FORMATIVE EVALUATION

In fall 2005, we conducted a formative user study for ETANA-DL. Many of the findings reported in the usability evaluation influenced the iterative design and implementation of ETANA-DL, aimed to achieve usability goals. In this section, instead of listing all the findings, we focus on findings that help validate the hypotheses related to browsing, searching, and visualization. When browsing service can be mapped to searching ($browsing \Rightarrow searching$), saved navigation paths can be viewed as searching history (which keeps track of user's information needs and helps reduce time and effort to achieve information seeking goals).

1. Evaluation methods and procedure

Twenty-eight graduate students from the computer science department at Virginia Tech participated in the evaluation experiment, which was posted with instructions online. The experiment was conducted through four sessions. Each user was required to:

- learn the online tutorial of ETANA-DL;

- complete a pre-evaluation questionnaire;

- perform tasks using ETANA-DL. After completion of each task, he (she) was asked to fill out a task-related questionnaire and give comments.

- provide subjective reactions using post-evaluation survey forms.

Users' interactions with ETANA-DL were logged by that system. The time to complete each task and the error rate for each task were measured automatically. At the completion of all the tasks, users were asked to rate the exploring services on a 5-point scale, where 1=poor, and 5=excellent. Our reason for measuring users' impressions about ETANA-DL services (five of them are listed in Table 2.1) stems from the following two pre-experimental hypotheses:

- Users significantly prefer integrated browsing and searching to browsing.

- Users significantly prefer integrated browsing and searching to searching.

2. Results and discussion

The median values for measuring users' impressions regarding five of the ETANA-DL services are shown in Table 2.1. Browsing, searching, and EtanaViz received four points on a 5-point scale, while searching within browsing context (abbreviated as SWBC) and saving navigation path (abbreviated as SNP) services received 4.5. Users commented that they appreciated SWBC and SNP because "SWBC is simple enough to understand and an excellent way of narrowing down a search …browsing through the different levels can be time consuming, so if we know that we will want to go to a given context a lot, it is useful to just be able to click on a link of SNP to get back to our context of interest …."

Table 2.1: Impression about ETANA-DL services (mean value). Adapted from [212, 214].

Browse	Search	EtanaViz	SNP	SWBC
4.0	4.0	4.0	4.5	4.5

We also did t-tests on the following four hypotheses:

- H1: Impression about SWBC is larger than that for browsing at significance level 0.05.

- H2: Impression about SWBC is larger than that for searching at significance level 0.05.

- H3: Impression about SNP is larger than that for browsing at significance level 0.05.

- H4: Impression about SNP is larger than that for searching at significance level 0.05.

The above four hypotheses were all accepted. The first two accepted hypotheses are associated with the two pre-experimental hypotheses mentioned above, i.e., users significantly prefer integrated browsing and searching to browsing (or to searching). To probe the last two hypotheses, we analyzed four of the seventeen tasks performed by users. For four tasks, users were asked to give the number of records retrieved, for specific information needs. The followings are those four tasks.

1. Use browsing to give the total number of pottery records excavated from tomb 007 in area A of the Bab edh-Dhra site.

2. Use searching to tell how many equus bones are from the Umayri site.

3. Use browsing to tell how many equus bones are from the Nimrin site.

4. Use saved navigation paths to give the total number of pottery records excavated from tomb 056 in area A of the Bab edh-Dhra site.

Fig. 2.10 shows the average time for each of the four tasks.

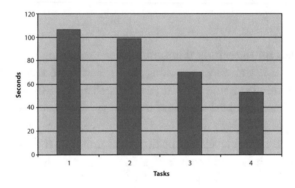

Figure 2.10:   Average time on tasks. Adapted from [212, 214].

Task 4 was completed significantly faster than either task 1 or task 2, at significance level 0.05. This showed that reusing saved navigation paths really improves users' performance. It saved users time during exploration. While similar information needs (e.g., task 1, 2, and 4) can be achieved through different ways (browsing, searching, or SNP), SNP keeps track of users' navigation history and helps reduce time and effort to achieve information seeking goals.

We expected that users would complete task 4 significantly faster than task 3. We also thought users would spend about the same time to complete the similar tasks, i.e., task 2 and task 3. However, our experimental results were somewhat surprising in that the average time on task 4 was not significantly less than that on task 3, and the average time on tasks 2 and task 3 was different. We did some follow-up interviews to probe the reasons. Our log file indicated that one user spent more than five minutes to complete task 4. We found that he was disconnected during the online experiment for task 4. Though task 2 and task 3 have similar information needs, users found it was difficult to find appropriate keywords to complete task 2, therefore, more time was needed to try more queries. We believe that since users gained experience and developed a searching strategy when doing task 2, they completed task 3 faster than task 2 (task 3 was performed after task 2).

Because our new service to organize searching results hierarchically was not implemented before we conducted the evaluation, we cannot yet report data about its efficiency and effectiveness. However, there is already evidence that information access is improved by posting search hits against an interactive tree structure [66, 67].

2.4   SUMMARY

Exploring services for digital libraries (DLs) include two major paradigms, browsing and searching, as well as other services such as clustering and visualization. We explain how 5S can be applied to digital libraries, in two ways. First, it covers the most important services of digital libraries: browsing, searching, discovery, and visualization. Second, 5S helped with the design, implementation, and evaluation of an integrated archaeological digital library, ETANA-DL.

2.5   EXERCISES AND PROJECTS

1. How does faceted search fit in with the integration of searching and browsing?

2. In addition to searching, browsing, clustering, and visualization, what other services and/or technologies might fit well as part of exploring? Why? How?

3. Multi-dimensional browsing was supported by ETANA-DL. What other application domain might benefit likewise? In such a case, what would the dimensions be, and how might they relate to each other?

4. Archaeology was used for the case study discussed in this chapter. What other application domain might similarly be served by a DL with services like those used to help with ETANA? How?

5. Consider the organization of results illustrated in Fig. 2.5. Consider a search in your favorite Web browser, with your favorite search system, for information about a recent event. How might the results be best organized, in a similar manner to what is shown in Fig. 2.5? What dimensions would you use? Why?

6. In Section 2.3.3, the use of a hyperbolic tree in EtanaViz was explained. What other visualization method might be used instead? Why? How? If your method was compared, through a user study, with a hyperbolic tree, which might give better results? For which types of tasks?

7. According to Table 2.1, some users like having browsing and searching integrated. Please explain why you think that might be. What do you think are the most important features of such an integration, that would lead to the most favorable impact?

8. What research or commercial system that you have worked with has the best integration of searching and browsing? Why do you think so? How does the integration work? How might it be improved further based on what you have learned in this chapter?

9. 5S can be used to describe digital libraries. Please give a 5S-oriented description of the support discussed in this chapter for archaeology. Be sure to cover each of the Ss separately, first. Then, consider combinations of pairs or triples of Ss too, as seems appropriate.

APPENDIX A

Mathematical Preliminaries

In this appendix, we briefly review the mathematical foundations necessary for this book. Since the goal is precision, all terms used in definitions must be carefully and unambiguously defined. Authors' definitions of terms even as basic as "function" often disagree, so (for completeness) we begin at the most fundamental level, with set notations, relations, functions, sequences, tuples, strings, graphs, and grammars [48]. Readers familiar with these concepts can skip this appendix or simply refer to it as needed when some of the concepts are used in other definitions.

Formally, *set* and $\in$ ("element of") are taken as undefined terms in the axioms of set theory. We remark that a set cannot contain itself and that the "set of all sets" does not exist. That x is an element of set S is denoted $x \in S$. There is an "empty" set ($\emptyset$). The notation $S = \{x \mid P(x)\}$ defines a set S of precisely those objects x for which the logical proposition $P(x)$ is true. Standard operations between sets A and B include union: $A \cup B = \{x \mid x \in A \text{ or } x \in B\}$; intersection: $A \cap B = \{x \mid x \in A \text{ and } x \in B\}$; and Cartesian product: $A \times B = \{(a, b) \mid a \in A \text{ and } b \in B\}$ where (a, b) is called an *ordered pair*. A is called a *subset* of B, denoted by $A \subset B$, if $x \in A$ implies $x \in B$. The set of all subsets of set S (including $\emptyset$) exists, is called the *power set* of S, and is denoted 2^S.

PR A.1   A binary **relation** R on sets A and B is a subset of $A \times B$. We sometimes write $(a, b) \in R$ as aRb. An n-ary relation R on sets $A_1, A_2, ..., A_n$ is a subset of the Cartesian product $A_1 \times A_2 \times ... \times A_n$.

PR A.2   Given two sets A and B, a **function** f is a binary relation on $A \times B$ such that for each $a \in A$ there exists $b \in B$ such that $(a, b) \in f$, and if $(a, b) \in f$ and $(a, c) \in f$ then $b = c$. The set A is called the domain of f and the set B is called the codomain of f. This is shown as $f : A \to B$. We write $b = f(a)$ as a common notation for $(a, b) \in f$. The set $\{f(a) \mid a \in A\}$ is called the range of f.

PR A.3   A **sequence** is a function f whose domain is the set of natural numbers or some initial subset $\{1, 2, ..., n\}$ of the natural numbers and whose codomain is any set.

PR A.4   A **tuple** is a finite sequence that is often denoted by listing the range values of the function as $\langle f(1), f(2), ..., f(n) \rangle$.

PR A.5   A **string** is a finite sequence of characters or symbols drawn from a finite set with at least two elements, called an **alphabet**. A string is often denoted by concatenating range values without punctuation. Let Σ be an alphabet. Σ^* denotes the set of all strings from Σ, including the empty string (an empty sequence ϵ). A **language** is a subset of Σ^*.

PR A.6   A **graph** G is a pair (V, E), where V is a nonempty set (whose elements are called **vertices**) and E is a set of two-item sets of vertices, $\{u, v\}, u, v \in V$, called **edges**. A **directed graph** (or digraph) G is a pair (V, E), where V is a nonempty set of vertices (or nodes) and E is a set of edges (or arcs) where each edge is an ordered pair of distinct vertices (v_i, v_j), with $v_i, v_j \in V$ and $v_i \neq v_j$. The edge (v_i, v_j) is said to be **incident** on vertices v_i and v_j, in which case v_i is **adjacent to** v_j, and v_j is **adjacent from** v_i.

Several additional concepts are associated with graphs. A **walk** in graph G is a sequence of not-necessarily distinct vertices such that for every adjacent pair $v_i, v_{i+1}, 1 \leq i < n$, in the sequence, $(v_i, v_{i+1}) \in E$. We call v_1 the origin of the walk and v_n the terminus. The **length** of the walk is the number of edges that it contains. If the edges of the walk are distinct, the walk is a **trail**. If the vertices are distinct, the walk is a **path**. A walk is **closed** if $v_1 = v_n$ and the walk has positive length. A **cycle** is a closed walk where the origin and non-terminal vertices are distinct. A graph is **acyclic** if it has no cycles. A graph is **connected** if there is a path from any vertex to any other vertex in the graph. A **tree** is a connected, acyclic graph. A **directed tree** or (DAG) is a connected, directed graph where one vertex—called the root—is adjacent from no vertices and all other vertices are adjacent from exactly one vertex. A graph $G' = (V', E')$ is a **subgraph** of $G = (V, E)$, if $V' \subseteq V$ and $E' \subseteq E$.

PR A.7   A **context-free grammar** is a quadruple (V, Σ, R, s_0) where V is a finite set of symbols called non-terminals, Σ is an alphabet of terminal symbols, R is a finite set of rules, and s_0 is a distinguished element of V called the **start** symbol.

A **rule**, also called a production, is an element of the set $V \times (V \cup \Sigma)^*$. Each production is of the form $A \rightarrow \alpha$ where A is a non-terminal and α is a string of symbols (terminals and/or non-terminals).

PR A.8   A **deterministic finite automaton** is a 5-tuple $(Q, q_0, A, \Sigma, \delta)$ where Q is a finite set of symbols called *states*, $q_0 \in Q$ is the **start** automaton state, $A \subseteq Q$ is a distinguished set of accepting states, Σ is an alphabet (defining what set of input strings the automaton operates on), and δ is a function from $Q \times \Sigma$ into Q, called the transition function of the automaton.

The finite automaton begins in state q_0 and reads characters of an input string one at a time. If after reading the string the automaton is in a state $q \in A$ the string is **accepted**.

PR A.9   Let X be a set. A σ-**algebra** is a collection $\mathbb{B}$ of subsets of X that satisfies the following conditions:

1. every union of a countable collection of sets in $\mathbb{B}$ is again in $\mathbb{B}$, *i.e.*, if $A_i \in \mathbb{B}$ ($i = 1, 2, 3, \ldots$), then $\bigcup_{i=1}^{\infty} A_i \in \mathbb{B}$;

2. if $A \in \mathbb{B}$, then $\tilde{A} \in \mathbb{B}$, where $\tilde{A}$ is the complement of A with respect to X.

One consequence of the definition of σ-algebra is that the intersection of a countable collection of sets in $\mathbb{B}$ is again in $\mathbb{B}$.

PR A.10 A **measurable space** is a tuple $(X, \mathbb{B})$ consisting of a set X and a σ-algebra $\mathbb{B}$ of subsets of X.

A subset A of X is called *measurable* (or *measurable with respect to* $\mathbb{B}$) if $A \in \mathbb{B}$. A *measure* μ on measurable space $(X, \mathbb{B})$ is a nonnegative real-valued function defined for all sets of $\mathbb{B}$ such that the following conditions are satisfied:

1. $\mu(\emptyset) = 0$ where $\emptyset$ is the empty set, and

2. $\mu\left(\bigcup_{i=1}^{\infty} A_i\right) = \Sigma_{i=1}^{\infty} \mu(A_i)$ for any sequence A_i of pairwise disjoint measurable sets.

PR A.11 A **measure space** $(X, \mathbb{B}, \mu)$ is a measurable space $(X, \mathbb{B})$, with measure μ defined on $\mathbb{B}$.

PR A.12 A **probability space** is a measure space $(X, \mathbb{B}, \mu)$, such that measure $\mu(X) = 1$.

PR A.13 A **vector space** is a set V (whose elements are called **vectors**) together with a field S of "scalars" [1] with an addition operation $+ : V \times V \to V$ and a multiplication operation $* : S \times V \to V$ such that if x, y, z are in V and α and β are in S then:

1. there is a unique vector $0 \in V$ such that $x + 0 = x$ for all $x \in V$ (additive identity);

2. for each vector $x \in V$ there exists a vector $-x \in V$ such that $x + (-x) = 0$ (additive inverse);

3. $(x + y) + z = x + (y + z)$ (associativity of $+$);

4. $x + y = y + x$ (commutativity of $+$);

5. $1 * x = x$ (identity);

6. $(\alpha * \beta) * x = \alpha * (\beta * x)$ (associativity of $*$);

7. $(\alpha + \beta) * x = \alpha * x + \beta * x$ (distributivity of $*$ over $+$, right); and

8. $\alpha * (x + y) = \alpha * x + \alpha * y$ (distributivity of $*$ over $+$, left).

[1] In this context, the field of real numbers.

PR A.14   A **topological space** is a pair $(X, \mathcal{T})$ consisting of a set X and a family $\mathcal{T} \subset 2^X$ of subsets of X such that:

1. $\emptyset$ (the empty set) $\in \mathcal{T}$ and $X \in \mathcal{T}$;

2. for any collection of sets in $\mathcal{T}$, $\{A_i \in \mathcal{T} | i \in I\}$, $\cup_{i \in I} A_i$ is also in $\mathcal{T}$, and if the *index set* I is finite, $\cap_{i \in I} A_i$ is in $\mathcal{T}$.

$\mathcal{T}$ is said to be a topology for X, and elements of $\mathcal{T}$ are called **open** sets. The complement of an open set is called a **closed** set.

APPENDIX B

Minimal Digital Library

B.1   5S FORMALIZATION

"DL development must move from an art to a science [and it needs] unifying and comprehensive theories and frameworks across the lifecycle of digital library (DL) information." [132] (p. 266)

In this appendix, we precisely and unambiguously formalize most of the informal digital library concepts introduced in previous parts of this book. Figure B.1 shows a map of the most important concepts and formal definitions. Each concept is associated with the corresponding definition number of its formal definition (e.g., Def. MI B.3 for "state', as given below); arrows indicate that a concept is formally defined in terms of previously defined concepts that point to it[1]. The mathematical preliminaries (Defs. PR A.1–A.14) are found in Appendix A. In the rest of this section we give one important definition (for system state), and provide semi-formal descriptions of many other key concepts related to digital libraries.

Probability studies the possible outcomes of given events (or experiments) together with their relative likelihood and distributions. Probability is defined in terms of a **sample space** S, which is a set whose elements are called **elementary events**. More formally, in terms of a probability space, the set of possible events for an experiment consists of the σ-algebra $\mathbb{B}$ and a sample space is defined as the largest set $S \in \mathbb{B}$. The measure μ is called a probability distribution.

Probabilistic information retrieval (PIR) takes a more subjective interpretation of probability, called the *bayesian* interpretation, which sees probability as a statistical procedure which endeavors to estimate parameters of an underlying probability distribution based on the observed distribution. In PIR the sample space is the set $Q \times D$ of all possible queries and documents and the probability distribution tries to estimate, given a query $q \in Q$, the probability that a document $d \in D$ will be **relevant** to the query, using any evidence at hand. Normally the words in the documents and in the query are the major sources of evidence. A precise definition of probability of relevance is dependent on the definition of relevance and different PIR models have different interpretations [51].

Vector spaces are the basis for a widely used information retrieval model, the Vector Space Model (VSM) [205]. In this model, a document space D is a vector space where a document $d_i \in D$ is represented by a t-dimensional vector $d_i = (w_{i1}, w_{i2}, ..., w_{it})$, w_{ij} being the weight (a numerical value) of the jth index term t_j of d_i, $w_{ij} \geq 0$. An *index term* is normally a word (or variant), occurring in the text of the document, whose semantics helps in defining the document's

---

[1]The notion of a tuple (Def. PR.A.4) is used in most definitions, so, for simplicity, we are not showing arrows coming out of that concept in Figure B.1. Other popular definitions are treated likewise.

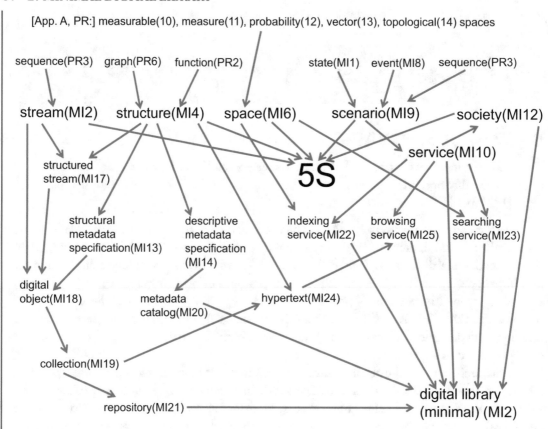

Figure B.1: 5S map of formal definitions. Adapted from [108].

main themes. However, in general, an index term may be any value describing some aspect of the document, such as a feature value (e.g., color, shape, elevation, temperature) or descriptor (e.g., element in a thesaurus or classification system), or concept, or complex linguistic expression (e.g., phrase, entry in a gazetteer). Furthermore, it is possible to use their representation vectors, i.e., their terms and term weights, to define a number of functions such as *degree of similarity* $s : D \times D \to \mathbb{R}$ between documents.

Vector spaces and measure spaces are often built on top of topological spaces, the latter being the more basic concept. Any use of the concept of distance implies an underlying **metric space**, which is a topological space whose open sets are defined by $\{y \mid d(x, y) < r\}$, where $d(x, y)$ is the distance between x and y.

MI B.1   A **system state** (from now on, just state) is a function $s : L \to V$, from labels L to values V. A **state set** S consists of a set of state functions $s : L \to V$.

Labels represent a logical *location* associated with some value in a particular state. Thus, $s_i(X)$ is the value, or the contents, of location X in state $s_i \in S$. The nature of the values related to contents in a system is granularity-dependent and is out of the scope of this chapter. Normally there are simple values of basic datatypes such as strings and numbers or higher-level DL objects such as digital objects and metadata specifications.

A transition event is not a *probabilistic* event [48]. Rather, it is more like the events in networked operating systems theory [217], transitions in finite state machines [57], those modeled by the Unified Modeling Language (UML) [24], or transitions between places in Petri Nets [177].

A condition is used to describe circumstances under which a state transition can take place. An action models a reference to an operation, command, subprogram or method, responsible to perform the actual state transition. Events and actions can have parameters that abstract data items associated with attributes (labels) of a state.

We also can interpret a scenario as a path in a directed graph $G = (S, \Sigma_e)$, where vertices correspond to states in the state set S and directed edges are equivalent to events in a set of events Σ_e (and correspond to transitions between states). (Technically, G is a pseudodigraph [2], since loops (s_i, s_i) are possible as events.)

Note that the scenarios defining a service can have shared states. Such a set of related scenarios has been called a "scenario view" [126] and a "use case" in the UML [24]. In this framework, a simple transmission service of streams can be formally specified.

Scenarios are *implemented* to make a working system and the so-called "specification-implementation" gap must be overcome [200]. Formally, the implementation of scenarios can be mapped to an abstract machine represented by a deterministic finite automaton (DFA). This automaton $M = (Q, \Sigma_e, \delta, q_0, F)$ is such that M is the user-perceived conceptual state machine of the system and accepts a language $L(M)$ over the set of events Σ_e. A grammar $G = (V, \Sigma_e, R, s_0)$ for the language $L(M)$ is such that the non-terminals set V corresponds to the state set S, the terminals are the finite set of events Σ_e, s_0 is a distinguished initial state initializing all locations in that state, and R is a finite set of rules. Each rule in R is of the form $s_i \rightarrow es_j$ and conveys the system from state s_i to s_j as a consequence of event e, or is of the form $s_i \rightarrow e$ when $s_j \in F$ is a final state. The grammar and the corresponding conceptual state machine make up the abstract formal model which the analyst uses to capture, represent, and display system behavior in terms of scenarios. Alternatively, denotational semantics [248] and object-oriented abstractions [199] offer a programming language perspective for the question of formal scenario implementation.

Societies often support collaboration as in the case of users and service managers engaged in performing DL services. Scenarios describe the service behavior exactly in terms of interactions among the involved societies. For example, an ETD submission service involves interactions between graduate students and an ETD submission workflow manager (an electronic member of a service managers society).

---

[2]A digraph which permits both loops and multiple edges between nodes.

B.2   FORMALIZATION OF MINIMAL DIGITAL LIBRARY

As is pointed out in previous parts of this book, there is no consensual definition of a digital library. This makes the task of formally defining this kind of application and its components extremely difficult. In this section, we approach this problem by constructively defining a "core" or a "minimal" digital library, i.e., the minimal set of components that make a digital library, without which, in our view, a system/application cannot be considered a digital library. Each component (e.g., collections, services) is formally defined in terms of an S construct or as combinations or compositions of two or more of them. The set-oriented and functional mathematical formal basis of 5S allows us to precisely define those components as functional compositions or set-based combinations of the formal Ss.

In the following we informally, and then, in Section B.3, formally define the concepts of *metadata (structural and descriptive), digital object, collection, catalog, repository, indexing service, searching service, browsing service*, and *digital library*.

Informally, a digital library involves a managed *collection* of information with associated *services* involving *communities* where information is stored in digital formats and accessible over a network. Information in digital libraries is manifest in terms of *digital objects*, which can contain textual or multimedia content (e.g., images, audio, video), and *metadata*. Although the distinction between data and metadata often depends on the context, metadata commonly appears in a structured way and covers different categories of information *about* a digital object. The most common kind of metadata is *descriptive metadata*, which occurs in catalogs and indexes and includes summary information used to describe objects in a DL. Another common characteristic of digital objects and metadata is the presence of some internal structure, which can be explicitly represented and explored to provide better DL services. Basic services provided by digital libraries are indexing, searching, and browsing. Those services can be tailored to different communities depending on their roles, for example, creators of material, librarians, patrons, etc.

The discussion above emphasizes the role of structural metadata as a representation or abstraction of relationships between digital objects and their component parts (cf. Def. 16). The graph-based representation of this type of metadata can be explicitly expressed, as in the case of markup [47], or implicitly computed [46, 168].

The definition for **descriptive metadata specifications,** is inspired by developments in the metadata area, mainly those related to the *Semantic Web* [20] and the Resource Description Framework (RDF) [234], and emphasizes the semantic relationships implied by the labeling function in a structure. Fig. B.2 illustrates the basic constructs. Statements, which are triples corresponding to a specific resource (the thing being described) together with a named property about the resource plus the value of that property for that resource, are promoted to first-class concepts. Figure B.2(b) shows an example of an instantiation of the construct for a descriptive metadata specification about an electronic thesis with four statements: Statement1 = (Thesis1, "author", "M.A.Goncalves"), Statement2 = (Thesis1, "degree", Degree1), Statement3 = (Degree1, "level", "doctoral"), and Statement4 = (Degree1, "grantor", "Virginia Tech"). Below we define the notions of **descriptive metadata specification** and **metadata format** more formally.

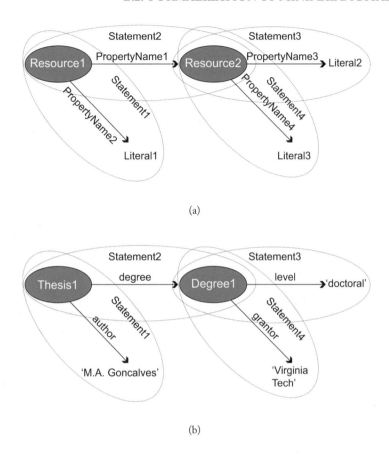

Figure B.2: Overview of descriptive metadata with example. Adapted from [108].

Therefore, a metadata format, through the property definition function, constrains the kinds of resources that can be associated together in statements of a metadata specification as well as the basic datatype domains, which are associated with pairs (resource-property) related to literals [40]. For example, for any set of labels $\mathcal{R}$ for resources, the Dublin Core metadata format defines that $\text{def}_{DC}(\mathcal{R}, \text{'title'}) = String$ and $\text{def}_{DC}(\mathcal{R}, \text{'subject'}) = SubjectTerms$ where $SubjectTerms$ is a finite set of labels for Resources corresponding to controlled terms.

A StructuredStream defines a mapping from nodes of a structure to segments of a stream. An example in a textual stream can be seen in Figure B.3. From the example, it can be deduced that several structures can be imposed over one stream and vice-versa. Also, it can be seen that segments associated with a node should include the segments of its children (in the case of a hierarchical tree), although it is not equal to the union of those, as "gaps" or "holes" can occur between child

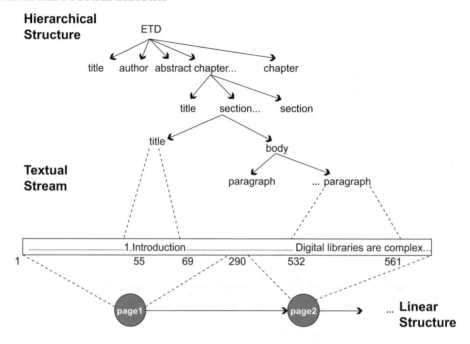

Figure B.3: A StructuredStream for an ETD. Adapted from [168].

segments [168]. Finally, it should be noted that this definition works also for multimedia streams like audio, video, and images.

Figure B.4 shows an example of a very simple digital object with one structure and several streams. Two important aspects must be pointed out about the definition of a digital object:

1. Any real implementation does not need to enforce physical containment of the several component parts of a digital object; for example, we could have pointers to external streams.

2. The definition does not consider active behavior of digital objects [169, 219] which supports operations like different disseminations or exporting of subparts. While there is no explicit restriction regarding this, the definition conforms to our minimalist approach.

Thus, a repository encapsulates a set of collections and specific services to manage and access the collections.

The interpretation of the index and the indexing service is dependent upon the underlying indexing space. Features of an indexing space can be words, phrases, concepts, or multimedia characteristics, like shape or color, appearing or associated with the content of a digital object (in its descriptive and structural metadata or streams). Normally, if a vector space is considered, terms are treated as unrelated, therefore defining orthogonal vectors that span a space $\mathcal{T}$ with dimension m. If

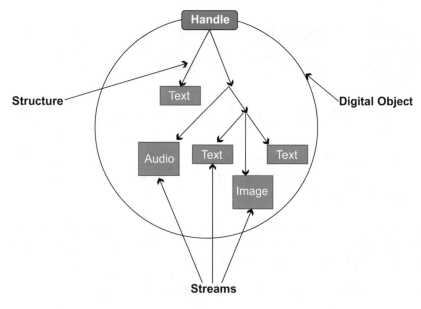

Figure B.4: A simple digital object. Adapted from [108].

a probabilistic space $p = (X, \mathbb{B}, \mu)$ is used, $\mathcal{T} = X$ is the set of distinct terms and is called a *sample space*. Also an index can be thought of as a mapping from an indexing space to a *document (digital object) space* defined by the collection.

The indexing service normally takes the shape of a *pipeline service* where scenarios themselves are executed in sequence and the final state of a scenario is the starting state of the next one. A very simple instance of such an indexing service is shown in Figure B.5 for indexing of textual material. The indexing service is composed of three scenarios organized as a pipeline of the following scenarios: 1) tokenization, which identifies unique terms inside the textual streams; 2) stopword removal, which filters out terms not useful for retrieval; and 3) stemming, which removes affixes and allows retrieval of syntactic variations of query terms [11]. Each one of the scenarios can be thought of as doing some transformation in the representations of digital objects in order to produce the index function. Note again that we are making use of our minimalist approach by not considering complex indexes, for example, defining locations inside streams of digital objects for phrase, proximity, or structural queries.

The components of a digital object do, are denoted by $do(1)$, $do(2)$, etc. Therefore, $do_k(2)$ denotes the second component, i.e., the stream set component of a digital object do_k, $do_k(3)$ its structural metadata set component (third component), and $do_k(4)$ its set of StructuredStreams functions (fourth component). Let also $G[v]$ denote the subgraph of a directed graph G containing node v and all points and edges reachable starting from v. A substructure defined by $G[v]$ inherits

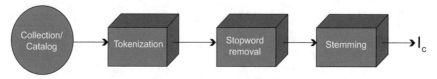

Figure B.5: Simple indexing service. Adapted from [108].

the labeling of the structure defined with G. Finally, let $f : A \rightarrow B$ and let $\mathcal{D}$ be any non-empty subset of A. The **restriction** of f to $\mathcal{D}$, denoted by $f|_{\mathcal{D}}$, is a subset of f and is a function from $\mathcal{D}$ to B. Then, for a collection C:

1. $AllStreams = (\cup_{do_k \in C} do_k(2))$ and $AllSubStreams = \cup_{sm_t \in AllStreams} \{sm_t[i, j] \mid sm_t = \langle a_0, a_1, \ldots, a_n \rangle, 0 \leq i \leq j \leq n) \}$ will be the set of all streams and substreams (segments of streams) of all digital objects in the collection C;

2. $AllSubStructuredStreams = \bigcup_{k,j}(SubStructuredStream_{k_j})$ where:

   (a) $d_k \in C$;

   (b) $G_{k_j} = (V_{k_j}, E_{k_j})$ is the first component of some structure $st_{k_j} \in d_k(3)$;

   (c) $\mathcal{H}_{k_j} = \{G_{k_j}[v_t] \mid vt \in V_{k_j}\}$ corresponds to the set of all substructures of st_{k_j};

   (d) $SubStructuredStream_{k_j} = \{S|_{V'} \mid (V', E') \in \mathcal{H}_{k_j}, S \in d_k(4)$ is a StructuredStream function defined from the structure st_{k_j}, and $S|_{V'}$ is the restriction of S to $V'\}$.

   Therefore, $AllSubStructuredStreams$ corresponds to the set of all possible substructures and their corresponding connections to streams inside digital objects of the collection.

   A hyperlink is an edge in the hypertext graph. Source nodes of a hyperlink are called "anchors" and are generally associated via function $\mathcal{P}$ with segments of streams. Two basic types of hyperlinks can be identified: *structural* and *referential* [235]. Structural hyperlinks allow navigation inside internal structures and across streams of digital objects. Referential hyperlinks usually have their target nodes associated with different digital objects or their subcomponents.

   Figure B.6 illustrates a hypertext. It is made using structural hyperlinks that follow the structural metadata and external referential links. Links originate from (segments of) streams. Link targets for, respectively, links 1, 2, and 3, are: an entire digital object, a portion of its StructuredStream function (in the figure, represented by the subgraph pointed to by the link and the associated streams), and one of its streams (in this case an image).

   An example of such a hypertext is the Web. The Web is a structure where hypertext links connect nodes that can be associated with: 1) complete HTML pages that can be considered digital objects; 2) substructures of an HTML page, for example, a section of the page; and 3) links to streams, e.g., images, audios, or text. The Distributed Graph Storage (DGS) system also implements similar ideas with structural and hyper-structural links representing, respectively, the internal structures of digital objects and hypertext constructs [210]. It should be noted that for the sake of brevity we are not describing links to services, for example, external plugins that can be invoked by browsers or Web forms.

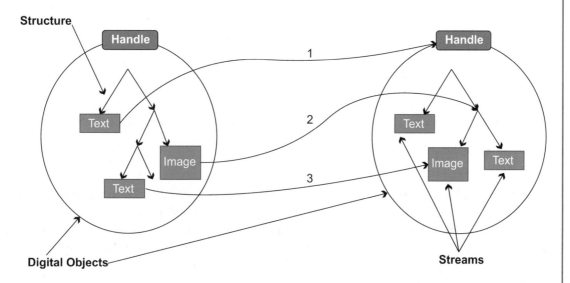

Figure B.6: A simple hypertext. Adapted from [108].

Thus, every browsing service is associated with an underlying hypertext construct. This view unifies the three modes of browsing defined by Baeza-Yates and Ribeiro-Neto [11]: flat browsing, structured guided, and navigational mode. The third one is the most general case and fits exactly our framework. The first two can be considered special cases. In flat browsing the hypertext has a flat organization, for example, an ordered list of documents or a set of points in an image, and the graph structure of the hypertext corresponds to a disconnected bipartite graph. In the second one, which includes classification hierarchies and directories, the hypertext graph is a tree. Many semi-structured wrapper algorithms disclose this hypertext "hidden" structure in the Web. Once revealed, this structure can be recorded in databases or represented in other semi-structured models to allow queries or transformations. Methodologies like PIPE [189] make use of this information to personalize Web sites. Note also that more sophisticated kinds of hypertext can be defined by extending the definition given below. For example, we could relax the function $\mathcal{P}$ to be a relation and associate different contents with the same node, which could be achieved by having different modes of traversing the same link in an extension of the *TraverseLink* function[3]. However, the present definition is simpler and serves well our minimalist approach[4].

B.3   FORMAL DEFINITIONS FOR DIGITAL LIBRARY

MI B.2   A **digital library** is a 4-tuple $(\mathcal{R}, Cat, Serv, Soc)$, where

- $\mathcal{R}$ is a repository;

- $Cat = \{DM_{C_1}, DM_{C_2}, ..., DM_{C_K}\}$ is a set of metadata catalogs for all collections $\{C_1, C_2, ..., C_K\}$ in the repository;

- Serv is a set of services containing at least services for indexing, searching, and browsing;

- Soc is a society.

We should stress that the above definition (illustrated in Fig. B.1) only captures the syntax of a digital library, i.e., what a digital library is. Many semantic constraints and consistency rules regarding the relationships among the DL components (e.g., how the scenarios in $Serv$ should be built from $\mathcal{R}$ and Cat and from the relationships among communities inside the society Soc, or what the consistency rules are among digital objects in collections of $\mathcal{R}$ and metadata records in Cat) are not specified here; please see Chapter 3.

MI B.3   A **stream** is a *sequence* whose codomain is a nonempty set.

MI B.4   A **structure** is a tuple $(G, L, \mathcal{F})$, where $G = (V, E)$ is a directed graph with vertex set V and edge set E, L is a set of label values, and $\mathcal{F}$ is a labeling function $\mathcal{F} : (V \cup E) \to L$.

MI B.5   A **substructure** of a structure $(G, L, \mathcal{F})$ is another structure $(G', L', \mathcal{F}')$ where $G' = (V', E')$ is a subgraph of G, $L' \subseteq L$ and $\mathcal{F}' : (V' \cup E') \to L'$.

MI B.6   A **space** is a measurable space, measure space, probability space, vector space, topological space, or a metric space [5].

---

[3]This extended approach also generalizes the notion of link directionality where bi-directional links or non-directional links correspond just to different ways of traversing the link (e.g., SOURCE_TO_SINK, SINK_TO_SOURCE, BOTH).
[4]Note also that libraries can support *serendipity* or "random links".
[5]See Appendix definitions 9-14 for formal definitions of each of these spaces.

MI B.7   A **system state** (from now on, just state) is a function $s : L \to V$, from labels L to values V. A **state set** S consists of a set of state functions $s : L \to V$.

MI B.8   A **transition event** (or simply **event**) on a state set S is an element $e = (s_i, s_j) \in (S \times S)$ of a binary relation on state set S that signifies the transition from one state to another. An event e is defined by a *condition* function $c(s_i)$ which evaluates a Boolean function in state s_i and by an *action* function p.

MI B.9   A **scenario** is a sequence of related transition events $\langle e_1, e_2, ..., e_n \rangle$ on state set S such that $e_k = (s_k, s_{k+1})$, for $1 \le k \le n$.

MI B.10   A **service, activity, task,** or **procedure** is a set of scenarios.

MI B.11   Let $T = \langle t_1, t_2, ..., t_n \rangle$ be a stream. Let event $e_{t_i} = (s_{t_i}, d_{t_i}{}^6)$ and event $a_{t_i} = (d_{t_i}, s_{t_{i+1}})$. A transmission of stream T is the scenario (sequence of related events) $e_T = \langle e_{t_1}, a_{t_1}, e_{t_2}, a_{t_2}, ... e_{t_n} \rangle$.

MI B.12   A **society** is a tuple (C, R), where

1. $C = \{c_1, c_2, ..., c_n\}$ is a set of conceptual communities, each community referring to a set of individuals of the same class or type (e.g., actors, service managers);

2. $R = \{r_1, r_2, ..., r_m\}$ is a set of relationships, each relationship being a tuple $r_j = (e_j, i_j)$, where e_j is a Cartesian product $c_{k_1} \times c_{k_2} \times \cdots \times c_{k_{n_j}}$, $1 \le k_1 < k_2 < \cdots < k_{n_j} \le n$, which specifies the communities involved in the relationship and i_j is an activity (cf. Def. 8) that describes the interactions or communications among individuals.

MI B.13   A **structural metadata** specification is a structure.

MI B.14   Let $\mathcal{L} = \bigcup D_k$ be a set of literals defined as the union of domains D_k of simple datatypes (e.g., strings, numbers, dates, etc.). Let also $\mathcal{R}$ and $\mathcal{P}$ represent sets of labels for resources and properties respectively. A **descriptive metadata specification** is a structure $(G, \mathcal{R} \cup \mathcal{L} \cup \mathcal{P}, \mathcal{F})$, where:

---

[6] d_{t_i} is the state that indicates that the destination has received stream item t_i

1. $\mathcal{F} : (V \cup E) \rightarrow (\mathcal{R} \cup \mathcal{L} \cup \mathcal{P})$ can assign general labels $\mathcal{R} \cup \mathcal{P}$ and literals from $\mathcal{L}$ to nodes of the graph structure;

2. for each directed edge $e = (v_i, v_j)$ of G, $\mathcal{F}(v_i) \in \mathcal{R} \cup \mathcal{L}$, $\mathcal{F}(v_j) \in \mathcal{R} \cup \mathcal{L}$ and $\mathcal{F}(e) \in \mathcal{P}$;

3. $\mathcal{F}(v_k) \in \mathcal{L}$ if and only if node v_k has outdegree 0.

The triple $st = (\mathcal{F}(v_i), \mathcal{F}(e), \mathcal{F}(v_j))$ is called a **statement** (derived from the descriptive metadata specification), meaning that the resource labeled $\mathcal{F}(v_i)$ has property $\mathcal{F}(e)$ with value $\mathcal{F}(v_j)$ (which can be designated as another resource or literal).

MI B.15   Let $D_{\mathcal{L}_{MF}} = \{D_1, D_2, ..., D_i\}$ be the set of domains that make up a set of literals $\mathcal{L}_{MF} = \bigcup_{j=1}^{i} D_j$. As for metadata specifications, let $\mathcal{R}_{MF}$ and $\mathcal{P}_{MF}$ represent sets of labels for resources and properties, respectively. A **metadata format** for descriptive metadata specifications is a tuple $MF = (V_{MF}, \mathrm{def}_{MF})$ with $V_{MF} = \{\mathcal{R}_1, \mathcal{R}_2, ..., \mathcal{R}_k\} \subset 2^{\mathcal{R}_{MF}}$ a family of subsets of the resource labels $\mathcal{R}_{MF}$ and $\mathrm{def}_{MF} : V_{MF} \times \mathcal{P}_{MF} \rightarrow V_{MF} \cup D_{\mathcal{L}_{MF}}$ is a property definition function.

MI B.16   A descriptive metadata specification $MS = (G_{MS}, \mathcal{R}_{MS} \cup \mathcal{L}_{MS} \cup \mathcal{P}_{MS}, \mathcal{F}_{MS})$ **conforms with** a metadata format $MF = (V_{MF}, \mathrm{def}_{MF})$ if $\mathcal{R}_{MS} \subseteq \mathcal{R}_{MF}, \mathcal{L}_{MS} \subseteq \mathcal{L}_{MF}, \mathcal{P}_{MS} \subseteq \mathcal{P}_{MF}$, and for every statement $st = (r, p, l)$ derived from MS, $r \in \mathcal{R}_k$ for some $\mathcal{R}_k \in V_{MF}$ and $p \in \mathcal{P}_{MS}$ implies $l \in \mathrm{def}_{MF}(\mathcal{R}_k, p)$.

MI B.17   Given a structure $(G, L, \mathcal{F})$, $G = (V, E)$ and a stream S, a **StructuredStream** is a function $V \rightarrow (\mathbb{N} \times \mathbb{N})$ that associates each node $v_k \in V$ with a pair of natural numbers (a, b), $a < b$, corresponding to a contiguous subsequence $[S_a, S_b]$ (segment) of the stream S.

MI B.18   A **digital object** is a tuple $do = (h, SM, ST, StructuredStreams)$ where

1. $h \in H$, where H is a set of universally unique handles (labels);

2. $SM = \{sm_1, sm_2, \ldots, sm_n\}$ is a set of streams;

3. $ST = \{st_1, st_2, \ldots, st_m\}$ is a set of structural metadata specifications;

4. $StructuredStreams = \{stsm_1, stsm_2, \ldots, stsm_p\}$ is a set of StructuredStream functions defined from the streams in the SM set (the second component) of the digital object and from the structures in the ST set (the third component).

MI B.19   A **collection** $C = \{do_1, do_2, \ldots, do_k\}$ is a set of digital objects.

MI B.20   Let C be a collection with k handles in H. A **metadata catalog** DM_C for C is a set of pairs $\{(h, \{dm_1, \ldots, dm_{k_h}\})\}$, where $h \in H$ and the dm_i are descriptive metadata specifications.

MI B.21   Let C be a collection with handles H. A **repository** is a tuple $(R, get, store, del)$, where $R \subset 2^C$ is a family of collections and the functions "get," "store," and "del" satisfy:

1. $get : H \to C$ maps a handle h to a digital object $get(h)$.

2. $store : C \times R \to R$ maps $(do, \tilde{C})$ to the augmented collection $\{do\} \cup \tilde{C}$.

3. $del : H \times R \to R$ maps $(h, \tilde{C})$ to the smaller collection $\tilde{C} - \{get(h)\}$.

MI B.22   Let $I : 2^{\mathcal{T}} \to 2^H$ be an index function where $\mathcal{T}$ is a set of indexing features and H is a set of handles. An **index** is a set of index functions. An **indexing service** is a single scenario $\{\langle is_1, is_2, \ldots, is_n \rangle\}$ comprised of pipelined scenarios $is_1, is_2, \ldots, is_n$ in which the starting state s_{k_0} of the first event of the initial scenario is_1 has a collection $s_{k_0}(K) = C$ and/or a metadata catalog $s_{k_0}(Y) = DM_C$ for collection C as its values and the final state s_{k_f} of the final scenario is_n has an index $I_C = s_{k_f}(Z)$ as its value (K, Y, and Z being labels of the respective states).

MI B.23   Let Q be a set of conceptual representations for user information needs, collectively called *queries*. Let $M_{I_C} : Q \times (C \times DM_C) \to \mathbb{R}$ be a matching function, associated with an index I_C, that associates a real number with a query $q \in Q$ and a digital object $do \in C$ and possibly its descriptive metadata specifications $ms \in DM_C$, indicating how well the query representation matches with the digital object, structurally, by content, or regarding the descriptive metadata specifications. A **searching service** is a set of searching scenarios $\{sc_1, sc_2, \ldots, sc_t\}$, where for each query $q \in Q$ there is a searching scenario $sc_k = \langle e_0, \ldots, e_n \rangle$ such that e_0 is the start event triggered by a query q and event e_n is the final event of returning the matching function values $M_I(q, d)$ for all $d \in C$.

MI B.24   Let $H = ((V_H, E_H), L_H, \mathcal{F}_H)$ be a structure and C be a collection. A **hypertext** $HT = (H, Contents, \mathcal{P})$ is a triple such that:

1. $Contents \subseteq C \cup AllSubStreams \cup AllSubStructuredStreams$ is a set of contents that can include digital objects of a collection C, all of their streams (and substreams) and all possible *restrictions* of the StructuredStream functions of digital objects.

2. $\mathcal{P} : V_H \to Contents$ is a function which associates a node of the hypertext with the node content.

MI B.25   A **browsing service** is a set of scenarios $\{sc_1, \ldots, sc_n\}$ over a hypertext (meaning that events are defined by edges of the hypertext graph (V_H, E_H)), such that traverse link events e_i are associated with a function $TraverseLink : V_H \times E_H \rightarrow Contents$, which given a node and a link retrieves the content of the target node, i.e., $TraverseLink(v_k, e_{k_i}) = \mathcal{P}(v_t)$ for $e_{k_i} = (v_k, v_t) \in E_H$.

APPENDIX C

Archaeological Digital Libraries

C.1   BACKGROUND ON THE 5S FRAMEWORK

Appendix B provides a formal framework for the DL field, summarized in Fig. B.1. A "minimal digital library" (Def. MI B.2, Appendix B, shown at the bottom right) was defined as the highest level concept. Fig. C.1 extends this to cover digital libraries for archaeology, as discussed in Chapter 2, but omits the top layer of definitions (specified in Appendix A), regarding mathematical foundations (e.g., graphs, sequences, and functions). Fig. C.1 begins with the 5 Ss (Streams, Structures, Spaces, Scenarios, and Societies), and key concepts of a DL (e.g., digital object, collection), and then adds in about archaeological objects and other essential concepts identified as we built the ETANA-DL [192, 194]. Arrows represent dependencies, indicating that a concept is formally defined in terms of previously defined concepts that point to it.

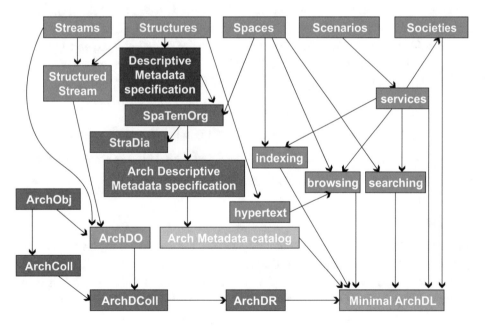

Figure C.1: 5S definitional structure extended for archaeology. Adapted from [212].

C.2   NOTATION AND DEFINITIONS

Notation: Let $DL_1, DL_2, \ldots, DL_i, \ldots, DL_n$ be n independent digital libraries; let Id_i be a unique identifier of DL_i; let C_{ij} be the jth collection of DL_i; let $C_i = \bigcup_{j=1}^{m} C_{ij}$, where m is the total number of collections of DL_i; let $UnionC = \bigcup_{i=1}^{n} C_i$ be a union collection of the n DLs; let H be a set of universally unique handles.

Following [108] we have $DL_i = (R_i, DM_i, Serv_i, Soc_i)$, where R_i is a network accessible repository, supporting some type of harvesting protocol to expose its metadata; DM_i is a set of metadata catalogs for C_i; $Serv_i$ is a set of services; and Soc_i is a society.

AR C.1   Let $Q = (H_q, Contents_q, P_q)$ be a set of conceptual representations for user information needs, where $H_q = ((V_q, E_q), L_q, F_q)$ is a structure (i.e., a directed graph with vertices V_q and edges E_q, along with labels L_q and labeling function F_q on the graph; see Def. MI. B.4 in Appendix B for details), $Contents_q$ can include digital objects and all of their streams, and P_q is a mapping function $P_q : V_q \longrightarrow Contents_q$.

AR C.2   An Exploration Space (**ESpa**) is a tuple, $\mathbf{ESpa} = (Q, Contents, OP_{Set})$, where Q is a set of conceptual representations for user information needs (see Def. AR. C.1), Contents can include digital objects of a collection C (C is a set of digital objects), all of their (sub)streams and all possible restrictions of the StructuredStream functions of digital objects, and OP_Set is a set of operations on Q and $Contents$. $OP_{viz}, OP_s, OP_b, OP_{clu} \subseteq OP\_Set$, where $viz, s, b,$ and clu, relate to visualization, search, browse, and cluster operations, respectively, and

1. $OP_{viz} = \{VisualMap_1, VisualMap_2, VisualMap_3\}$, where

   $VisualMap_1 : 2^C \longrightarrow VSpa$ associates a set of digital objects with a set of vectors;

   $VisualMap_2 : 2^C \longrightarrow VisualM$ associates a set of digital objects with a visual mark;

   $VisualMap_3 : Base \longrightarrow VisualMP$ associates a basis vector with a visual property of a visual mark.

   Examples of OP_{viz}:

   A special case is that there is only one digital object, a document in the set. Given a vector space $VSpa$ of three dimensions, the document is mapped to a vector of three elements, i.e., its length, date published, and number of citations, by function $VisualMap_1$. It is mapped to a visual mark: a point in 2D space by function $VisualMap_2$. The first two base vectors in $VSpa$ are associated with the position of the point in 2D space, while the third base vector may be mapped to another visual property of the point, its gray scale (e.g., a document represented by a black point has more citations than a document represented by a gray point).

   Fig. C.2 shows another example of OP_{viz}. A set of digital objects contains three bone records in the ETANA-DL bone collection. Each of these records is mapped to a vector in a vector space $VSpa$ by function $VisualMap_1$ and mapped to a special visual mark: rows of text by function $VisualMap_2$. Two base vectors in $VSpa$ are associated with the position of the rows of text in a 2D user interface.

Nimrin **Bone** **ID** 1   **Partition** NW   **Subpartition** N40/W25   **Locus** 178   **Container** 212   **PIECES** 3
AGES IRON II   **AGE** 900-800 BC
BONE METAPODIAL   **ANIMAL** SHEEP / GOAT
COMMENTS
[View complete record] [Add to Items of Interest] [Share Item]

Nimrin **Bone** **ID** 1169   **Partition** NW   **Subpartition** N40/W25   **Locus** 159   **Container** 77   **PIECES** 1
AGES IRON II   **AGE** 850-800 BC / L 9BC
BONE METAPODIAL   **ANIMAL** MEDIUM MAMMAL
COMMENTS UNIDENTIFIED,IM
[View complete record] [Add to Items of Interest] [Share Item]

Nimrin **Bone** **ID** 1370   **Partition** NW   **Subpartition** N35/W20   **Locus** 64   **Container** 168   **PIECES** 1
AGES IRON II   **AGE** 800-700 BC
BONE METAPODIAL   **ANIMAL** MEDIUM MAMMAL
COMMENTS UNIDENTIFIED
[View complete record] [Add to Items of Interest] [Share Item]

Figure C.2: Example of OP_{viz} [212].

2. $OP_{clu} : (2^C \times 2^C) \times Sim_{clu} \longrightarrow 2^{Contents}$, where $Sim_{clu} = \{OP_{clu1}(cluster_x, cluster_y)|$ $cluster_x \in 2^C, cluster y \in 2^C\}$, where $OP_{clu1} : 2^C \times 2^C \longrightarrow R$ is a matching function that associates a real number with a pair of subsets of C. Sim_{clu} is a set of numerical values measuring the similarity between each pair of subsets of C. Similarity measures between clusters are called linkage methods. The three most popular linkage methods (single-link, complete-link, and group-average) were presented in [202]. The range of OP_{clu} is a set of the *Contents* associated with collection C. Note that OP_{viz} may be applied on the result of OP_{clu}.

Example of OP_{clu} :

C is a set of all the digital objects in ETANA-DL; $cluster_x$ and $cluster_y$ are subsets of C, and they are bone records from the Nimrin site and Umayri site, respectively, as shown in Fig. C.3. If the similarity between $cluster_x$ and $cluster_y$ is above a predefined threshold, OP_{clu} returns the contents associated with a new cluster, $cluster_x \cup cluster_y$, i.e., a set of all bone records. $cluster_x$ has 7419 records and $cluster_y$ has 2122 records; while the clustering result, $cluster_x \cup cluster_y$, has 9541 records as shown in Fig. C.4.

3. $OP_s : (Q \times C) \times Sim_s \longrightarrow 2^{Contents}$, where

$Sim_s = \{OP_q(q, do)|q \in Q, do \in C\}$, where $OP_q : Q \times C \longrightarrow R$ is a matching function that associates a real number with $q \in Q$ and a digital object $do \in C$. The range of function

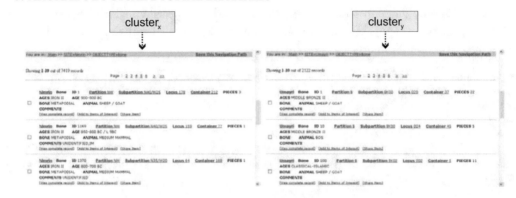

Figure C.3: Example of *cluster_x* and *cluster_y* in ETANA-DL. Adapted from [212].

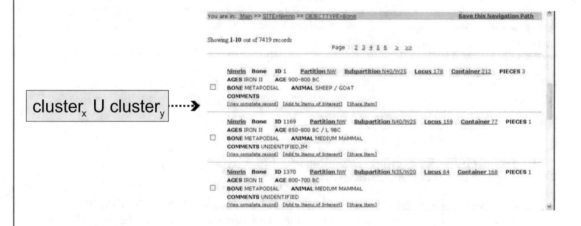

Figure C.4: Example of clustering result. Adapted from [212].

OP_s is the Contents associated with collection C. We consider the retrieved results as (a subset of) the *Contents*. OP_{viz} and OP_{clu} may be applied on the result of OP_s.

Example of OP_s:

q is a structured query named "animal bones from the Nimrin site" as illustrated in Fig. D.2; C is a set of all the digital objects in ETANA-DL; Sim_s is a set of numerical values measuring the similarity between q and each digital object using the vector space model (cosine similarity) [203]. Based on Sim_s, OP_s returns the contents associated with a set of digital objects whose similarity between q is above a predefined threshold. There are 7419 animal bone records similar to the query; OP_{viz} is applied to the result of function OP_s and the retrieved results are shown in Fig. C.5.

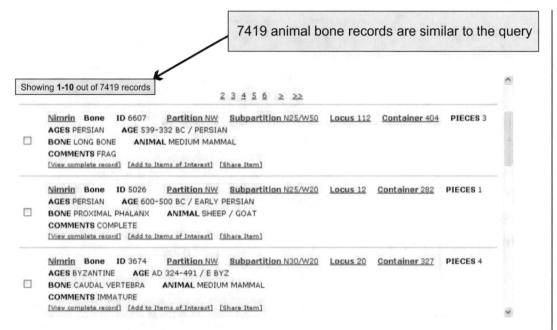

Figure C.5: Example of function OP_s in ETANA-DL. Adapted from [212].

4. $OP_b : E_H \longrightarrow 2^{Contents}$ is a function which, given a link, retrieves the content of the target node, where E_H is a set of edges of the digraph defined for a hypertext.

   The *TraverseLink* function discussed in Section B.2 and specified in Def. MI B.25 of Section B.3 was intended to achieve the same result as OP_b. We think both the domain and range of *TraverseLink* function may need to be refined. The domain of *TraverseLink* function can be generalized and the range of it is not proper. The domain of *TraverseLink* is $V_H \times E_H$, while the domain of OP_b is E_H. Since $\forall e = (v_s, v_t) \in E_H$ is an directed edge having a start vertex v_s and an end (target) vertex v_t, the input of OP_b can be simplified as e instead of a pair (v_s, e) as required by *TraverseLink*. The output of OP_b is a set of *Contents*, therefore, the range of OP_b is $2^{Contents}$ instead of *Contents* as the range of function *TraverseLink*. Note OP_{viz} may be applied to the result of function OP_s as well.

   Example of OP_b:

   $edge = (v_s, v_t)$ is labeled as "Member Collections," where v_s is labeled as "ETANA-DL," v_t is labeled as "ETANA-DL's Member Collections," $v_s, v_t \in V_q$, and $v_s, v_t \in V_H$. $OP_b(edge)$ is the content of the target node v_t, i.e., the user's new information need represented by the webpage describing ETANA-DL's member collections (see Fig. C.6).

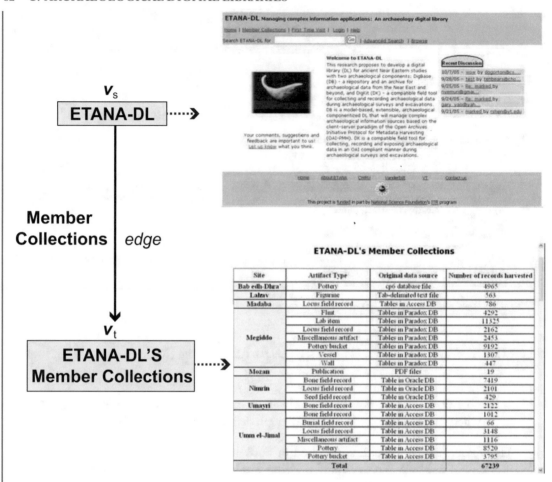

Figure C.6: Example of function OP_b in ETANA-DL. Adapted from [212].

AR C.3   An exploring service **(ESer)** is a set of scenarios $\{sc_1, \ldots, sc_n\}$ over an exploration space $ESpa$. Each scenario is a sequence of events. An event e_i is associated with one or more of the operations in $ESpa$.

AR C.4   A Union Repository **(UnionRep)** of n DLs $(DL_1, \ldots, DL_n)$ is a DL repository ([108]) with a $getDL\_Id$ function: $UnionRep = (CollSet, getDL\_Id, get, store, del)$, where
    1) $CollSet \subseteq 2^{\{UnionC\}}$;
    2) $getDL\_Id : UnionC \rightarrow \{Id_1, Id_2, \ldots, Id_i, \ldots, Id_n\}$ maps a digital object do to the DL it belongs to;

3) $get : H \to UnionC$ maps a handle h to $do = get(h)$;

4) $store : UnionC \times CollSet \to CollSet$ maps $(do, \tilde{C})$ to the augmented collection $\{do\} \bigcup \tilde{C}$;

5) $del : H \times CollSet \to Collset$ maps $(h, \tilde{C})$ to the smaller collection $\tilde{C} - get(h)$;

AR C.5   A Union Catalog **UnionCat** $= DM_{UnionC}$ is a metadata catalog for $UnionC$.

AR C.6   Minimal Union Services (**MinUnionServ**) $= \{harvesting, mapping\} \bigcup (\bigcup_{i=1}^{n} Serv_i)$.

The *harvesting* service provides a mechanism to gather metadata from each DL_i; the mapping service supports transforming information organized by local schema to information structured according to the global schema. The harvesting service is formally defined in [108]; the mapping is defined as follows (see Defs. AR C.7-C.10):

AR C.7   A schema is a structure [108] with a domain D of data types (e.g., strings, numbers, dates, etc.). **schema** $= ((V, E), L, F, D, M)$, where (V, E) is a graph with vertex set V and edge set E, L is a set of label values, F is a labeling function $F : (V \cup E) \longrightarrow L$, and M is a function $M : V \longrightarrow D$.

AR C.8   Given a schema $((V, E), L, F, D, M)$, its element set $=(v, F(v))(e, F(e))$.

AR C.9   1-1 mapping
Let S and T be two element sets, of S_Schema and T_Schema, respectively. 1-1 mapping is a function: $M_{1-1} : S \times T \longrightarrow Sim$, where $\forall sim \in Sim, 0 \leq sim \leq 1$. A tuple (s, t, sim) indicates element s of S is similar to element t of T with confidence score sim. The higher a confidence score, the more semantically similar are s and t.

AR C.10   complex mapping
Let S and T be two element sets, of S_Schema and T_Schema, respectively; let O be a set of operators that can be applied to elements of S and T, according to a set of rules R, to construct formulas; and let $Formu_s$ and $Formu_t$ be two sets of formulas constructed from the elements of S and T, using O. Complex mapping is a function: $M : (S \bigcup Formu_s) \times (T \bigcup Formu_t) \longrightarrow Sim$, where $\forall sim \in Sim, 0 \leq sim \leq 1$.

AR C.11   A Union Society **UnionSoc** $= \bigcup_{i=1}^{n} Soc_i$

AR C.12   A Minimal Union Digital Library integrated from n DLs is given as a four-tuple: **MinUnionDL** $= (R_{union}, DM_{union}, Ser_{union}, Soc_{union})$, where R_{union}, DM_{union}, Ser_{union}, Soc_{union} are Union Repository, Union Catalog, Minimal Union Services, and Union Society. A Union DL is a superset of a **MinUnionDL**. "Integrated DL" and "Union DL" can be used interchangeably.

AR C.13   DL Integration Problem Definition

Given n individual digital libraries $(DL_1, DL_2, \ldots, DL_n)$, each defined as described above, to integrate the n DLs is to create a Union DL.

C.3   ARCHITECTURE OF AN INTEGRATED DL

As above (Def. AR. C.12), an integrated DL is a 4-tuple consisting of a union repository, a union catalog, union services, and a union society. There are three popular integration architectures to deal with regarding the first two components of the definition, namely: 1) a centralized union catalog along with a centralized union repository; 2) a centralized union catalog for a decentralized union repository; and 3) a middle ground between the above two extremes of the spectrum, i.e., a centralized union catalog with a partially centralized union repository.

Decision on the architecture to be used to develop an integrated DL is based on 1) what contents (metadata, digital objects, or both) the DLs to be integrated would like to share; and 2) what the integrated DL is harvesting. The former relates to copyrights and publication rights. The latter may involve issues such as scalability, consistency, and preservation.

Having both a centralized union catalog and a centralized union repository in an integrated DL can guarantee adequate performance at information seeking time. No burden is placed on the remote DLs to retrieve results. Storing digital objects in the integrated DL redundantly can help preservation. However, delivery of the most current information to users cannot always be guaranteed. Changes to the metadata and digital objects by the individual DLs need to be propagated to the integrated DL. Assumed for a decentralized union repository is that the metadata contains links to concrete realizations of digital objects. The main disadvantage is that retrieval of digital objects relies on remote DLs. CITIDEL [183] is a DL that has a centralized catalog and decentralized repository; sustainability of the centralized portion of such a system also can be a challenge.

A partially decentralized union repository may store the digital objects that will not be changed frequently. The architecture of ETANA-DL [192, 193, 194] consists of a centralized catalog and partially decentralized repository. As shown in Fig. C.7, ETANA-DL integrates several DLs:

1. Member DLs of ETANA-DL

2. Architecture of ETANA-DL, with centralized catalog and partially decentralized repository

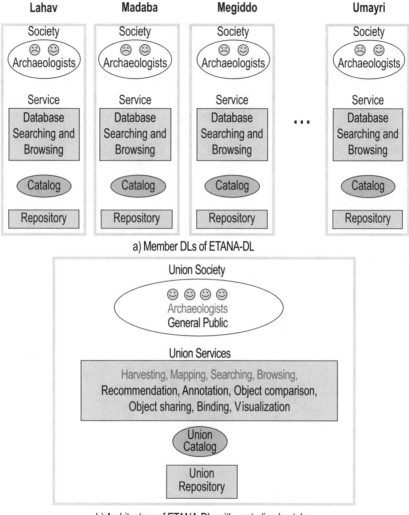

Figure C.7: An example of an integrated DL: ETANA-DL. Adapted from [212].

To create a centralized catalog, ETANA-DL provides a harvesting service and a mapping service. Beside these two, it should provide all the services supported by its member DLs (e.g., searching and browsing), and other services (e.g., clustering and visualization). The visualization service may integrate searching, browsing, and clustering. EtanaViz [216] is an example of such an integrated service. It provides a visual interface to ETANA-DL. Search results can be classified by predefined classes. Grouped documents are displayed in several ways to help browsing.

The union services illustrated in Fig. C.7 aim to satisfy users of ETANA-DL's member DLs. The user society in an integrated DL may be simplified as a union of the users of the DLs to be integrated. However, special cases need to be considered, e.g., how to deal with the situations where a user (or her partners) belongs to different user groups of various DLs to be integrated.

APPENDIX D

5S Results: Lemmas, Proofs, and 5SSuite

D.1 EXPLORING SERVICE FORMALIZATION

Notation: Let C be a collection (a collection is a set of digital objects; see Def. MI B.19 in Appendix B for details), and 2^C be the set of all subsets of C. Let ϕ be an empty set. Let $HT = (H, Contents, P)$ be a hypertext, where

1. $H = ((V_H, E_H), L_H, F_H)$ is a structure (i.e., a directed graph with vertices V_H and edges E_H, along with labels L_H and labeling function F_H on the graph; see Def. MI B.4 in Appendix B.

2. $Contents \subseteq C \cup AllSubStreams \cup AllSubStructuredStreams$ can include digital objects of a collection C, all of their (sub)streams (a stream is a sequence whose codomain is a nonempty set; see Def. MI B.3 in Appendix B) and all possible restrictions of the StructuredStream (see Def. MI B.17 in Appendix B) functions of digital objects.

3. $P : V_H \longrightarrow 2^{Contents}$ is a function which associates a node of the hypertext with the node content. Note that the range of P is $2^{Contents}$ instead of $Contents$ as defined in Def. MI B.24 in Appendix B.

According to the definition of a minimum DL in Appendix B, a DL has hypertext and so can be a Web accessible information system. Therefore, $\forall C$, $\exists HT$, i.e, for each collection C in a DL, there exists a hypertext (statically or dynamically created) associated with C.

If $subC \in 2^C$ and $subC \neq \phi$, $subC$ can be partitioned into a set of (non)overlapping clusters (groups) $\{cluster_1, cluster_2, \ldots, cluster_k\}$, where $cluster_i$ is denoted as a cluster belonging to $subC$, and $\bigcup_{i=1}^{k} cluster_i = subC$.

Contents of $subC$ is denoted $CluCon(subC) = \{cluCon_1, cluCon_2, \ldots, cluCon_k\}$, where $cluCon_i$ is the contents associated with $cluster_i$.

Let $VSpa$ be a vector space (see Def. PR A.13 in Appendix A) and $Base$ be a set of basis vectors in $VSpa$. Let $VisualM$ be a set of visual marks (e.g., points, lines, areas, volumes, and glyphs) and $VisualMP$ be a set of visual properties (e.g., position, size, length, angle, slope, color, gray scale, texture, shape, animation, blink, and motion) of visual marks.

Examples:

The notion of *conceptual representations* for user information needs was used in Appendix B to define searching service, however, it was not formally defined. Def. AR C.1 in Appendix C is a formal definition for conceptual representations for user information needs. Based on Def. AR C.1, we can define not only searching, but also browsing services. The examples illustrated below show conceptual representations for user information needs related to textual and image retrieval, and hypertext navigation.

Examples of user information needs: $q = (H_q, Contents_q, P_q) \in Q$

Examples from a) through c) show that conceptual representation for user information needs are materialized into a query specification.

1. Example a): Textual retrieval: q is a keyword named "energy."

   A user's information need is something about energy, she may explicitly express it as a key word "energy."

   $q = ((V_q, E_q), L_q, F_q), Contents_q, P_q)$, where $V_q = \{v_1\}, Eq = \phi, Lq = \phi, F_q : V_q \longrightarrow L_q, Contents_q$ is the stream of string "energy," and $P_q : V_q \longrightarrow Contents_q$.

   In this case, $H_q = ((V_q, E_q), L_q, F_q)$ is a one-node graph (see Fig. D.1), and P_q maps that node to its contents, i.e., string "energy" (indicated by the dashed arrows in Fig. D.1).

Figure D.1: q is a keyword named "energy." Adapted from [212].

2. Example b): Textual retrieval: q is a structured query named "animal bones from the Nimrin site."

   A user wants to find records about animal bones from the Nimrin Site from ETANA-DL (an integrated archaeological DL [213]). q is a structured query represented as '$+objectType : Bone + site : Nimrin$' based on the query language of ETANA-DL. "$+objectType : Bone$" means that the object type of the user's interested records should be bone (i.e., the attribute *objectType* should contain value *Bone*); "$+site : Nimrin$" means that the records should be from site Nimrin (i.e., the attribute site should contain value Nimrin.). $q = ((V_q, E_q), L_q, F_q), Contents_q, P_q)$, where $V_q = \{v_1, v_2\}, E_q = \phi, L_q = \{object\ type, site\}, F_q : V_q \longrightarrow L_q, Contents_q$ is the stream of strings "animal bones" and "Nimrin," and $P_q : V_q \longrightarrow Contents_q$.

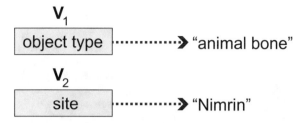

Figure D.2: q is a structured query named "animal bones from the Nimrin site." Adapted from [212].

In this case, $H_q = ((V_q, E_q), L_q, F_q)$ is a two-node graph with "object type" and "site" as labels for these two nodes (see Fig. D.2), and P maps each node to its contents, i.e., string "animal bones" and "Nimrin," respectively, (indicated by the dashed arrows in Fig. D.2).

Structured query q was defined as a set of attribute-value pairs: $q = \{A_1 : value_{1q}, \ldots, A_k : value_{kq}, \ldots, A_n : value_{nq}\}$, where A_k is an attribute or metadata field and each $value_{kq}$ a value belonging to the domain of A_k [106]. We find that this definition can be derived from Def. AR C.1 (definition of a set of conceptual representations for user information needs). By Def. AR C.1, we get $A_k = F_q(v_k)$ and $value_{kq} = P_q(v_k)$, i.e., A_k is the label of node v_k and $value_{kq}$ is the contents associated with v_k.

3. Example c): Image retrieval: q itself is an image, which contains five spatially related sub-images (objects).

   A user wants to find some images similar to an existing one as shown in Fig. D.3 (a). $q = ((V_q, E_q), L_q, F_q), Contents_q, P_q)$,   where $V_q = \{v_1, v_2, v_3, v_4, v_5\}, E_q = \{e_1, e_2, e_3, e_4, e_5\}, L_q = \{`fire', `earth', `metal', `water', `wood', `produce'\}, F_q : V_q \cup E_q \longrightarrow L_q, Contents_q$ is the stream of the five spatially related sub-images with their location information, and $P_q : V_q \longrightarrow Contents_q$.

   In this case, H_q is a graph of five nodes with labels 'fire', 'earth', 'metal', 'water', 'wood', and 'produce', respectively, as illustrated in Fig. D.3 (b). P_q maps each node to its contents, i.e., the associated sub-image with its spatial information (indicated by the dashed arrows in Fig. D.3). This kind of query representation has been used to retrieve images according to spatial relationships of objects or layout representations (e.g., [21, 209]).

4. Example d) Navigation starting point

   $q = ((V_q, E_q), L_q, F_q), Contents_q, P_q)$,   where $V_q = \{v_1\}, E_Q = \phi, L_q = \{`ETANA - DL'\}, F_q : V_q \longrightarrow L_q, Contents_q$ is the homepage of ETANA-DL, and $P_q : V_q \longrightarrow Contents_q$.

   In this case, $H_q = ((V_q, E_q), L_q, F_q)$ is a one-node graph with "ETANA-DL" as label for that node (see Fig. D.4), and P_q maps that node to its contents, i.e., the ETANA-DL homepage

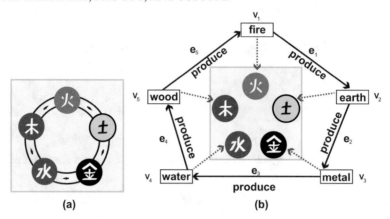

Figure D.3: q is an image of 5 spatially related sub-images. Adapted from [212].

(indicated by the dashed arrows in Fig. D.4). In this situation, a user does not have an explicit information need like a query though she may have a conceptual information need. She wants to know something about ETANA-DL. She goes to its homepage and her navigation start point represents her initial information need.

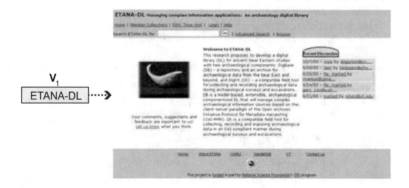

Figure D.4: q is a user's navigation start point. Adapted from [212].

Fig. D.5 shows two constructs of an exploring service. The left part of Fig. D.5 is a state diagram, which consists of events. The dashed arrow means an event e_i has associated operations(s) in the set of operations, denoted by OP_Set. Characterized by its associated operations(s) in $ESpa$, an exploring service can be a searching, browsing, clustering, or visualization service as illustrated in the following theorems and lemmas according to Def. AR C.1, Def. AR C.2, and Def. AR C.3. A sequence of events may be associated with a sequence of operations, e.g., OP_s is followed by OP_{clu}, OP_{viz}, and OP_{clu} as illustrated by the three arrows numbered 1, 2, and 3, respectively, (see Fig. D.6).

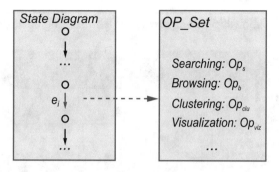

Figure D.5: Constructs for an exploring service. Adapted from [212, 214].

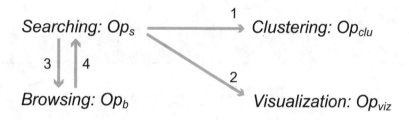

Figure D.6: Sequence of operations. Adapted from [212].

D.2   PROOFS

Table D.1 shows the relationships among the theorems (lemmas), operations, and the sequence of these operations. If an operation is used for a theorem (lemma), there will be a check mark in the corresponding cell. Theorem 1 and Theorem 2 state searching and browsing services separately; Theorem 3 and Theorem 4 propose post retrieval clustering and visualization services, respectively; Lemma 1 and Lemma 2 argue that searching and browsing can be mapped to each other under certain conditions; Lemma 3 and Lemma 4 demonstrate switching between searching and browsing.

Theorem 1: If $\forall e_i$, the associated operation with event e_i is OP_s, then an exploring service is a searching service.

The event e_i in Fig. D.7 illustrates that a user issues a query $query_i$. The event then triggers operation OP_s, as indicated by the dashed arrow. The patterned arrow denotes the output of OP_s, i.e., searching results for $query_i$. If the searching result is empty or the user does not think the result is related to her information need, then we consider the user is not satisfied with the searching service.

Proof: $\forall q \in Q$, where Q is a set of conceptual representations for user information needs (see Def. AR C.1), there is a searching scenario having a final event of returning the matching function

Table D.1: Relationship among theorems (lemmas) and operations. Adapted from [212].

Theorems and Lemmas	Searching OP_s	Browsing OP_b	Clustering OP_{clu}	Visualization OP_{viz}
Theorem 1	X			
Theorem 2		X		
Theorem 3 (OP_s followed by OP_{clu})	X		X	
Theorem 4 (OP_s followed by OP_{viz})	X			X
Lemma 1	X	X		
Lemma 2	X	X		
Lemma 3 (OP_b followed by OP_s)	X	X		
Lemma 4 (OP_s followed by OP_b)	X	X	X	

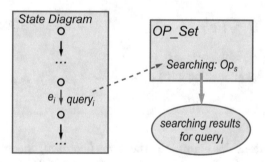

Figure D.7: An exploring service is a searching service. Adapted from [212, 214].

value $sim_s = OP_q(q, do)$ for each digital object $do \in C$ and $\{OP_s((q, do), Sim_s)\}$, the contents of the retrieved digital objects for query q.

Searching services may need indexing services provided by a DL to speed up the performance. We do not discuss indexing services here. Note that the OP_{viz} function may be applied on searching results.

Theorem 2: If $\forall v \in V_q$, $v \in V_H$, and e_i, the associated operation with event e_i is OP_b, then an exploring service is a browsing service.

By Def. MI B.25 of Appendix B, a browsing service is associated with an underlying hypertext construct. Event e_i in Fig. D.8 models a path through a website a user follows to access the target node. It invokes operation OP_b defined in Def. AR C.2 of Appendix C. The output of OP_b is the

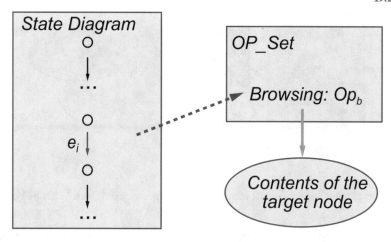

Figure D.8: An exploring service is a browsing service. Adapted from [212, 214].

contents of the target node. A sequence of target nodes, $v_{t\_0}, v_{t\_1}, \ldots, v_{t\_i}, \ldots, v_{t\_k}$, associated with a sequence of events, $e_0, e_1, \ldots, e_i, \ldots, e_k$, is denoted as a user's navigation path π.

Since $\forall v \in V_q$, $v \in V_H$, each node v in a user's information need $((V_q, E_q), L_q, F_q)$ is included in the hypertext, therefore the user's navigation path π is a (sub)structure of the hypertext. If $\exists v \in V_q$, $v \in V_H$, and the contents associated with v are related to the user's information need, then we consider the user is satisfied with the browsing service. Otherwise, either contents in the hypertext or contents associated with nodes in the user's navigation path π are not related to the user's information need. Both lead to an unpleasant browsing experience. In the latter case, there may be a node associated with relevant contents in the hypertext; however, the vertex does not belong to V_q (i.e., the node is not included in the user's navigation path π). Therefore, the user is lost in the hypertext when browsing.

Proof: given a node v_s and a link (v_s, v_t), where $v_s, v_t \in V_q$ and $v_s, v_t \in V_H$, according to Def. AR C.2, each link traversal event e_i is associated with a function $OP_b : E_H \longrightarrow 2^{Contents}$, $OP_b(v_s, v_t) = P(v_t)$, and P is a function which associates a node of the hypertext with the node context, i.e., given a node v_s and a link (v_s, v_t) retrieves the contents of target node v_t. Therefore, the exploring service is a browsing service.

Theorem 3: If $\forall e_i$, the associated operations with event e_i are OP_s followed by OP_{clu}, then an exploring service is a post retrieval clustering service.

The event e_i in Fig. D.9 associates operation OP_s, as indicated by the one dashed arrow. The two patterned arrows (numbered 1 and 3, respectively) point to the output of OP_s and OP_{clu}, respectively. Searching results for $query_i$ provide the input to OP_{clu} (shown by the arrow numbered 2).

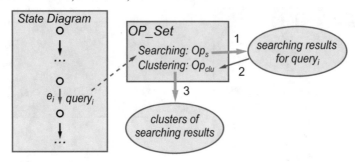

Figure D.9: An exploring service is post retrieval clustering. Adapted from [212, 214].

Proof: $\forall q \in Q$, there is a searching scenario returning C_{retr}, a set of retrieved digital objects, and a post retrieval clustering scenario having a final event of returning the matching function value $sim_{clu} = OP_{clu1}(cluster_x, cluster_y)$ for each pair of clusters and the contents of the clustering results $\{OP_{clu}((cluster_x, cluster_y), sim_{clu})\}$, where $cluster_x, cluster_y \subseteq C_{retr}$. Note that if $C_{retr} = C$, then the exploration service also is a clustering service on a whole collection C.

Lemma 1: Let $Espa_{browse} = (Q_{browse}, Contents_{browse}, OP\_Set_{browse})$ be the exploration space of a browsing service $Eser_{browse}$, where $OP_b \in OP\_Set_{browse}$; let $Espa_{search} = (Q_{search}, Contents_{search}, OP\_Set_{search})$ be the exploration space of a searching service $Eser_{search}$, where $OP_s \in OP\_Set_{search}$; let π be a user's navigation path, a sequence of target nodes consisting of v_{t_k-1} and v_{t_k} as the last two nodes; let Π be as a set of π, where π is a user's navigation path, a sequence of target nodes, $v_{t\_0}, v_{t\_1}, \ldots, v_{t\_i}, \ldots, v_{t\_k}$, associated with a sequence of events, $e_0, e_1, \ldots, e_i, \ldots, e_k$.

1. $Eser_{browse}$ can be converted to $Eser_{search}$, denoted $Eser_{browse} \Rightarrow Eser_{search}$, if $\exists M_1 : \Pi \longrightarrow Q_{search}$, such that $\forall \pi \in \Pi$, $M_1(\pi) = q \in Q_{search}$, and $OP_b(v_{t\_k-1}, v_{t\_k}) = P(v_{t\_k}) = OP_s(q)$, where $P(v_{t\_k})$ is the contents associated with the last target node $v_{t\_k} \in V_{q_{browse}}$ and $OP_s(q)$ is the content associated with retrieved digital objects for query $q \in Q_{search}$.

2. $Eser_{search}$ can be converted to $Eser_{browse}$, denoted $Eser_{search} \Rightarrow Eser_{browse}$, if $\exists M_2 : Q_{search} \longrightarrow \Pi$, such that $\forall q \in Q_{search}$, $M_2(q) = \pi \in \Pi$, and $OP_b(v_{t\_k-1}, v_{t\_k}) = P(v_{t\_k}) = OP_s(q)$, where $P(v_{t\_k})$ is the contents associated with the last target node $v_{t\_k} \in V_q$ and $OP_s(q)$ is the content associated with retrieved digital objects for query $q \in Q_{search}$.

Proof:

1. $\forall \pi \in \Pi$, $M_1(\pi) = q \in Q_{search}$, and the results of the operations associated with each link traversal event are the contents of retrieved digital objects for query q. Therefore, $Eser_{browse} \Rightarrow Eser_{search}$.

2. $\forall q \in Q_{search}$, $M_2(q) = \pi \in \Pi$, and the results of the operations associated with the event of issuing query q are the contents of the last target node v_{t_k} in the user?s navigation path π. Therefore, $Eser_{search} \Rightarrow Eser_{browse}$.

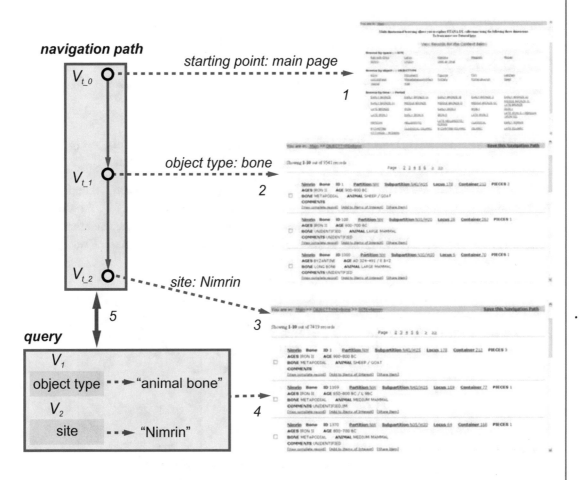

Figure D.10: Example of mapping between navigation path and a structured query. Adapted from [212].

Example:

The rectangle shown in Fig. D.10 represents a navigation path of a user. It consists of three nodes. The first one v_{t_0} is the starting point, which is associated with the main page of ETANA-DL's multi-dimensional browsing interface (illustrated by an arrow numbered 1 in Fig. D.10); the second one v_{t_1} is related to a page about 9541 bone records (illustrated by an arrow numbered 2 in Fig. D.10); the page about 7419 bone records from the Nimrin site is the contents of the last target node v_{t_1} (illustrated by an arrow numbered 3 in Fig. D.10) and it displays the retrieved results for a structured query (illustrated by an arrow numbered 4 in Fig. D.10). The bidirectional arrow numbered 5 in Fig. D.10 denotes that the navigation path and the structured query can be mapped to each other.

Lemma 2: Given $Q_{search} = \{q_1, q_2, \ldots, q_n\}$, $\Pi = \{\pi_1, p\pi_2, \ldots, \pi_n\}$, where π_i is a user's navigation path, a sequence of target nodes consisting of $v_{i\_t\_k-1}$ and $v_{i\_t\_k}$ as the last two nodes, $OP_s(q_i) = OP_b(v_{i\_t\_k-1}, v_{i\_t\_k}) = contents_i \in 2^{Contents}$ (see Def. AR C.2), $OP_s^{-1}(contents_i) = q_i$, and $P_b^{-1}(contents_i) = \pi_i$, then $\exists M_1, \exists M_2, Eser_{browse} \Rightarrow Eser_{search}$, and $Eser_{search} \Rightarrow Eser_{browse}$.

Proof:

1. $\exists M_1, \forall \pi_i \in \Pi, M_1(\pi_i) = OP_s^{-1}(OP_b(v_{i\_t\_k-1}, v_{i\_t\_k})) = OP_s^{-1}(contents_i) = q_i$, therefore, according to Lemma 1, $\exists M_1 : \Pi \longrightarrow Q_{search}$ and $Eser_{browse} \Rightarrow Eser_{search}$.

2. $\exists M_2, \forall q \in Q_{search}, M_2(q_i) = OP_b^{-1}(OP_s(q_i)) = OP_b^{-1}(contents_i) = \pi_i$, therefore, according to Lemma 1, $\exists M_2 : Q_{search} \longrightarrow \Pi$ and $Eser_{search} \Rightarrow Eser_{browse}$. As shown in Fig. D.11, both "$query_i$" and "π_i" are associated with the same results, therefore, $\exists M_1 : M_1(query_i) = \pi_i, \exists M_2 : M_2(\pi_i) = query_i, Eser_{browse} \Rightarrow Eser_{search}$ and $Eser_{search} \Rightarrow Eser_{browse}$.

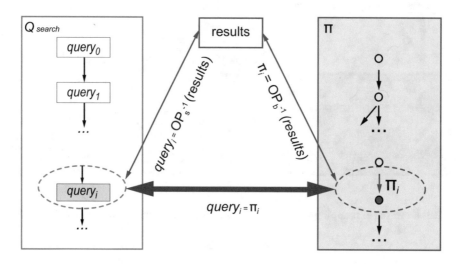

Figure D.11: "$query_i$" and "p_i" are associated with the same results. Adapted from [212, 214].

Example:

There are 3 records about acacia seed in ETANA-DL. They are associated with the query "acacia seed" (represented as '$+objectType : seed + name : acacia$' based on the query language of ETANA-DL) and with a navigation path (represented as '$Main >> OBJECTTYPE =$

Seed >> *Name* = *Acacia*') as shown in Fig. D.12. In this example, searching results are displayed along with the query *q* and browsing results are displayed along with the corresponding navigation path π. Therefore, there exists function M_1 and M_1, such that $OP_s^{-1}(results) = q$ and $OP_b^{-1}(results) = \pi$, where *results* are represented by the 3 acacia seed records.

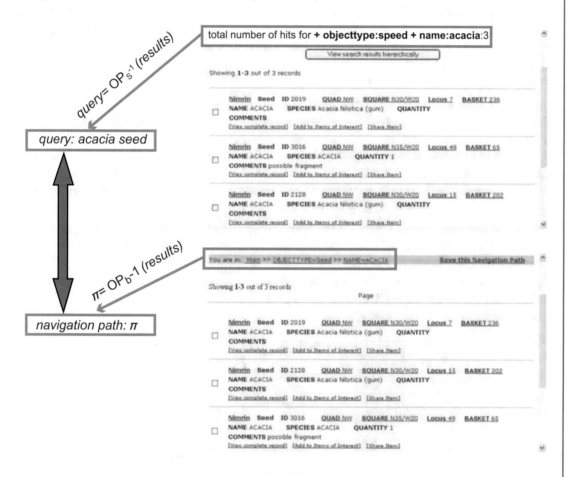

Figure D.12:   Example of Lemma 2. Adapted from [212]

PESTO [37], DataWeb [162], and MIX [165] are cases where browsing can be converted to searching. Because of PESTO's "query-in-place" paradigm, DataWeb's hierarchically browsing, and MIX's navigation commands of the standard DOM API, the navigation paths of each of them can be mapped to queries. Therefore, $Eserbrowse \Rightarrow Esersearch$.

Lemma 3: Let $Espa_{postBrowse} = (Q_{postBrowse}, Contents_{postBrowse}, OP\_Set_{postBrowse})$ be the exploration space of an exploring service $Eser_{postBrowse}$ occurring after $Eser_{browse}$, where

$Contents_{postBrowse} = OP_b(v_{t\_i-1}, v_{t\_i})$ is the contents associated with edge (v_{t_i-1}, v_{t_i}), v_{t_i-1} and v_{t_i} are the last two nodes of a user's navigation path $\pi_i \in \Pi$ in $Eser_{browse}$, $C_{postBrowse}$ is a set of digital objects associated with $Contents_{postBrowse}$, and $OP_b \in OP\_Set_{postBrowse}$. According to Theorem 1, $Eser_{postBrowse}$ is a searching service (i.e., browsing service $Eser_{browse}$ leads to searching service $Eser_{postBrowse}$), if $OP_s : (Q_{postBrowse} \times C_{postBrowse}) \times Sim_s \longrightarrow 2^{Contents}$, where $Sim_s = \{OP_q(q, do)|q \in Q_{postBrowse}, do \in C_{postBrowse}$, where $OP_q : Q_{postBrowse} \times C_{postBrowse} \longrightarrow R$ is a matching function that associates a real number with $q \in Q_{postBrowse}$ and a digital object $do \in C_{postBrowse}$.

Proof:

$\forall q \in Q_{postBrowse}$, $\{OP_s((q, do), Sim_s)\}$ is the contents of the retrieved digital objects for query q, where $Sim_s = OP_q(q, do)$, therefore, by Theorem 1, $Eser_{postBrowse}$ is a searching service.

The switch from browsing to searching in PESTO [37], DataWeb [162], and MIX [165] can be generalized as shown in Fig. D.13. The arrow numbered 1 points to the browsing results associated with navigation path π_i. Since π_i and $query_i$ can be mapped to each other in these systems as discussed before (indicated by the arrow numbered 3), they are associated with the same results, $Contents_{postBrowse}$. Therefore, the arrow numbered 2 also points to $Contents_{postBrowse}$. After browsing, a user searches $Contents_{postBrowse}$ for a new query $query$. Searching results for $query_{i+1}$ then is a subset of $Contents_{postBrowse}$. It is illustrated as the circle and pointed to by the arrow numbered 4 in Fig. D.13. Therefore, $query_{i+1}$ is a new query refined from $query_i$ as indicated by the arrow numbered 5. So switching from browsing to searching in this situation is a query refining or expansion process.

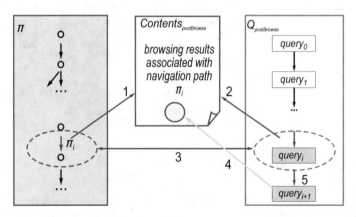

Figure D.13: "$query_{i+1}$" is refined from "$query_i$" after browsing. Adapted from [212, 214].

Lemma 4: Let $Espa_{postRetr} = (Q_{postRetr}, Contents_{postRetr}, OP\_Set_{postRetr})$ be the exploration space of an exploring service $Eser_{postRetr}$ occurring **after** $Eser_{search}$, where $Q_{postRetr} =$

$\{((V_{q_{postRetr}}, E_{q_{postRetr}}), L_{q_{postRetr}}, F_{q_{postRetr}}), Contents_{q_{postRetr}}, P_{q_{postRetr}}\}$ (see Def. AR C.1), $Contents_{postRetr}$ is associated with C_{retr}, a set of retrieved digital objects for query $q \in Q_{search}$ in $Eser_{search}$. According to Theorem 2, Lemma 1, and Lemma 2, $Eser_{postRetr}$ is a browsing service (i.e., searching service $Eser_{search}$ leads to browsing service $Eser_{postRetr}$), if $OP\_Set_{postRetr} = \{OP_s, OP_{clu}\}$, $cluCon_{retr} = \{OP_{clu}((cluster_x, cluster_y), sim_{clu})|cluster_x, cluster_y \subseteq C_{retr}\} = \{cluCon_{retr\_1}, cluCon_{retr\_2}, \dots, cluConretr\_i, \dots, cluCon_{retr\_z}\}$ is the contents of clustered retrieved results, where $sim_{clu} = OP_{clu1}(cluster_x, cluster_y)$ (see Def. AR C.2), $\Pi = \{\pi_1, \pi_2, \dots, \pi_i, \dots, \pi_z\}$, where $\pi_i = (v_0, v_i)$ is a navigation path consisting of only two nodes, $v_0, v_i \in V_{q_{postRetr}}$, and $\exists M_{b\_cluster} : \Pi \longrightarrow cluCon_{retr}$.

The event e_i of issuing $query_i$ triggers the operation OP_s, as indicated by the dashed arrow numbered 1 in Fig. D.14. The patterned arrow numbered 2 denotes the output of OP_s, i.e., $Contents_{postRetr}$ (searching results for $query_i$). OP_{clu} takes $Contents_{postRetr}$ as input and yields as output the contents of clusters as shown by the arrows numbered 3 and 4. The arrow numbered 5 represents the mapping from each navigation path to the contents of a cluster. Therefore, the contents of the last target nodes of these navigation paths are the contents of clusters and the mapping function $M_{b\_cluster}$ can be viewed to be OP_b for browsing.

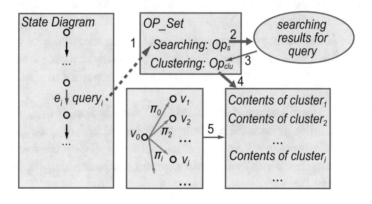

Figure D.14: Switch from searching to browsing. Adapted from [212, 214].

Proof:

$\exists v \in V_{q_{postRetr}}$, $v \in V_H$, and e_i, the associated operation with event e_i is $OP_b((v_0, v_i)) = M_{b\_cluster}(\pi_i) = cluCon_{retr\_i}$, where v_i is the target node of π_i, therefore, by Theorem 2, $Eser_{postRetr}$ is a browsing service.

Categorizing or clustering searching results is a case of switching searching to browsing. ScentTrails [180] can be viewed as a special case as $|cluCon_{retr}| = 1$, i.e., each cluster is a singleton having one item from the retrieved result list.

Theorem 4: If $\forall e_i$, the associated operations with e_i are OP_s followed by OP_{viz}, then an exploring service is a post retrieval visualization service.

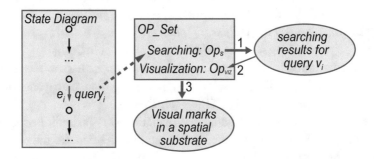

Figure D.15:   An exploring service is a visualization service. Adapted from [212, 214].

The event e_i in Fig. D.15 associates operation OP_s, as indicated by the dashed arrow. The two patterned arrows (numbered 1 and 3, respectively) point to the output of OP_s and OP_{viz}, respectively. Searching results for $query_i$ is the input to OP_{viz} (shown by the arrow numbered 2). Proof:

$\forall q \in Q$, there is a searching scenario returning a set of retrieved digital objects C_{retr} and a post retrieval visualization scenario having a final event of visually mapping a set of digital objects (or each digital object) of C_{retr} to a visual mark with visual properties in a spatial substrate of n dimensions.

If $n = 2$, it is 2-D visualization; if $n = 3$, it is 3-D visualization. If $C_{retr} = C$, the exploring service also is a visualization service for a whole collection. If $\exists M_2(q)$, the exploring service is a visualization service for browsing. Vector graphics and raster display are two different types of display used for representation. Virtually all modern current computer video displays translate vector representations to a raster format.

D.3   INTEGRATION TOOLKIT: 5SSUITE

The 5S framework allows a new approach to DL development (see Fig. D.16). 5SGraph [261, 262] supports analysis and specification, while 5SGen [140] melds together suitable components from a large software pool to yield a running system. To semi-automatically build an integrated DL, we extend this approach and develop 5SSuite to cover the process of union DL generation, including requirements gathering (see Fig. D.16 step 1), conceptual modeling (see Fig. D.16 step 2), rapid prototyping (see Fig. D.16 step 3), and code generation (see Fig. D.16 step 4 and Fig. D.17). 5SSuite consists of 5SGraph, 5SGen, and SchemaMapper (see the Mapping Tool in Fig. D.17, described further in book 2 of this series), which plays an important role during integration; it has been extended with additional software for logging and quality assessment, as is discussed in book 2.

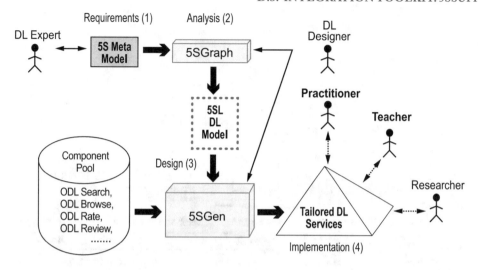

Figure D.16: 5S related tools and their use in developing DLs. Adapted from [105].

A DL designer interacts with the 5SGraph tool to model the DLs to be integrated and the union DL, when a metamodel is fed to 5SGraph. Each produced DL model (described using 5SL) contains a structure sub-model and a scenario sub-model as well as the other three sub-models (i.e., stream, space, and society sub-models). Schemas (metadata formats) are described in the structure sub-model, whereas services are described in the scenario sub-model.

A DL designer interacts with SchemaMapper, which maps a local schema into a global schema for a union DL and generates a wrapper for the DL to be integrated. The wrapper transforms the metadata catalog of its DL to one conforming to the global schema. The converted catalogs are stored in the union catalog, so that the union DL has a global metadata format and union catalog. The mapping process is iterative. When another DL needs to be integrated, the DL designer may use SchemaMapper to help complete mapping and updating of the union catalog. The complexity of the mapping and updating processes can be affected by several factors, such as knowledge of the application domain, the number of elements in the local schema, and the size of the collection to be integrated. Further, there may be users added who administer and/or assess the quality of the integration processes.

To integrate domain specific DLs, a metamodel for that particular domain needs to be developed based on the 5S formal theory. In book 2 of this series, we describe an archaeological DL (ArchDL) metamodel and the use of 5SGraph to model ArchDLs, as well as further details regarding 5SSuite.

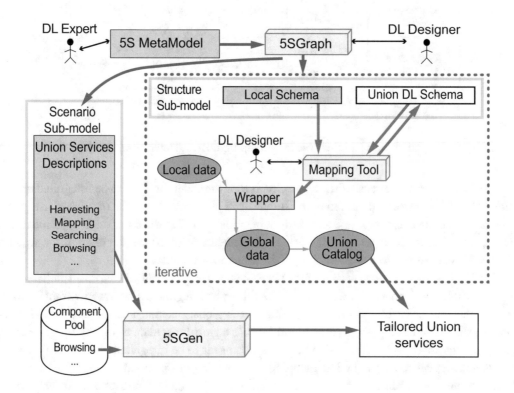

Figure D.17: 5S related integration toolkit and process. Adapted from [212].

APPENDIX E

Glossary

5S A framework for digital libraries, building upon five constructs that each start with the letter 'S': Societies, Scenarios, Spaces, Structures, and Streams.

5SGen Software for generating a digital library, using a pool of components, based on a description in XML using the 5S language (5SL).

5SGraph A graphical user interface allowing a digital library designer to load a metamodel for a class of digital libraries, according to the 5S framework, and then to specify details of a particular digital library, so that 5SGen can generate that digital library.

5SL An XML-based language used to specify a digital library.

5SQual A software toolkit to assess the quality of a (federated) digital library, building upon the 5S framework.

5SSuite The suite of tools supporting digital library work according to the 5S framework.

Access control The prevention of unauthorized use of a resource (e.g., determining who has access to a resource, under what conditions access can occur, and what those accessing the resource are allowed to do).

Algorithm A step by step procedure for solving a specific problem.

Analysis of content A method through which some given data or information is processed, to identify structure, extract entities, determine distributions, prepare summaries, or otherwise develop characterizations, decompositions, or descriptions.

Analyst (user) A person, in some cases connected with intelligence work, who engages in analysis of content, often on individual documents as well as on content collections, to promote understanding, such as for identification of anomalies or trends, early spotting of potential problems, or summarization of a situation.

Anchor A source node of a hyperlink.

Animation A visual portrayal of an activity or process, often involving multiple entities, sometimes based on simulation, typically where motion is perceived from the rendering of a series of images.

Annotation A textual or graphical indication of what is typically a small amount of content, that describes or is otherwise associated with, a part or the whole of another (multimedia) document.

Annotator (user) A person who marks annotations on streams of content or individual documents.

API An Application Program Interface, i.e., a specification of how to work with some program or service, often through a set of protocols used by software components to communicate with each other.

Archive (institution) An organization supporting a collection of content where permanence is highly valued, typically implemented by mechanisms for selection of important works, description of items or aggregates of items, and long-term preservation.

Archive (open) A collection of metadata records, including links or pointers to works of interest, sometimes with those works also included in the archive, together with software services supporting processes like harvesting, listing of (subsets of) records, and retrieval of metadata.

Assignment (in education) Work that a learner should undertake, typically in a course, as required by an instructor.

Assignment (in programming) Assigning a value to a given variable.

Audio What can be heard with the ears – a sound wave in the frequency range suitable for hearing.

Authentication Verification of the identity of an entity, often in the context of electronic communications.

Authorization Affording access rights to a resource for an entity.

Availability A property of a system allowing it to be accessible and usable upon demand by an authorized entity.

Base document Information existing as a whole document for which subdocument(s) have been defined. A digital object becomes a base document upon creation of the first asssociated subdocument.

Browse A type of exploring for information, typically using some logical or visual organization as an aid, as in the WWW, or in a digital or other media collection of documents. See also Chapter 2, which explains that browsing is closely connected with searching, as well as other approaches to exploring. For a precise explanation, see Def. MI B.25.

Catalog A collection of descriptive metadata specifications or records, each of which points to a digital object in a repository; in turn, each digital object should have at least one associated metadata record in the catalog. If multiple metadata formats are included, then there can be one metadata record for each particular format, for a given digital object. For a precise explanation, see Def. MI B.20.

CBIR See Content-based image retrieval below.

Classify To arrange cases according to their category or based on mutual similarity, typically considering several features.

CLIR See Cross language information retrieval below.

Cluster A group of related data or information, often occurring close to each other in some space. Usually the elements of a cluster are similar to each other but not that similar to elements of other clusters.

CMS See Content Management System below.

Collaboration A group of people or other intelligent entities working together to achieve a common goal.

Collection A set of entities, e.g., a set of digital objects found in a digital library. For a precise explanation, see Def. MI B.19.

Community A group of people with common practices, e.g., shared use of a resource (collection), or with common activities (often in the same locality).

Complex object A digital object serving as a logical whole but that is described using a network of digital objects (each an entity in its own right), usually within a repository, as in a digital library.

Compound object An object with more than one constituent part (e.g., a metadata record that is present in multiple versions according to different representation standards, or an image represented using several file formats).

Composite object Many objects bundled together and presented as a single object (e.g., a training package that is made of many parts, such as presentations, assignments, and reading materials).

Comment A remark or observation added to, or otherwise associated with, some document or other type of digital object. In computer science, comments are used for documentation purposes, and should be liberally placed inline in the code.

Completeness A pervasive quality dimension that is associated with many digital library concepts, reflecting if everything appropriate is included. One approach to assess completeness quantitatively is to divide the number of units of some type that are associated with a concept, by the ideal number of units for that concept.

Compress To reduce the size of the representation of some type of content, e.g., reducing the bits required in storage and/or transmission. Lossless (invertible) compression methods allow the original to be perfectly reconstructed from the compressed representation. Lossy methods usually result in a representation (much) smaller than is possible with a lossless method, and allow reconstruction of an approximation of the original that suffices for desired scenarios, but does not allow perfect reconstruction of the original.

Consistency The integrity, validity, and accuracy of a collection of data and/or information, reflecting one aspect of its freedom from errors, such that values fit together according to all relevant correspondences, rules, and patterns, e.g., no value falsifies other values, as when a total reflects the summation of all elements, or a person's first and last names are correctly paired.

Content-based image retrieval (CBIR) Supporting querying from an image collection, using the actual content of the image such as color or shape, instead of using supporting data such as keywords or tags.

Content Management System (CMS) Software (often a type of digital library) that manages information represented in a collection of digital objects, often with a usable interface, commonly supporting submission and search, sometimes with a set of workflows integrated to enable a collaborative environment.

Copyright A legally binding statement of ownership covering a concrete manifestation or rendering of person's creation(s), e.g., novels, paintings, papers, poems, programs, songs, etc. If a piece of work is neither in the public domain nor the permission to use it has been acquired from the creator (or copyright owner), then using the work (other than according to fair use stipulations) or disseminating copies of it would be in violation of copyright law.

Course A unit of instruction and/or learning, aimed to help someone (or a group, as in an academic class) to achieve an educational goal, often requiring at least weeks.

Courseware A program or module developed to assist with learning, usually associated with an educational course.

Coverage The extent of the cases covered by a process or by a content collection.

Crawl Go through all of the parts and elements of (a defined portion of) an archive or the Web (or other hypertext/hypermedia collection) automatically with the help of some computer program, often to collect copies or information.

Crawler A computer program which crawls an archive or the Web or other hyperbase in a methodical, automated manner.

Cross language information retrieval (CLIR) Querying, searching, and accessing information written in a natural language different from the language of a user's query.

Curation Organizing and maintaining (digital) data.

Curriculum A designed course or set of courses aimed to help students specialize in a certain field of study. In higher education, a curriculum often includes specialized courses as well as general courses within a field.

Database A structured collection of data held on a computer or servers for future access, usually through a database management system, such as one supporting SQL queries, that typically also allows additions, updates, and various kinds of transactions.

Data confidentiality The protection of data from unauthorized disclosure.

Data integrity The assurance that the data received is exactly as sent by an authorized entity (i.e., contains no improper modification, insertion, deletion, or replay).

Denial of Service (DoS) A security attack that prevents the normal use of communications or computing facilities, usually involving overwhelming those facilities with spurious requests or transmissions.

Descriptor In information retrieval, a term capturing a topic that characterizes a document, e.g., the preferred term in a controlled vocabulary, often used in a metadata record to indicate the subject.

Digital object An object whose main component is digital material, e.g., a document or multimedia file. For a precise explanation, see Def. MI B.18 as well as Fig. B.4.

Digital library A collection of digital objects which is accessible by computers, with at least the minimal characteristics (see Appendix B), such as services supporting searching and browsing, as well as a repository of digital content, along with an index and a catalog. More comprehensive digital libraries (see Appendix C) give us new ways to deal with data, information, and knowledge.

Digital library administrator (user) A person who manages the operation of a digital library, such as: cleaning datasets or metadata, curating content, managing accounts, and evaluating existing components.

Digitize To transform something into digital form; thus, scanners are widely used to transform photographs into image files, or paper books into digital books.

Digital rights management (DRM) The protection of content from the different logical security attacks and abuses relating to disrespecting intellectual property rights.

Dimension An aspect or particular component or facet of a situation or a problem; in mathematics, some attribute of a space, like one of the spatial directions.

Dimensionality reduction A method of reducing the number of (random) variables in a data representation, often done by techniques such as Principal Component Analysis (PCA). In information retrieval, the document by term matrix might have hundreds of thousands of columns which could be approximately mapped down to hundreds of dimensions, sometimes each covering an aggregate semantic aspect (as through LSA – see below).

Dissemination The transmission or broadcasting of information with the help of some medium or mechanism, without necessarily getting direct feedback from the receivers.

DRM See Digital rights management above.

Dublin Core A metadata format used for describing electronic resources, consisting of the following 15 fields for each resource: title, creator, subject, description, publisher, contributor, date, type, format, identifier, source, language, relation, coverage, and rights. This resulted from a meeting connected with OCLC, in Dublin, Ohio, USA; the Dublin Core Metadata Initiative now has responsibility.

Education A process whereby learning takes place, usually leading to an enhancement of knowledge and/or skills, sometimes supported by digital multimedia related technologies.

Educational institution A school, college, university, or other organization dedicated to educating people.

Entity Something that has a separate existence, typically either concrete or abstract. In data modeling or in an ontology, an entity is a unit of data or a concept such as a person, place, or thing. Relationships may exist among entities.

Evaluation A process of assessment, typically involving measuring quality against some criteria or standard(s), e.g., determining a digital library's utility, usability, effectiveness, efficiency, and cost.

Explore Search, browse, investigate, study, or analyze for the purpose of discovery, e.g., pursuing truth or facts about something.

Explorer (user) A user who explores collections or experimental streams of documents.

Experiment A procedure, often part of the scientific method, to test some hypothesis, model, rule, or idea. Typically, this involves attempting something, making measurements, collecting data, and determining if the test was successful.

Faceted classification system An approach to organizing a collection of objects that each can be described by multiple characteristics or attributes, whose values are distinct, thus effecting a partitioning. In digital libraries, common facets include date, author name, language, or city of publication. See also Search, faceted.

Functionality The ability to produce desired results from suitable inputs in a particular situation or environment. Usually this involves a program or system demonstrating a capability that it is expected to fulfill. For example, a digital library should be able to store and retrieve information of interest.

Feature A prominent characteristic of an entity. Thus, we describe people using features like height, weight, hair color, or age. Documents often are characterized by features like length and date, or by the terms or concepts related to their content. Software features typically relate to their functionality or the scenarios supported; e.g., search is a feature of digital libraries through which one can locate interesting metadata in the digital library.

Feature extraction Transforming data into feature vectors, e.g., representing documents in a vector space where each column represents a distinct term, or representing images as a concatenation of sets of features for each of color, shape, and texture.

Feedback Information, often provided by humans, giving some assessment of the results of a system performing a task. In the context of information retrieval, a human gives judgments on the relevance of the entries in a result set. In the context of the Web, logs aggregate information on what documents are viewed, what links are clicked on, and what sites are visited.

Filter Selecting what to pass through from a stream. In a pipeline of software routines, each routine only includes in its output a suitable portion of its input. In a system for Selective Dissemination of Information, each client only receives personalized information.

Gazetteer A geographical index or geographical database. Thus, GeoNames is a gazetteer which contains country names and over 8 million place names.

Generation Referring to societies, a time period during which something is of interest, e.g., when a given technology is widely used, or when people grew up with the WWW in place (i.e., the Net Generation – sometimes called Generation Z or M). Referring to information retrieval, computational linguistics, modeling, or probabilities, a process of producing something, often in accordance with a (generative) model, grammar, design, or distribution.

Geo-coding A process associating a document with some specific latitude and longitude based on locations recognized, e.g., by geo-parsing. Thus, a document is mapped to a location on Earth (e.g., preparation is made to support queries like: "Give me all documents that refer to parks in the Blacksburg vicinity.").

Geo-parsing A process analyzing documents to recognize references to locations, while ignoring false references (e.g., names that might refer to places but actually refer to the name of an organization or person).

Geographic entity An entity which occupies space and has geographical attributes such as latitude and longitude (e.g., city, country, lake, etc.).

Geographic relationship The connection of some entity to a geographic location (e.g., relating a university to its locality), or the specification of how two geographic entities are associated (e.g., USA is north of Brazil). In the case of Web search from a mobile device, e.g., when looking for food, results might be given priority when identifying a restaurant located near to where the query was submitted.

Geographic query A request or question posed that should return information about geographic locations.

Grammar A set of rules used to represent linguistic, logical, or mathematical sentences. In linguistics, each natural language can be partially characterized by its syntax, that includes its grammar. In computer science, every programming language has a specific, and usually relatively simple, grammar. For a precise explanation of one type of grammar, see Def. PR A.7.

Graph A mathematical structure made of nodes, along with links (arcs) that connect (some of) the nodes. This can be visually rendered in a diagram with circles or dots, connected by lines (sometimes with arrows, in the case of a directed graph). For a precise explanation, see Def. PR A.6.

Harvest (metadata) In the case of the Open Archives Initiative (OAI), the gathering of some or all of the metadata in a repository, often into another repository, using a specialized protocol (e.g., Protocol for Metadata Harvesting).

Hierarchy A structure or organization in which every entity (except the root or topmost entity) has a (single) other entity as parent (i.e., one that points to it), as in an organization chart, or a military command structure.

Hyperbase A broad term that encompasses both hypertext and hypermedia collections of documents, analogous to a database or knowledge base, but distinguished by providing support for hyperlinks.

Hyperlink A reference or link from a document in a hypertext or hypermedia collection to some other information that can be accessed electronically, usually in the same collection; note that one such popular hypermedia collection is the WWW. See also Link.

Hypermedia A collection of multimedia documents (e.g., texts, audio, graphics, images, or videos) in which (some) resources are linked together, so that, by selecting a link from one document, the target (destination) of that link can be accessed (almost) immediately.

Hypertext A collection of digital texts in which (some) resources are linked together, so that, by selecting a link from one text, the target (destination) of that link can be accessed (almost) immediately. For a precise explanation, see Def. MI B.24.

IDF See Inverse document frequency below.

Image A representation of something that can be seen visually, like a graphic or photograph, typically a two-dimensional picture, that is represented as a matrix with entries that have values, e.g., binary (for black and white), integer (for grayscale), or a tuple of integers (for color).

Index A collection of indicators or pointers, e.g., used in digital libraries for finding records. Often entries in an index are pairs, with some value (e.g., a term found in documents) coupled with a set of pointers (e.g., to the documents having that term). For a precise explanation, see Def. MI B.22 as well as Fig. B.5.

Indexing A process that produces an index. Though historically many indexes were produced manually, most today are produced automatically by a group of programs that: analyze texts, identify words or other tokens (sometimes convert to stems), and then prepare the index. Often this involves sorting or other manipulations of suitable data structures. For a precise explanation, see Def. MI B.22 as well as Fig. B.5.

Intellectual property rights (IPR) Legally enforceable control of use of some creation of the human mind, commonly resulting from a patent, copyright, or license agreement.

Interoperate The working together of different systems, e.g., when the parts of a federated digital library operate as if they were a single digital library.

IPR See Intellectual property rights above.

Inverse document frequency (IDF) A value, typically used to compute the weight of an entry (term) in the vector space used to represent a document collection, based on the inverse document frequency, e.g., the logarithm of the ratio that is the total number of documents in the collection divided by the number of documents containing a particular term.

Knowledge base A collection of data, information, and/or knowledge along with services which allow such content to be collected, managed, searched, utilized, and shared – in support of scenarios typically associated with artificial intelligence. Often, high level representations like rules or frames make up the knowledge base, and support inference.

Latent Dirichlet Allocation (LDA) A generative probabilistic model, applied in information retrieval to build a topic model for documents, where each word occurrence is attributable to a topic, where each document is a mixture of a small number of topics, and where the topic distribution is assumed to have a Dirichlet prior. This latter assumption distinguishes LDA from PLSA (see below).

Latent semantic analysis (LSA) Sometimes called LSI, i.e., latent semantic indexing, a technique in information retrieval or natural language processing, that uses the singular value decomposition (SVD), commonly applied to a vector space representation, to reduce the dimensionality (number of columns) based on the assumption that words that co-occur are close in meaning. Thus, a pair of documents, one having words related to those in the other, might, after LSI, yield high similarity, even though there are few words that occur in both documents.

LDA See Latent Dirichlet Allocation above.

Learner A person who is undergoing a positive change in the state of their knowledge. Digital resources made available through educational digital libraries often are collected to serve learners.

Lecture An educational lesson from speaker to audience, often enhanced through interaction and discussion. Though commonly occurring with all participants present together in a classroom, telecommunications allows lectures at a distance, while digital libraries allow recordings of lectures to be viewed remotely at a future time.

Lexicon In linguistics, a language's vocabulary or collection of lexemes, which are roughly the same as the root forms of words (plus compounds), often represented through a dictionary, though more completely covered when additional relationships are integrated, such as lexical/semantic relations and inflectional morphology groupings. In specialized domains, there are tailored lexicons (or simpler constructs like thesauri), like the Unified Medical Language System (UMLS), covering medical and biomedical terms.

Link A digital reference to some other information, which can be electronically accessed by following or traversing the link to its target or destinarion, often, as in hyperbases, by clicking on the anchor that designates the source or origin of the link. See also Hyperlink.

Location In geographic systems, a name of a place or a latitude-longitude description. In information systems, an address or a position for a particular element of data or information (e.g., record) in a database or the Web.

LSA See Latent semantic analysis above.

Mapping Associating each of the elements of one set with one or more elements of the other.

Mark A visible sign placed to distinguished a place or span of content.

Metadata A set of data, often in the form of a record, that provides information about other data, e.g., a digital object. For a precise explanation, see Defs. MI B.13, B.14, and B.15.

Metadata extraction The process of creating a metadata description of a digital object (e.g., an image file, sound file, video, or PDF or Microsoft Office document), through content analysis (e.g., natural language processing) that identifies information like author, publisher, date, etc.

MIT OpenCourseWare An initiative from the Massachusetts Institute of Technology to take educational material from the university and make it readily available through digital technologies.

Module In the context of education, a portion of a curriculum, aimed to help students gain knowledge about a certain area of study, typically describing lesson plans, lectures, exercises, evaluations of student achievements, etc.

Modeling Constructing an abstract model of a process or system, that documents and organizes data, e.g., to support simulation, prediction, or other computation that is related to the underlying process or system.

Multimedia Media that involves multiple content forms, e.g., animation, image, video, audio, text, or other descriptive or interactive content forms.

Multi-modal search A search which uses more than one mode to get results for a search, e.g., using a textual description as well as a sketch to find an image.

National Science Digital Library (NSDL) A project launched early in the 21st Century by the US National Science Foundation (NSF), to provide a broad range of educational resources, generally related to Science, Technology, Engineering, or Mathematics (STEM), while preserving the identity of the individual collections and their associated curation practices.

Navigate In digital libraries, to move through a series of steps, as when browsing, or following a scenario through a user interface, or traversing a sequence of links in a hyperbase.

Non-repudiation Providing protection against denial, of having participated in all or part of a communication, by one of the entities involved in the communication.

NSDL See National Science Digital Library above.

OAI The Open Archives Initiative, originating in 1999 at a meeting in Santa Fe, which aims to support interoperability, especially related to metadata, digital libraries, and content repositories.

OAI-ORE Open Archives Initiative Object Reuse and Exchange, a specification from OAI, defining standards for the exchange of aggregations of Web resources, i.e., compound digital objects, using URIs, resource maps, and proxies.

OAI-PMH Open Archives Initiative Protocol for Metadata Harvesting, a specification from OAI, supporting metadata repository interoperability by having repositories respond to a small set of types of requests, aimed to facilitate sharing of metadata records.

Ontology In information science, a formal representation (model) of knowledge in a domain as a set of relevant concepts along with relationships, usually more comprehensive than a taxonomy, sometimes including definitions and properties associated with the concepts.

Parse To break information into components, along with a description of their syntactic roles, as when a compiler analyzes a computer program, or a natural language processing system applies a grammar to enhance the understanding of a query or document.

PDF Portable Document Format, originally developed by Adobe, also described by the standard ISO 32000-1:2008, used to represent fixed layout documents, facilitating interchange across computer hardware and software systems, building upon Adobe's PostScript language, that can be read (in any of its versions) by the free software package Adobe Reader, with open specifications so other software can support it as well.

PDF/A A version of the Portable Document Format specialized for archiving, e.g., for digital preservation of documents, described by the standard ISO 19005-1:2005.

Personalization A process that allows a computer system to be tailored to a particular individual, usually incorporating user profiles, user preferences, navigation profiles, logs of user actions, and/or the relationships between all these types of information.

PLSA Probabilistic latent semantic analysis (indexing), that adds statistical rigor to LSA (see above), through a mixture decomposition (of conditionally independent multinomial distributions) derived from a latent class model. In information retrieval it yields a low dimensional topic distribution of a document, that contrasts with the high dimensional representation commonly employed in the vector space model (see below).

Policy A set of accepted rules for actions.

Precision A state of exactness. In information retrieval, typically regarding a result set, the ratio of the number relevant retrieved to the total number retrieved.

Presentation specification A descriptive metadata specification for a presentation-based metadata format, that explains how the content in a digital object is rendered, thus yielding a particular view/presentation.

Preserve A process of data/information conservation, so that content can be accurately understood in the future, often over the long term, when the hardware, software, and formats may be radically different, and storage media may be difficult to read correctly.

Privacy A situation or condition whereby data and information about a particular entity (e.g., person) has restricted access, enforcing that entity's desire to limit what is known about them, sometimes supported by legislation as well as cultural norms.

Probability In mathematics, especially probability theory, a measure in the range zero to one, that reflects the likelihood or confidence that an event will occur. Typical interpretations are objective, as when frequencies are observed during experiments, or subjective, as in Bayesian approaches, when expert knowledge and other considerations lead to a priori distributions.

Profile An instance for a particular entity (e.g., person or system) of a descriptive template that gives suitable values for that entity, as in a user profile, which characterizes a given user in terms of values for each of the parts of the description.

Provenance Information about a content object (e.g., original painting) that documents the history of ownership, transactions related to changes in location or situation, and other events of interest relative to authenticity, property rights, and the ability to examine – often covering from creation to the present.

Quality A concept used to assess an entity based on the values of parameters that describe its characteristics – often using some measures to compare to perfection or the ideal, so that generally higher quality is desired. In the case of digital libraries, quality often is evaluated regarding functionality, content collections, objects, and/or services.

Query A request for information, as from a digital library, typically given using some concrete representation.

Query expansion In information retrieval, the process of reformulating a query, usually adding terms and/or weights, so it more accurately reflects a user's interest, sometimes based on feedback provided (explicitly or else implicitly).

Ranking In information retrieval, the ordering of results, as for a query, typically so they appear in decreasing order of their estimated relevance.

Rating A process of assessing, according to some measure of quality or other characteristic, often leading to a small integer value. In digital libraries, a digital object or service might be rated by different users, so that statistical summaries, or even suitable recommendations, based on the set of available ratings, are given to other users.

RDF See Resource Description Framework below.

Recall In information retrieval, the percentage of what is relevant in a collection, that has already been retrieved. In machine learning, the ratio of true positive documents (with class correctly identified), to the sum of the true positive and false negative documents (with class wrongly discarded) identified by the classifier.

Recommend In information retrieval, to give to a user suggestion(s) as to what might be of interest, typically based on the user's prior behavior (e.g., clicks on result sets provided in response to queries), their user profile, as well as the behavior of those considered similar to the user, or at least the general trends that characterize community actions.

Record A complete item of information, as in a metadata record used to describe a digital object. Typically, a record has fields, each containing an appropriate value, as when the name of the author of a work goes in the creator field.

Reducing In digital libraries, to lower the range of operation performed during a specific process, as when the scope of a search is limited by specifying a small set of acceptable values for publication date. In information retrieval, as in dimensionality reduction, decreasing the number of dimensions for the sake of efficiency and/or shifting to a more conceptual rather than word/feature oriented representation.

Regular expression In formal language theory (a branch of linguistics or computer science), an expression in a regular language, specified by a regular grammar, that corresponds to the class of languages accepted by deterministic finite state automata. In computer science practice, an expression used to identify/match common (simple) patterns of characters, where the grammar allows standard characters as well as additional special characters like: |, ?, *, +, and parentheses (for grouping).

Relationships Connections between different entities, e.g., concepts of digital library, often assigned labels, types and/or values, reflecting how they fit together or are otherwise associated.

Relevance A relationship, in the context of an expression of an information need or interest, indicating that an entity, such as a document, might satisfy that need or relate to that interest.

Repository A network-accessible logical storage system in which digital objects may be stored for possible subsequent access or retrieval, as when a handle or other identifier is supplied when requesting an object of interest. Another sense in the context of digital libraries refers to a digital library having some special type and/or collection of content. For a precise explanation, see Def. MI B.21.

Representation In the digital domain, how some instance of some type of content is specified, e.g., using bits, i.e., a description of the structure, using bits or higher level groupings like bytes or words. For example, an integer might be represented in a 64-bit computer word as a binary value with the least significant bit on the right, or a grayscale image with resolution X-by-Y might be given as an X-by-Y matrix of binary values using 8 bits per value, reflecting a range from zero (black) to 256 (white).

Resource Description Framework (RDF) A recommendation for the Semantic Web by the World Wide Web Consortium (W3C), giving specifications for a metadata data model, as well as for modeling of the relationships among Web resources. These usually involve statements in the form of triples, typically designating subject-predicate-object expressions, where the predicate expresses a relationship between the subject and object, sometimes indicating traits or aspects of resources. A collection of RDF statements can represent a labeled and directed multi-graph, and may be managed by a Triplestore.

Result The outcome of a process, such as search.

Retrieval A process to obtain stored information, as in digital libraries.

Robustness The ability of a hardware and/or software system to operate properly in a variety of situations, i.e., to not break down easily, or to recover quickly from problems, or to manage well in spite of bugs or attacks.

Scenario A description of interactions among a collection of human users and/or computerized systems. For a precise explanation, see Def. MI B.9.

Schema A (formal) description of structure, as of a relational or XML database, sometimes given in levels, as when conceptual, logical, and physical schema are each given for a database, so together they can model real-world entities in a way suitable for a database management system. In a relational database, the description covers tables, fields, relationships, views, indexes, etc.

Score A value, e.g., a similarity, that characterizes how alike are two objects.

Search In information retrieval, the process of taking a query and working to identify relevant documents. In digital libraries, a type of exploring that involves processing queries when seeking relevant metadata objects and/or digital objects. See also Chapter 2, which explains that searching is closely connected with browsing, as well as other approaches to exploring. For a precise explanation, see Def. MI B.23.

Search, faceted In information retrieval, an approach to exploring that often integrates searching and browsing, using a faceted classification system (see above). Queries may include desired values for one or more facets, and may be developed incrementally through a sequence of searching and/or browsing steps where selection of facet values helps constrain or filter prior results.

Search, weighted In information retrieval, search where documents, and/or queries, include weights that reflect the importance of terms, based on occurrence frequencies and other statistics.

Search engine A program or system which seeks and retrieves information found in a collection of digital objects, as in a digital library or the WWW, based on queries supplied by users, usually by estimating similarity between a query and a document, but sometimes considering other factors/signals, like document importance, preferences of similar users, geographic proximity, etc.

Security The ability to protect, enabling confidence in safety, often based on support by people and systems and tools, that are aimed to protect entities (e.g., data and/or information) and to thwart attacks.

Security policies In digital libraries, the different regulations and procedures that govern how a system stores, manages, protects, and distributes sensitive information.

Semantic Web An extension of the WWW, based on a collaborative movement, so that Web content can be used meaningfully by computers as well as people, thus provided greatly expanded services. This requires common formats for integration and combination of data drawn from diverse sources, as well as mechanisms (e.g., RDF, OWL) for recording how the data relates to real world objects.

Semantic network A representation of knowledge in a graph or network, which explicitly represents relationships (using links) between different concepts (nodes).

Sequence A specific order in which entities (e.g., numbers, processes, etc.) follow each other.

Service In digital libraries or the WWW, a capability to carry out desired activities in support of users or computers, usually involving accepting some data or information, implementing some functionality, and returning results or changing the environment (or other external conditions). For a precise explanation, see Def. MI B.10.

Similarity In information retrieval, a measure of the relatedness between digital objects.

Similarity function In information retrieval, a mathematical formula or a routine that operates on a pair of digital objects and returns a value which reflects their relatedness.

Simulation The running of a model of some process or system, that aims to show what would occur if the system or process being modeled were to operate under the conditions described in the model. When carried out by computers, this can support experimentation and lead to predictions that might not be possible to obtain otherwise, or that might be carried out more quickly or less expensively; applications include the spread of disease, the prediction of weather, assessing the impact of earthquakes on structures, or the movement of planes or spacecraft.

Singular value decomposition (SVD) A factorization of a real or complex matrix, used in information retrieval as part of Latent Semantic Analysis (Indexing) – see above.

Smoothing A technique often used to fill in gaps with values that reflect a more pleasing fit, as when Bézier curves connect a set of points, or a moving average is applied to a sequence of values.

Social network A social structure, usually involving people and organizations that are inter-related, which can be described in a computer using a network or graph, where nodes represent entities and links designate relationships, and that can support key operations of systems like Facebook and LinkedIn.

Society A set of entities and the relationships between them. The entities include humans as well as hardware and software components, which either use or support digital library services. For a precise explanation, see Def. MI B.12.

Space A set of objects, with operations on the objects, that follow certain constraints. For a precise explanation, see Def. MI B.6.

Spam A security attack whereby an attacker (spammer) sends deceptive, irrelevant, or inappropriate messages to a large number of recipients on the Internet.

Span In hyperbases, a representation of the extent of an anchor, as when an annotation applies just to a limited portion of text. In the context of computer performance, the duration of a process from start to end, sometimes used to determine response time.

Stem In information retrieval, the main part of a word, usually an approximation of its root form, often computed by a simple program (stemmer) that applies rules tailored to a particular natural language.

Stemmer A program that reduces words to their stem (i.e., an approximation of the root form), e.g., converts "runs" and "running" to "run," but also converts "operate," "operative," and "operational" to "oper."

Stream A sequence whose co-domain is a nonempty set. In the context of educational digital libraries, there are streams of characters, pixels, audio, and video. For a precise explanation, see Def. MI B.3.

Structure A specific way in which parts of a whole are arranged or organized. In digital libraries, structures can represent databases, hypertexts, taxonomies, system connections, and user relationships. For a precise explanation, see Def. MI B.4.

Study designer (user) In the context of simulations or scientific digital libraries, a study designer may generate new model schemas as well as updated versions; enter, validate, load, execute, or save input configurations and sub-configurations; search or browse; or monitor experiment progress.

Subdocument A digital object that is part of a base document, usually described by an address, which indicates a range or span in the base document.

Superimposed document A complex object, in which at least one of the constituent digital objects is a subdocument.

SVD See Singular value decomposition above.

Tagging Assigning a label or tag to a record in a digital library so that, when searched with that tag, the record can be retrieved easily. Multiple tags may be assigned to a record, and the assignment of tags may expand during the course of system use.

Tag cloud A visual representation of a text, also called a "word cloud," that presents more frequent words with bigger font sizes (and less frequent words with smaller font sizes), thus emphasizing the potential importance of popular words.

Taxonomy A classification system or categorization of entities, sometimes with the categories taking the form of a tree, as in biological taxonomies, such that new cases or descriptions can be classified (e.g., based on their similarity to a class or category) into the appropriate category.

Teacher An instructor or other educator aiming to promote learning, typically (re)using educational resources, as might be found in an educational digital library.

Text An ordered sequence of words in a natural language, that, if of sufficient length, may be organized into sentences, and that may take the form of a document, like a paper, report, or book.

Term In information retrieval, an entity that is (derived from) an element of, or that describes, some digital object like a document. Examples include words, stems, lemmas, phrases, concepts, and descriptors.

Term extraction In information retrieval, the algorithmic identification of terms that should be associated with a document, often used in the index of a document collection. Simple approaches may employ tokenization and stemming, while more sophisticated approaches may involve natural language processing methods like named entity recognition.

TF The term frequency for a term (e.g., word), i.e., the count of the number of times that term appears, typically in a query or a document.

Thesaurus A list of groups of terms, wherein each group includes semantically related entries and usually relates to a concept. Common semantic relations incorporated include: synonym, antonym, broader term (hyperonym), narrower term (hyponym), part-whole (meronyms and holonyms), used for, and related term. Thesauri may be for a natural language or for a specialized domain, like Art and Architecture. In information retrieval they may describe a controlled vocabulary and be utilized in search.

Threshold A value that designates the boundary between classes, as in threshold of interest, or in minimal similarity (below which entities are not considered similar).

Token A string of characters which together constitute some entity that has significance, e.g., a word, name, integer, social security number, or programming language keyword. Often a token has an assigned type, based on what kind of entity has been identified.

Tokenizer In computational linguistics or computer science, a program that converts a string of characters into a string of tokens. Often, the process of tokenization uses regular expressions or more advanced parsing techniques, and may involve lookups in a lexicon or controlled vocabulary so that tokens of interest are properly identified (and classified).

Topic In information retrieval, usually a noun phrase that expresses what is being talked about, or that conveys a concept or idea discussed in a sentence, paragraph, section, chapter, or document.

Topic spotting A natural language processing technique that identifies a potential topic (or topics) from a given input text.

Transaction In computing, an interactive process that acts as a unit (e.g., a scenario), typically involving a series of steps, such as responding to user's request, handling a cash withdrawal from an ATM, or buying some goods.

Tree A connected, acyclic graph, where each node has at most one parent node, as well as (zero or more) children nodes. The usual presentation is as a hierarchy, with the "root" at the top.

Trust A relationship among entities, were an entity is said to "trust" a second entity when the first entity assumes the second entity behaves exactly as the first entity expects.

Tweet A post (also called a status update) into a system like Twitter, constituting a short microblog writing, which can be a maximum of 140 characters long.

URI A Uniform Resource Identifier, i.e., a string of characters used to identify (serve as handle for) a resource or a name, usually in the form of a URL or URN, as in the WWW (see RFCs 1630 and 3986).

URL A Uniform Resource Locator, i.e., a type of URI, in the form of a string of characters used to identify (serve as handle for) a Web resource. The syntax generally used is protocol://domainname:port/path but there also may be more at the end, as in ?querystring (when a query is submitted to a search engine) or #partid (when a section of a page gives additional specificity). For different protocols (schemes – see RFCs 2717 and 2718), formats are given in RFCs 1738, 2255, 2368, 2397, 5092, etc.

URN A Uniform Resource Name, i.e., a type of URI, specified in RFCs 1737 and 2141, i.e., a string of characters used to identify (serve as handle for) or name, in a location-independent (hence persistent) manner. The general syntax is urn:namespaceid:namespaceentry, where common identifiers of namespaces include ietf, isbn, issn, mpeg, and oid; the syntax of the entry in that namespace is specific to the namespace.

User Interface A way for users to communicate with computers, as in a graphical user interface (like what is found in Windows or Macintosh systems) or a command line interface (as with basic Unix or Linux). For a particular digital library there usually is a suitably designed user interface supporting all types of access.

Usability In digital libraries, a quality of the system (or part thereof) concerning how well the user is able to perform desired tasks or carry out appropriate scenarios.

Vector In mathematics, an element of a vector space, that can be multiplied by a scalar or added to another vector. In computer programming, generally a one-dimensional array. In the case of feature vectors, a list of values (e.g., real numbers) for each of the features of interest.

Vector space In mathematics (i.e., linear algebra), over a field, a set of vectors satisfying eight axioms, with the two operations of adding vectors together, and multiplication (scaling) of a vector by a number (scalar). In a particular vector space, a vector is often represented as a list of numbers, whose length corresponds to the dimensionality of that vector space (e.g., two, for Eucliean space). In the case of feature vectors, each dimension may correspond to a particular type of feature (e.g., for images: color, texture, or shape).

Vector space model In information retrieval, VSM, an approach to describing key aspects of a document collection, where documents and queries are each represented as a vector in a vector space, thus allowing the similarity between a query and a document (or a pair of documents) to be easily computed (e.g., as the cosine of the angle between the vectors). Commonly, each dimension (column) of the vector space corresponds to a term (e.g., stem, word, tag, phrase, thesaurus category, topic, or concept) and each vector (row) corresponds to a document (or query). Consequently, entries in a vector may designate the importance or weight (e.g., a binary value, or tf-idf, a real number computed as term frequency multiplied by inverse document frequency – so words occurring frequently in a document, or rarely in a corpus, are emphasized) for a term in a document (query).

Video In multimedia, a set of images (frames) played rapidly together (often with an accompanying audio stream) so that the computer rendering leads to viewers perceiving it as a movie or motion picture.

View-in-context A type of browsing that involves referencing and viewing a subdocument in situ – i.e., a service enabling a subdocument to be viewed in the original context of its containing base document.

Visualize In digital libraries, to render content or the result of analysis into a form that can be viewed, with the aim of improving understanding, often leading to a picture, video, graph, animation, etc.

W3C World Wide Web Consortium, the main standards organization for the Web.

Web (WWW) The World Wide Web, launched in the early 1990s, a network of information that can be accessed by computers using Web browsers, generally following the standards specified by W3C.

Web service A software system accessible through the WWW, supporting computer to computer interaction, generally fitting in with a service-oriented architecture (SOA), commonly making use of standards like WSDL, SOAP, REST, and XML.

Weighting scheme A method used to determine the weight or importance of different components in a process. In information retrieval, a way to assign values in a vector space, or to give priority to fields of documents, or to specify the relative values of different signals considered when assigning similarity scores.

Wild card In information retrieval, a special symbol (e.g., an asterisk) used in a regular expression or query, to designate that various (or any) characters are all considered acceptable.

WordNet A database of English words (classified by part of speech, like noun, verb, adjective, or adverb), grouped into synsets (connected according to semantics), providing a great deal of linguistic information, widely used to aid with natural language processing. It was developed at Princeton University but is freely and publicly available.

XML Extensible Markup Language, a standard developed by W3C, using tagging for encoding documents, so important aspects of their structure are made explicit, and can be readily analyzed by software systems.

Bibliography

[1] S. Abiteboul, P. Buneman, and D. Suciu. *Data on the Web: From Relations to Semistructured Data and XML*. Morgan Kaufmann, San Francisco, CA, 1999. Cited on page(s) 27

[2] S. Abiteboul, D. Quass, J. McHugh, J. Widom, and J. L. Wiener. The Lorel Query Language for Semistructured Data. *Int. Journal on Digital Libraries*, 1(1):5–19, April 1997. Cited on page(s) 27

[3] M. Agosti, S. Berretti, G. Brettlecker, A. del Bimbo, N. Ferro, N. Fuhr, D. Keim, C.-P. Klas, T. Lidy, M. Norrie, P. Ranaldi, A. Rauber, H.-J. Schek, T. Schreck, H. Schuldt, B. Signer, and M. Springmann. DelosDLMS – the Integrated DELOS Digital Library Management System. In *Proc. DELOS Conference on Digital Libraries*, pages 71–80, Pisa, Italy, 2007. DOI: 10.1007/978-3-540-77088-6_4 Cited on page(s) 11

[4] M. Agosti and N. Ferro. A formal model of annotations of digital content. *ACM Transactions on Information Systems (TOIS)*, 26(1):1–55, 2008. DOI: 10.1145/1292591.1292594 Cited on page(s) 41

[5] M. Akbar, W. Fan, C. A. Shaffer, Y. Chen, L. N. Cassel, L. M. L. Delcambre, D. D. Garcia, G. W. Hislop, F. M. Shipman III, R. Furuta, B. S. Carpenter II, H. wei Hsieh, B. Siegfried, and E. A. Fox. Digital Library 2.0 for Educational Resources. In *Proc. TPDL 2011, Berlin, GE, Sept. 2011, LNCS 6966*, pages 89–100. Springer, Sept. 2011. DOI: 10.1007/978-3-642-24469-8_11 Cited on page(s) 23

[6] J. Andre, R. Furuta, and V. Quint. *Structured Documents*. Cambridge University Press, Cambridge, 1989. Cited on page(s) 25

[7] ANSI. Information retrieval (Z39.50): Application service definition and protocol specification: The Z39.50 maintenance agency official text for Z39.50-1995. Technical report, Library of Congress, 1995. 1995. Cited on page(s) 22

[8] W. Y. Arms. *Digital Libraries*. MIT Press, Cambridge, MA, 2000. Cited on page(s) 1, 12

[9] W. F. Atchison, S. D. Conte, J. W. Hamblen, T. E. Hull, T. A. Keenan, W. B. Kehl, E. J. McCluskey, S. O. Navarro, W. C. Rheinboldt, E. J. Schweppe, W. Viavant, and J. David M. Young. Curriculum 68: Recommendations for academic programs in computer science: a report of the ACM curriculum committee on computer science. *CACM*, 11(3):151–197, 1968. DOI: 10.1145/362929.362976 Cited on page(s) 18

126 BIBLIOGRAPHY

[10] R. Baeza-Yates and G. Navarro. XQL and proximal nodes. *J. Am. Soc. Inf. Sci. Technol.*, 53(6):504–514, 2002. DOI: 10.1002/asi.10061 Cited on page(s) 27

[11] R. Baeza-Yates and B. Ribeiro-Neto. *Modern Information Retrieval.* Addison-Wesley, Harlow, England, 1999. Cited on page(s) 69, 71

[12] M. Q. W. Baldonado. A user-centered interface for information exploration in a hetero-geneous digital library. *J. American Society for Information Science*, 51(3):297–210, 2000. DOI: 10.1002/(SICI)1097-4571(2000)51:3%3C297::AID-ASI8%3E3.0.CO;2-N Cited on page(s) 45, 46

[13] K. D. Bayley. *Typologies and Taxonomies – An Introduction to Classification Techniques.* SAGE Publications, Thousand Oaks, California, 1994. Cited on page(s) 34

[14] M. Bayraktar, C. Zhang, B. Vadapalli, N. Kipp, and E. A. Fox. A Web Art Gallery. In *Proc. Digital Libraries '98, The Third ACM Conf. on Digital Libraries*, pages 277–278. ACM, Pittsburgh, PA, 1998. DOI: 10.1145/276675.276727 Cited on page(s) 29

[15] C. Beeri. A formal approach to object-oriented databases. *IEEE DKE*, 5:353–382, December 1990. DOI: 10.1016/0169-023X(90)90020-E Cited on page(s) 26

[16] N. Belkin. Anomalous states of knowledge as the basis for information retrieval. *Canadian Journal of Inf. Sci.*, 5:133–143, 1980. Cited on page(s) 43

[17] N. Belkin, P. Marchetti, and C. Cool. BRAQUE: Design of an interface to support user interaction in information retrieval. *Information Processing and Management*, 29(3):325–344, 1993. DOI: 10.1016/0306-4573(93)90059-M Cited on page(s) 43

[18] N. J. Belkin, R. N. Oddy, and H. M. Brooks. ASK for information retrieval. *Journal of Documentation*, 33(2):61–71, 1982. DOI: 10.1108/eb026726 Cited on page(s) 33

[19] BEPress. BEPress Repository Technology, http://www.bepress.com/repositories.html [last visited july 4, 2012], 2005. Cited on page(s) 21

[20] T. Berners-Lee, J. Hendler, and O. Lassila. The Semantic Web. *Scientific American*, 284(5), May 2001. DOI: 10.1038/scientificamerican0501-34 Cited on page(s) 66

[21] S. Berretti, A. D. Bimbo, and E. Vicario. Spatial arrangement of color in retrieval by visual sim-ilarity. *Pattern Recognition*, 35(8):1661–1674, 2002. DOI: 10.1016/S0031-3203(01)00161-3 Cited on page(s) 89

[22] A. P. Bishop, N. A. V. House, and B. P. Buttenfield. *Digital library use: social practice in design and evaluation.* MIT Press, Cambridge, Mass., 2003. Cited on page(s) 1, 12

[23] R. Boisvert. The architecture of an intelligent virtual mathematical software repository system. *Mathematics and Computers in Simulation*, 36:269–279, 1994. DOI: 10.1016/0378-4754(94)90062-0 Cited on page(s) 21

[24] G. Booch. UML in action. *Communications of the ACM*, 42(10):26–28, 1999. DOI: 10.1145/317665.317672 Cited on page(s) 65

[25] C. Borgman. UCLA-NSF Social Aspects of Digital Libraries Workshop, Feb. 15-17, 1996. `http://is.gseis.ucla.edu/research/dig%5Flibraries/UCLA%5FDL %5FReport.html` [last visited July 4, 2012]. Cited on page(s) 3

[26] C. L. Borgman. Social aspects of digital libraries. In *DL'96: Proceedings of the 1st ACM International Conference on Digital Libraries*, D-Lib Working Session 2A, pages 170–171, 1996. DOI: 10.1145/226931.226964 Cited on page(s) 1, 2

[27] C. L. Borgman. What are digital libraries? Competing visions. *Information Processing and Management*, 35(3):227–243, 1999. DOI: 10.1016/S0306-4573(98)00059-4 Cited on page(s) 3

[28] C. L. Borgman. *From Gutenberg to the global information infrastructure: Access to information in the networked world*. MIT Press, Cambridge, MA, 2003. Cited on page(s) 1, 12, 14

[29] C. L. Borgman. *Scholarship in the Digital Age: Information, Infrastructure, and the Internet*. MIT Press, Cambridge, MA, Sept. 2010. Cited on page(s) 1, 12

[30] P. Borlund and P. Ingwersen. The development of a method for the evaluation of interactive information retrieval systems. *Journal of Documentation*, 53(3):225–250, June 1997. DOI: 10.1108/EUM0000000007198 Cited on page(s) 33

[31] C. M. Bowman, P. B. Danzig, D. R. Hardy, U. Manber, and M. F. Schwartz. The Harvest information discovery and access system. *Computer Networks and ISDN Systems*, 28(1):119–126, 1995. DOI: 10.1016/0169-7552(95)00098-5 Cited on page(s) 22

[32] C. M. Bowman, P. B. Danzig, D. R. Hardy, U. Manber, M. F. Schwartz, and D. P. Wessels. Harvest: A scalable, customizable discovery and access system. Technical Report CU-CS-732-94, Department of Computer Science, University of Colorado, Boulder, August 1994. Cited on page(s) 22

[33] V. Bush. As we may think. *Atlantic Monthly*, 176:101–108, July 1945. DOI: 10.1145/227181.227186 Cited on page(s) 10

[34] F. Can, E. A. Fox, C. Snavely, and R. K. France. Incremental clustering for very large document databases: Initial MARIAN experience. *Information Systems*, 84:101–114, 1995. DOI: 10.1016/0020-0255(94)00111-N Cited on page(s) 23

[35] L. Candela, D. Castelli, N. Ferro, Y. Ioannidis, G. Koutrika, C. Meghini, P. Pagano, S. Ross, D. Soergel, M. Agosti, M. Dobreva, V. Katifori, and H. Schuldt. The DELOS Digital Library Reference Model - Foundations for Digital Libraries. Version 0.98, 2008. http://www.delos.info/files/pdf/ReferenceModel/DELOS%5FDLReferenceModel%5F0.98.pdf [last visited July 4, 2012]. Cited on page(s) 4, 22, 34, 40

[36] L. Candela, D. Castelli, Y. Ioannidis, G. Koutrika, P. Pagano, S. Ross, H.-J. Schek, and H. Schuldt. The Digital Library Manifesto. In *DELOS, A Network of Excellence on Digital Libraries – IST-2002-2.3.1.12, Technology-enhanced Learning and Access to Cultural Heritage.* http://146.48.87.21:80/OLP/UI/1.0/Disseminate/1341413785AuhMwSP6aI/a221341413785YIxt7eI8 [last visited 2012, July 4], September 2006. Cited on page(s) 22

[37] M. Carey, L. Haas, V. Maganty, and J.Williams. PESTO: An integrated query/browser for object databases. In *Proceedings of VLDB*, pages 203–214, 1996. Cited on page(s) 45, 48, 97, 98

[38] J. M. Carroll, editor. *Minimalism Beyond the Nurnberg Funnel.* MIT Press, Cambridge, MA, 1988. Cited on page(s) 20

[39] D. Castelli and P. Pagano. A Flexible Repository Service: the OpenDLib Solution. In *Proc. ELPUB*, pages 194–202, 2002. Cited on page(s) 21

[40] D. Castelli and P. Pagano. OpenDLib: A Digital Library Service System. In *Research and Advanced Technology for Digital Libraries, Proceedings of the 6th European Conference, ECDL 2002, Rome, Italy, September*, pages 292–308. ECDL, 2002. DOI: 10.1007/3-540-45747-X_22 Cited on page(s) 67

[41] CC2001. Computing Curricula 2001: Computer Science (IEEE Computer Society and Association for Computing Machinery Joint Task Force on Computing Curricula). *Journal on Educational Resources in Computing (JERIC)*, 1(3es), 2001. Cited on page(s) 18

[42] CC2001. Computing Curriculum 2001 (Web Site), 2001. http://www.acm.org/education/curric%5Fvols/cc2001.pdf [last visited July 4, 2012]. Cited on page(s) 2

[43] CCSDS. Reference Model for an Open Archival Information System (OAIS): Recommendation for Space Data System Standards : CCSDS 650.0-B-1. Technical report, Consultative Committee for Space Data Systems, January 2002. Cited on page(s) 21

[44] S. Chaudhuri and L. Gravano. Optimizing Queries over Multimedia Repositories. In *Proceedings of the 1996 ACM SIGMOD International Conference on Management of Data*, pages 91–102, Montreal, Quebec, 1996. DOI: 10.1145/233269.233323 Cited on page(s) 21

[45] P. Chen. The Entity–Relationship Model – Towards a Unified View of Data. *ACM Transactions on Database Systems (TODS)*, 1(1):9–36, 1976. DOI: 10.1145/320434.320440 Cited on page(s) 9

[46] C. L. Clarke, G. V. Cormack, and F. J. Burkowski. An algebra for structured text search and a framework for its implementation. *The Computer Journal*, 38:43–56, 1995. Cited on page(s) 66

[47] J. H. Coombs, A. H. Renear, and S. J. DeRose. Markup systems and the future of scholarly text processing. *Communications of the ACM*, 30(11):933–947, 1988. DOI: 10.1145/32206.32209 Cited on page(s) 25, 66

[48] T. H. Cormen, C. E. Leiserson, and R. L. Rivest. *Introduction to Algorithms*. MIT Press, 1990. Cited on page(s) 59, 65

[49] A. Crabtree, M. B. Twidale, J. O'Brien, and D. M. Nichols. Talking in the library: implications for the design of digital libraries. In *Proc. of the 2nd ACM Int. Conf. on Digital Libraries*, pages 221–229, New York, July 1997. Cited on page(s) 29

[50] A. Crespo and H. Garcia-Molina. Archival storage for digital libraries. In *DL'98: Proceedings of the 3rd ACM International Conference on Digital Libraries*, pages 69–78, 1998. DOI: 10.1145/276675.276683 Cited on page(s) 17

[51] F. Crestani, M. Lalmas, C. J. v. Rijsbergen, and I. Campbell. "Is this document relevant? Probably": A survey of probabilistic models in information retrieval. *ACM Computing Surveys*, 30(4):528–552, 1998. DOI: 10.1145/299917.299920 Cited on page(s) 63

[52] W. Croft and R. Thompson. A New Approach to the Design of Document Retrieval Systems. *JASIS*, 38(6):389–404, 1987.
DOI: 10.1002/(SICI)1097-4571(198711)38:6%3C389::AID-ASI1%3E3.0.CO;2-4 Cited on page(s) 45

[53] CUDL. University of Colorado System Digital Library (CUDL), June 2012. `https://www.cu.edu/digitallibrary/images/headerleft/header1.jpg` [last visited July 4, 2012]. Cited on page(s) 18

[54] F. Curbera and al. Unraveling the Web services web: An introduction to SOAP, WSDL, and UDDI. *IEEE Distributed Systems Online*, 3(4), 2002. DOI: 10.1109/4236.991449 Cited on page(s) 22

[55] F. A. Das Neves and E. A. Fox. A study of user behavior in an immersive virtual environment for digital libraries. In *Proceedings of the Fifth ACM Conference on Digital Libraries: DL '00, June 2-7, 2000, San Antonio, TX*, pages 103–111. ACM Press, New York, 2000. DOI: 10.1145/336597.336648 Cited on page(s) 29

[56] D. Davis, Fedora 3.5 Documentation, available at `https://wiki.duraspace.org/display/fedora35/fedora+3.5+documentation`, 2011. Cited on page(s) 21

[57] M. D. Davis, R. Sigal, and E. J. Weyuker. *Computation, Complexity, and Languages (second edition)*. Academic Press, 1994. Cited on page(s) 65

[58] E. S. de Moura, G. Navarro, N. Ziviani, and R. A. Baeza-Yates. Fast and flexible word searching on compressed text. *ACM Trans. Inf. Syst.*, 18(2):113–139, 2000. DOI: 10.1145/348751.348754 Cited on page(s) 29

[59] H. V. de Sompel and C. Lagoze. The Santa Fe Convention of the Open Archives Initiative. *D-Lib Magazine*, 6(2), Feb. 15, 2000. `http://www.dlib.org/dlib/february00/vandesompel-oai/vandesompel-oai.html` [last visited July 4, 2012]. DOI: 10.1045/february2000-vandesompel-oai Cited on page(s) 10, 23

[60] DELOS. Sixth DELOS Workshop: Preservation of Digital Information, Tomar, Portugal, June 17-19, 1998. ERCIM-98-W003 INESC, `http://www.ercim.eu/publication/ws-proceedings/DELOS6/delos6.pdf` [last visited July 4, 2012]. Cited on page(s) 17

[61] DLIB. D-Lib Magazine: The Magazine of Digital Library Research, 1995. `http://www.dlib.org/` [last visited July 4, 2012]. Cited on page(s) 1, 12

[62] DSpace. DSpace homepage, 2003. `http://www.dspace.org/` [last visited July 4, 2012]. Cited on page(s) 11, 22

[63] L. Duranti. The long-term preservation of accurate and authentic digital data: the Inter-PARES project. *Data Science Journal*, 4:106–118, 2005. DOI: 10.2481/dsj.4.106 Cited on page(s) 17

[64] DuraSpace. DuraSpace.org, 2011. `http://www.duraspace.org/` [last visited July 4, 2012]. Cited on page(s) 23

[65] N. Dushay, J. C. French, and C. Lagoze. Using query mediators for distributed searching in federated digital libraries. In *Proceedings of the Fourth ACM Conference on Digital Libraries (DL '99, August 11-14, 1999)*, pages 171–178. ACM, Berkeley, CA, 1999. Aug. Cited on page(s) 22

[66] D. Egan, J. Remde, T. Landauer, C. Lochbaum, and L. Gomez. Behavioral evaluation and analysis of a hypertext browser. In *Proceedings of CHI*, pages 205–210, 1989. DOI: 10.1145/67449.67490 Cited on page(s) 57

[67] D. E. Egan, J. R. Remde, L. M. Gomez, T. K. Landauer, J. Eberhardt, and C. C. Lochbaum. Formative design evaluation of Superbook. *ACM Trans. Inf. Syst.*, 7(7):30–57, 1989. DOI: 10.1145/64789.64790 Cited on page(s) 57

[68] D. Ellis. The physical and cognitive paradigms in information retrieval research. *Journal of Documentation*, 48:45–64, 1992. DOI: 10.1108/eb026889 Cited on page(s) 33

[69] European Commission. Commission Recommendation of 24 August 2006 on the digitisation and online accessibility of cultural material and digital preservation. *Official Journal of the European Union, OJ L 236, 31.8.2006*, 49:28–30, August 2006. Cited on page(s) 21

[70] D. J. Foskett. Thesaurus. In A. Kent, H. Lancour, and J. Daily, editors, *Encyclopedia of Library and Information Science - Volume 30*, pages 416–462. Marcel Dekker, New York, 1980. Cited on page(s) 35

[71] E. Fox. The digital libraries initiative: Update and discussion: Guest editor's introduction to special section. *Bulletin of the American Society of Information Science*, 26(1):7–11, 1999. Cited on page(s) 11

[72] E. Fox, R. Moore, R. Larsen, S. Myaeng, and S. Kim. Toward a Global Digital Library: Generalizing US-Korea Collaboration on Digital Libraries. *D-Lib Magazine*, 8(10), October 2002. DOI: 10.1045/october2002-fox Cited on page(s) 16, 17

[73] E. A. Fox. Development of the CODER system: A testbed for artificial intelligence methods in information retrieval. *Information Processing and Management*, 23(4):341–366, 1987. DOI: 10.1016/0306-4573(87)90022-7 Cited on page(s) 23

[74] E. A. Fox. Digital Library Source Book. Technical Report TR-93-35, Virginia Tech Dept. of Computer Science, Blacksburg, VA, 1993. http://fox.cs.vt.edu/DLSB.html [last visited July 4, 2012]. Cited on page(s) 1, 11, 12

[75] E. A. Fox. IR Curriculum: Information Engineering to Digital Libraries. In *Information Retrieval 2000 — Workplace Needs and Curricular Implications, Drexel University hosted Workshop/Symposium sponsored by the W.K. Kellogg Foundation*, Marriott Hotel, Philadelphia PA, 1996. Invited presentation. Cited on page(s) 18

[76] E. A. Fox. Digital Library Research Laboratory (DLRL home page), 2011. http://www.dlib.vt.edu [last visited July 4, 2012]. Cited on page(s) 12

[77] E. A. Fox, R. Akscyn, R. Furuta, and J. Leggett. Guest editors' introduction to digital libraries. *Communications of the ACM*, 38(4):22–28, 1995. 88, April 1995. DOI: 10.1007/s00799-011-0068-6 Cited on page(s) 35

[78] E. A. Fox, Y. Chen, M. Akbar, C. A. Shaffer, S. H. Edwards, P. Brusilovsky, D. D. Garcia, L. M. Delcambre, F. Decker, D. W. Archer, R. Furuta, F. Shipman, S. Carpenter, and L. Cassel. Ensemble PDP-8: Eight Principles for Distributed Portals. In *Proc. JCDL/ICADL 2010, June 21-25, Gold Coast, Australia*, pages 341–344. ACM, 2010. DOI: 10.1145/1816123.1816174 Cited on page(s) 23

[79] E. A. Fox and K. Garach. CITIDEL collection building. Technical Report TR-03-14, Computer Science, Virginia Tech, 2003. http://eprints.cs.vt.edu/archive/00000660/ [last visited July 4, 2012]. Cited on page(s) 23, 47

[80] E. A. Fox, L. S. Heath, and D. Hix. Project Envision Final Report: A User-Centered Database from the Computer Science Literature. Technical report, Virgina Tech Dept. of Computer Science, Blacksburg, VA, 1995. Cited on page(s) 13

[81] E. A. Fox, R. S. Heller, A. Long, and D. Watkins. CRIM: Curricular Resources in Interactive Multimedia. In *Proceedings ACM Multimedia '99*. ACM, Orlando, 1999. Oct. 30 - Nov. 5, 1999. DOI: 10.1145/319463.319474 Cited on page(s) 18

[82] E. A. Fox, D. Hix, L. Nowell, D. Brueni, W. Wake, L. Heath, and D. Rao. Users, user interfaces, and objects: Envision, a digital library. *J. American Society Information Science*, 44(8):480–491, 1993. 98, Sept. 1993.
DOI: 10.1002/(SICI)1097-4571(199309)44:8%3C480::AID-ASI7%3E3.0.CO;2-B   Cited on page(s) 13

[83] E. A. Fox and L. Kieffer. Multimedia curricula, courses and knowledge modules. *ACM Computing Surveys*, 27(4):549–551, 1995. 90. DOI: 10.1145/234782.234787   Cited on page(s) 18

[84] E. A. Fox, D. Knox, L. Cassel, J. A. N. Lee, M. Pérez-Quiñones, J. Impagliazzo, and C. L. Giles. CITIDEL: Computing and Information Technology Interactive Digital Educational Library, 2002. http://www.citidel.org [last visited July 4, 2012]. Cited on page(s) 23, 47

[85] Fox, E. A. et al. Curriculum on Digital Libraries. http://en.wikiversity.org/wiki/Curriculum%5Fon%5FDigital_Libraries [last visited July 4, 2012]. Cited on page(s) 18

[86] Fox, E. A. et al. Digital Libraries Curriculum Development. http://curric.dlib.vt.edu [last visited July 4, 2012]. Cited on page(s) 18

[87] R. K. France, , M. A. Gonçalves, and E. A. Fox. MARIAN digital library system, 2002. http://www.dlib.vt.edu/products/marian.html [last visited July 4, 2012]. Cited on page(s) 23

[88] J. C. French, A. L. Powell, C. L. Viles, T. Emmitt, and K. Prey. Evaluating database selection techniques: A testbed and experiment. In *Proc. 21st International Conf. on R&D in Information Retrieval (ACM SIGIR'98)*, pages 121–129. ACM, Melbourne Australia, 1998. Aug. DOI: 10.1145/290941.290976 Cited on page(s) 22

[89] J. C. French and C. L. Viles. Ensuring retrieval effectiveness in distributed digital libraries. *J. Visual Communication and Image Representation*, 7(1):61–73, 1996. March. DOI: 10.1006/jvci.1996.0006 Cited on page(s) 22

[90] T. L. Friedman. *The World Is Flat 3.0: A Brief History of the Twenty-first Century*. Picador, New York, 2007. Cited on page(s) 15

[91] N. Fuhr. XIRQL - An Extension of XQL for Information Retrieval. In *Proc. of the ACM SIGIR 2000 – Workshop on XML and Information Retrieval*, Athens, Greece, 2000. Cited on page(s) 27

[92] N. Fuhr and K. Grobjohann. XIRQL - an XML query language based on information retrieval concepts. *ACM Transactions on Information Systems*, 22(2):313 – 356, Apr. 2004. DOI: 10.1145/984321.984326 Cited on page(s) 27

[93] N. Fuhr, C.-P. Klas, A. Schaefer, and P. Mutschke. Daffodil: An Integrated Desktop for Supporting High-Level Search Activities in Federated Digital Libraries. In *ECDL 2002*, pages 597–612. Springer-Verlag, 2002. http://link.springer.de/link/service/series/0558/bibs/2458/24580597.htm [last visited July 4, 2012]. Cited on page(s) 22

[94] K. Fullerton, J. Greenberg, M. McClure, E. Rasmussen, and D. Stewart. A digital library for education: the PEN-DOR project. *Electronic Library*, 17(2):75–82, 1999. DOI: 10.1108/02640479910334279 Cited on page(s) 21

[95] G. Furnas and S. Rauch. Considerations for Information Environments and the NaviQue Workspace. In *Proceedings of ACM Digital Libraries 1998*, pages 79–88, 1998. http://sr-hercules01.iat.sfu.ca/CzSawVA/images/2/28/Furnas%5Fnavique.pdf [last visited July 4, 2012]. DOI: 10.1145/276675.276684 Cited on page(s) 43

[96] R. Furuta. Defining and using structure in digital documents. In J. L. Schnase, J. J. Leggett, R. K. Furuta, and T. Metcalfe, editors, *Proceedings of Digital Libraries'94: The First Annual Conference on the Theory and Practice of Digital Libraries*, pages 139–145, College Station, TX, 1994. Cited on page(s) 25

[97] E. Garfield. From 1950s documentalists to 20th century information scientists - and beyond. *Bulletin of the American Society for Information Science*, 26(2), 2000. December / January. DOI: 10.1002/bult.148 Cited on page(s) 10

[98] G. Geisler and G. Marchionini. The Open Video Project: A Research-Oriented Digital Video Repository. In *Proceedings of the Fifth ACM Conference on Digital Libraries: DL '00, June 2-7, 2000, San Antonio, TX*, pages 258–259. ACM Press, New York, 2000. DOI: 10.1145/336597.336693 Cited on page(s) 21

[99] P. Ginsparg. arXiv.org e-Print archive, 2000. http://arxiv.org/ [last visited July 4, 2012]. Cited on page(s) 21

[100] H. M. Gladney and A. Cantu. Authorization management for digital libraries. *Communications of the ACM*, 44(5):63–65, 2001. DOI: 10.1145/374308.374343 Cited on page(s) 39

[101] J. Gleick. *Chaos: Making a New Science*. Penguin Books, 1987. Cited on page(s) 6

[102] R. Godement. *Algebra*. Kershaw Publ. Co. Ltd, London, 1969. Cited on page(s) 28

[103] C. F. Goldfarb and P. Prescod. *The XML Handbook*. Prentice-Hall PTR, Upper Saddle River, NJ 07458, USA, 1998. Cited on page(s) 25

[104] G. Golovchinsky. Queries? links? is there a difference? In *Proc. CHI'97*, pages 407–417, 1997. DOI: 10.1145/258549.258820 Cited on page(s) 43

[105] M. A. Goncalves. *Streams, Structures, Spaces, Scenarios, and Societies (5S): A Formal Digital Library Framework and Its Applications*. PhD thesis, Virginia Tech, Blacksburg, VA, 2004. http://scholar.lib.vt.edu/theses/available/etd-12052004-135923/ [last visited July 4, 2012]. Cited on page(s) xx, 40, 44, 46, 101

[106] M. A. Gonçalves, E. A. Fox, A. Krowne, P. Calado, A. H. F. Laender, A. S. da Silva, and B. Ribeiro-Neto. The Effectiveness of Automatically Structured Queries in Digital Libraries. In *Proc. of the 4th Joint Conf. on Digital Libraries (JCDL'2004)*, pages 98–107, Tucson, Arizona, June 7-11, 2004. DOI: 10.1145/996350.996377 Cited on page(s) 89

[107] M. A. Gonçalves, E. A. Fox, L. T. Watson, and N. A. Kipp. Streams, structures, spaces, scenarios, societies (5S): A formal model for digital libraries. Technical Report TR-03-04, Computer Science, Virginia Tech, Blacksburg, VA, 2003. http://eprints.cs.vt.edu/archive/00000653/ [last visited July 4, 2012]. DOI: 10.1145/984321.984325 Cited on page(s) 35

[108] M. A. Gonçalves, E. A. Fox, L. T. Watson, and N. A. Kipp. Streams, structures, spaces, scenarios, societies (5S): A formal model for digital libraries. *ACM Transactions on Information Systems*, 22(2):270–312, 2004. DOI: 10.1145/984321.984325 Cited on page(s) 36, 37, 38, 40, 44, 46, 64, 67, 69, 70, 71, 78, 82, 83

[109] M. A. Gonçalves, R. K. France, and E. A. Fox. MARIAN: Flexible Interoperability for Federated Digital Libraries. *Springer Lecture Notes in Computer Science*, 2163:173–186, 2001. http://link.springer-ny.com/link/service/series/0558/bibs/2163/21630173.htm [last visited July 4, 2012]. DOI: 10.1007/3-540-44796-2_16 Cited on page(s) 23

[110] M. A. Gonçalves, R. K. France, E. A. Fox, and T. E. Doszkocs. MARIAN: Searching and Querying Across Heterogeneous Federated Digital Libraries. In *Proceedings of the First DELOS Network of Excellence Workshop on Information Seeking, Searching and Querying in Digital Libraries, Dec. 11-12*. DELOS, Zurich, Switzerland, 2000. Cited on page(s) 22, 23

[111] M. A. Gonçalves, P. Mather, J. Wang, Y. Zhou, M. Luo, R. Richardson, R. Shen, L. Xu, and E. A. Fox. Java MARIAN: From an OPAC to a modern digital library system. In *Proc. of SPIRE'02*, pages 194–209, Lisbon, Portugal, September 11-13 2002. DOI: 10.1007/3-540-45735-6_18 Cited on page(s) 23

[112] M. A. Gonçalves, B. L. Moreira, E. A. Fox, and L. T. Watson. What is a good digital library? - defining a quality model for digital libraries. *Information Processing & Management*, 43(5):1416–1437, 2007. DOI: 10.1016/j.ipm.2006.11.010 Cited on page(s) 40

[113] M. A. Gonçalves, L. T. Watson, and E. A. Fox. Towards a Digital Library Theory: A Formal Digital Library Ontology. In S. Dominich and C. J. van Rijsbergen, editors, *ACM SIGIR Mathematical/Formal Methods in Information Retrieval Workshop(MF/IR 2004)*. http:// www.dcs.vein.hu/CIR/cikkek/MFIR%5FDLOntology4.pdf [last visited 2007, March 23], 2004. Cited on page(s) 8, 40

[114] D. Gorton. Practical Digital Library Generation into DSpace with the 5S Framework. Master's thesis, Virginia Tech, 2007. Committee Chairman E. A. Fox, http://scholar.lib. vt.edu/theses/available/etd-04252007-161736/ [last visited July 4, 2012]. Cited on page(s) 23

[115] Greenstone. Greenstone Digital Library Software homepage, 2011. http://www. greenstone.org/ [last visited July 4, 2012]. Cited on page(s) 22

[116] S. Griffin. NSF/DARPA/NASA Digital Libraries Initiative: A Program Manager's Perspective, 2000. Reprint of paper in July/August 1998 D-Lib Magazine, http://www.ideals.illinois.edu/bitstream/handle/2142/25479/griffin %5Fnsf%5F004.pdf?sequence=2 [last visited July 4, 2012]. Cited on page(s) 11

[117] A. L. Hammond. *Which World?: Scenarios for the 21st Century*. Earthscan, 1998. http:// books.google.com/books/about/Which_World.html?id=YGN4bUUX4bQC [last visited July 4, 2012]. Cited on page(s) 31

[118] S. Harnad. CogPrints archive, 2000. http://cogprints.org/ [last visited July 4, 2012]. Cited on page(s) 23

[119] S. Harnad. The self-archiving initiative – freeing the refereed research literature online. *Nature*, 411(6837):522, 2001. May 31. DOI: 10.1038/35074210 Cited on page(s) 10

[120] S. Harnad, W. Hall, L. Carr, P. Ginsparg, J. Halpern, and C. Lagoze. Integrating and Navigating ePrint Archives through Citation-Linking: The Open Citation (OpCit) Linking Project, 1999. NSF / JISC - eLib Collaborative Project: International Digital Libraries Research Programme, University of Southampton, http://users.ecs.soton.ac.uk/ harnad/citation.html [last visited July 4, 2012]. Cited on page(s) 21

[121] S. Harum. Digital Library Initiative (DLI) website, 1998. http://dli.grainger.uiuc.edu/national.htm [last visited July 4, 2012]. Cited on page(s) 11

[122] R. Hassan. *The Information Society*. Polity Press, Cambridge, UK, 2008. Cited on page(s) 32

[123] B. M. Hemminger, J. Fox, and M. Ni. Improving the ETD submission process through automated author self contribution using DSpace. In *7th International Symposium on Electronic Theses and Dissertations (ETD 2004) - Lexington, Kentucky, USA, 3-5 June*. NDLTD, 2004. Cited on page(s) 23

[124] T. Hey, S. Tansley, and K. Tolle, editors. *The Fourth Paradigm: Data-Intensive Scientific Discovery*. Microsoft Research, 2009. Cited on page(s) 17

[125] D. Holmgren. *Future Scenarios: How Communities Can Adapt to Peak Oil and Climate Change*. Chelsea Green Publishing, 2009. Cited on page(s) 31

[126] P. Hsia, J. Samuel, J. Gao, D. Kung, Y. Toyoshima, and C. Chen. Formal approach to scenario analysis. *IEEE Software*, 11(2):33–41, Mar. 1994. DOI: 10.1109/52.268953 Cited on page(s) 30, 65

[127] J. Hunter and S. Choudhury. Implementing Preservation Strategies for Complex Multimedia Objects. In *Proc. 7th European Conf. Research and Advanced Technology for Digital Libraries, ECDL 2003*, pages 473–486, Trodheim, Norway, August 17-22, 2003. DOI: 10.1007/978-3-540-45175-4_43 Cited on page(s) 17

[128] J. Hunter and S. Choudhury. A semi-automated digital preservation system based on semantic web services. In *Proceedings of the Fourth ACM/IEEE-CS Joint Conference on Digital Libraries*, pages 269–278, Tucson, Arizona, 2004. DOI: 10.1145/996350.996415 Cited on page(s) 17

[129] IFLA. Functional requirements for bibliographic records, 2009. http://www.ifla.org/en/publications/functional-requirements-for-bibliographic-records [last visited July 4, 2012]. Cited on page(s) 9

[130] J. Impagliazzo. Using CITIDEL as a Portal for CS Education. In *CCSCNE Conference*, 2002. Panel Presentation and Chair (with L. Cassel and D. Knox). Cited on page(s) 23, 47

[131] InternetArchive. Internet Archive, 2000. http://www.archive.org/ [last visited July 4, 2012]. Cited on page(s) 21

[132] Y. Ioannidis, D. Maier, S. Abiteboul, P. Buneman, S. Davidson, E. A. Fox, A. Halevy, C. Knoblock, F. Rabitti, H.-J. Schek, and G. Weikum. Digital library information-technology infrastructures. *International Journal on Digital Libraries*, 5(4):266–274, 2005. DOI: 10.1007/s00799-004-0094-8 Cited on page(s) 63

[133] Y. E. Ioannidis, D. Milano, H. J. Schek, and H. Schuldt. DelosDLMS. *International Journal on Digital Libraries*, 9(2):101–114, 2008. DOI: 10.1007/s00799-008-0044-y Cited on page(s) 11, 22

[134] R. K. Johnson. Institutional repositories: Partnering with faculty to enhance scholarly communication. *D-Lib Magazine*, 8(11), 2002. Cited on page(s) 21

[135] W. Jones and J. Teevan, editors. *Personal Information Management*. University of Washington Press, 2007. Cited on page(s) 1

[136] B. Kahin and H. R. Varian. *Internet Publishing and Beyond: The Economics of Digital Information and Intellectual Property*. MIT Press, Cambridge, Massachusetts, 2000. Cited on page(s) 33

[137] R. Kahn and R. Wilensky. A framework for distributed digital object services. Technical report cnri.dlib/tn95-01, CNRI, Reston, VA, May 1995. http://www.cnri.reston.va.us/k-w.html [last visited 2011]. DOI: 10.1007/s00799-005-0128-x Cited on page(s) 21

[138] N. Kampanya, R. Shen, S. Kim, C. North, and E. A. Fox. Citiviz: A visual user interface to the CITIDEL system. In *Proc. European Conference on Digital Libraries (ECDL) 2004, September 12-17, University of Bath, UK*. Springer, 2004. DOI: 10.1007/b100389 Cited on page(s) 23, 43, 47

[139] H. Kautz, B. Selman, and M. Shah. Referral Web: Combining social networks and collaborative filtering. *Communications of the ACM*, 40(3):63–65, 1997. DOI: 10.1145/245108.245123 Cited on page(s) 39

[140] R. Kelapure. Scenario-Based Generation of Digital Library Services. Master's thesis, Virginia Tech Dept. of Computer Science, 2003. http://scholar.lib.vt.edu/theses/available/etd-06182003-055012/ [last visited July 4, 2012]. Cited on page(s) 100

[141] D. Krafft. The NCore Platform: An Open-Source Suite of Tools and Services for Implementing Digital Libraries. In *Third International Conference on Open Repositories 2008, 1-4 April, Southampton, UK*, 2008. Cited on page(s) 7

[142] D. B. Krafft, A. Birkland, and E. J. Cramer. NCore: architecture and implementation of a flexible, collaborative digital library. In *JCDL '08: Proceedings of the 8th ACM/IEEE-CS joint conference on Digital libraries*, pages 313–322, New York, NY, USA, 2008. ACM. http://doi.acm.org/10.1145/1378889.1378943 [last visited July 4, 2012]. DOI: 10.1145/1378889.1378943 Cited on page(s) 7

[143] M. Kying. Creating contexts for design. In *Scenario-Based Design: Envisioning Work and Technology in System Development*. John Wiley & Sons, New York, NY, USA, 1995. Cited on page(s) 30

[144] A. Laender, B. Ribeiro-Neto, A. da Silva, and J. Teixeira. A brief survey of web data extraction tools. *ACM SIGMOD Record*, 31(2):84–93, 2002. DOI: 10.1145/565117.565137 Cited on page(s) 27

[145] C. Lagoze. A Secure Repository Design for Digital Libraries. *D-Lib Magazine*, 1(12), December 1995. http://www.dlib.org/dlib/december95/12lagoze.html [last visited July 4, 2012]. DOI: 10.1045/december95-lagoze Cited on page(s) 21

[146] A. V. Lamsweerde and L. Willemet. Inferring declarative requirements specifications from operational scenarios. *IEEE Trans. on Soft. Engineering*, 24(12):1089–1114, December 1998. DOI: 10.1109/32.738341 Cited on page(s) 30

[147] R. L. Larsen and H. D. Wactlar. *Knowledge Lost in Information: Report of the NSF Workshop on Research Directions for Digital Libraries, June 15-17, 2003, Chatham, MA.* University of Pittsburgh, Pittsburgh, 2004. Cited on page(s) 5

[148] W. G. LeFurgy. PDF/A: Developing a File Format for Long-Term Preservation. *RLG DigiNews*, 7(6), 2003. Cited on page(s) 17

[149] M. Lesk. Perspectives on DLI-2 – Growing the Field. *D-Lib Magazine*, 5(7/8), 1999. DOI: 10.1002/bult.136 Cited on page(s) 11

[150] M. Lesk. *Understanding Digital Libraries, 2nd ed.* San Francisco: Morgan Kaufmann, 2004. Cited on page(s) 1, 12

[151] D. M. Levy. Heroic measures: reflections on the possibility and purpose of digital preservation. In *DL'98: Proceedings of the 3rd ACM International Conference on Digital Libraries*, pages 152–161, Pittsburgh, PA, 1998. DOI: 10.1145/276675.276692 Cited on page(s) 17

[152] D. M. Levy and C. C. Marshall. Going Digital: A Look at Assumptions Underlying Digital Libraries. *Communications of the ACM*, 38:77–84, April 1995. DOI: 10.1145/205323.205346 Cited on page(s) 31

[153] Library of Congress. MARC homepage, March 1998. http://lcweb.loc.gov/marc/marc.html [last visited July 4, 2012]. Cited on page(s) 21

[154] J. C. R. Licklider. *Libraries of the Future.* MIT Press, Cambridge, Massachusetts, 1965. Cited on page(s) 1, 12, 28

[155] R. A. Lorie. Long term preservation of digital information. In *JCDL 2001*, pages 346–352, Roanoke, VA, 2001. ACM. DOI: 10.1145/379437.379726 Cited on page(s) 17, 33

[156] R. A. Lorie. A methodology and system for preserving digital data. In *JCDL 2002*, pages 312–319, Portland, Oregon, 2002. ACM. DOI: 10.1145/544220.544296 Cited on page(s) 33

[157] C. A. Lynch. The Z39.50 Information Retrieval Standard Part I: A Strategic View of Its Past, Present and Future. *D-Lib Magazine*, 3(4), 1997. April. DOI: 10.1045/april97-lynch Cited on page(s) 22

[158] C. A. Lynch. Institutional Repositories: Essential Infrastructure for Scholarship in the Digital Age. *ARL Bimonthly Report*, 226, February 2003. Cited on page(s) 21

[159] W. E. Mackay and M. Beaudouin-Lafon. DIVA exploratory data analysis with multimedia streams. In *Proc. of CHI-98*, pages 416–423, Los Angeles, CA, USA, Apr. 18-23, 1998. DOI: 10.1145/274644.274701 Cited on page(s) 24

[160] U. Manber, M. Smith, and B. Gopal. Webglimpse: Combining browsing and searching. In *Proceedings of Usenix Technical Conference*, pages 195–206, 1997. Cited on page(s) 45

[161] G. Marchionini. *Information Seeking in Electronic Environments*. Cambridge University Press, Cambridge, 1995. DOI: 10.1017/CBO9780511626388 Cited on page(s) 43

[162] R. Miller, O. Tsatalos, and J. Williams. DataWeb: Customizable Database Publishing for the Web. *Multimedia, IEEE*, 4(4):14–21, 1997. DOI: 10.1109/93.641875 Cited on page(s) 45, 97, 98

[163] R. Mirandola and D. Hollinger. A New Approach to Performance Modelling of Client/Server Distributed Data Base Architectures. *Performance Evaluation*, 29(4):255–272, 1997. DOI: 10.1016/S0166-5316(96)00047-8 Cited on page(s) 22

[164] C. S. Mooers. Coding information retrieval and the rapid selector. *American Documentation*, 1(4):225–29, 1950. Cited on page(s) 10

[165] P. Mukhopadhyay and Y. Papakonstantinou. Mixing Querying and Navigation in MIX. In *Proceedings of ICDE*, pages 245–254, 2002. DOI: 10.1109/ICDE.2002.994714 Cited on page(s) 45, 97, 98

[166] K. D. Munroe and Y. Papakonstantinou. BBQ: A Visual Interface for Integrated Browsing and Querying of XML. In *Proceedings of VDB*, pages 277–296, 2000. http://db.ucsd.edu/publications/bbq.ps [last visited July 4, 2012]. Cited on page(s) 45

[167] NASA (Jet Propulsion Laboratory, California Institute of Technology). CW Leo Space Image. http://photojournal.jpl.nasa.gov/jpeg/PIA15417.jpg [last visited July 4, 2012]. Cited on page(s) 29

[168] G. Navarro and R. Baeza-Yates. Proximal nodes: A model to query document databases by content and structure. *ACM Transactions on Information Systems*, 15(4):400–435, 1997. DOI: 10.1145/263479.263482 Cited on page(s) 66, 68

[169] M. L. Nelson and K. Maly. Buckets: Smart objects for digital libraries. *Communications of the ACM*, 44(5):60–61, 2001. DOI: 10.1145/374308.374342 Cited on page(s) 68

[170] S. Nestorov, S. Abiteboul, and R. Motwani. Inferring structure in semistructured data. *SIGMOD Record*, 26(4):39–43, 1997. DOI: 10.1145/271074.271084 Cited on page(s) 27

[171] NISO. Information Retrieval (Z39.50): Application Service Definition and Protocol Specification (ANSI/NISO Z39.501995). Technical report, NISO (National Information Standards Organization) Press, 1995. Cited on page(s) 22

[172] P. Noerr. *The Digital Library Toolkit*. Sun Microsystems, Inc., Palo Alto, CA, 2nd edition, March 2000. Cited on page(s) 23

[173] P. Norris. *Digital Divide: Civic Engagement, Information Poverty, and the Internet Worldwide*. Cambridge University Press, Cambridge, UK, 2001. DOI: 10.1017/CBO9781139164887 Cited on page(s) 13

[174] OAI. The Open Archives Initiative Protocol for Metadata Harvesting – Version 2.0. Eds. Lagoze, C., Van De Sompel, H., Nelson, M., Warner, S., http://www.openarchives.org/OAI/openarchivesprotocol.html [last visited July 4, 2012], October 2004. Cited on page(s) 10

[175] OAI. Open Archive Initiative, http://www.openarchives.org/, 2005. Cited on page(s) 10

[176] D. Oard, C. Peters, M. Ruiz, R. Frederking, J. Klavans, and P. Sheridan. Multilingual Information Discovery and AccesS (MIDAS): A Joint ACM DL'99 / ACM SIGIR'99 Workshop. *D-Lib Magazine*, 5(10), Oct. 1999. http://www.dlib.org/dlib/october99/10oard.html [last visited July 4, 2012]. DOI: 10.1045/october99-oard Cited on page(s) 33

[177] A. Oberweis and P. Sander. Information system behavior specification by high level Petri nets. *ACM Transactions on Information Systems*, 14(4):380–420, 1996. DOI: 10.1145/237496.237498 Cited on page(s) 24, 65

[178] OCLC. SRW/U, 2010. http://www.oclc.org/research/activities/srw/default.htm [last visited July 4, 2012]. Cited on page(s) 22

[179] R. Ogawa, H. Harada, and A. Kaneko. Scenario-based hypermedia: A model and a system. In *Proc. of the ECHT'90 European Conf. on Hypertext*, pages 38–51, 1990. Cited on page(s) 31

[180] C. Olston and E. Chi. ScentTrails: Integrating browsing and searching on the Web. *ACM Trans. Comput.-Hum. Interact*, 10(3):177–197, 2003. DOI: 10.1145/937549.937550 Cited on page(s) 43, 45, 99

[181] A. M. B. Pavani. Digital Reference Center - the Maxwell Project. In *Proceedings of the 1999 International Conference on Engineering Education*. INEER, 1999. Cited on page(s) 22

[182] S. Payette and C. Lagoze. Flexible and Extensible Digital Object and Repository Architecture (FEDORA). In *ECDL '98: Proceedings of the Second European Conference on Research and Advanced Technology for Digital Libraries*, pages 41–59, London, UK, 1998. Springer-Verlag. Cited on page(s) 21

[183] S. Perugini, K. McDevitt, R. Richardson, M. Perez-Quinones, R. Shen, N. Ramakrishnan, C. Williams, and E. A. Fox. Enhancing usability in CITIDEL: Multimodal, multilingual, and interactive visualization interfaces. In *Proceedings Fourth ACM/IEEE-CS Joint Conference on Digital Libraries (JCDL2004), Tucson, AZ, June 7-11*, pages 315–324. IEEE-CS, 2004. DOI: 10.1145/996350.996424 Cited on page(s) 23, 47, 84

[184] J. Pomerantz, S. Oh, B. Wildemuth, S. Yang, and E. A. Fox. Digital library education in computer science programs. In *Proc. 7th ACM/IEEE-CS Joint Conference on Digital Libraries, Vancouver, British Columbia, Canada, June 18-23*. ACM, 2007. DOI: 10.1145/1255175.1255208 Cited on page(s) 19

[185] J. Pomerantz, S. Oh, S. Yang, E. A. Fox, and B. Wildemuth. The Core: Digital Library Education in Library and Information Science Programs. *D-Lib Magazine*, 12(11), 2006. DOI: 10.1045/november2006-pomerantz Cited on page(s) 19

[186] J. Pomerantz, B. Wildemuth, E. A. Fox, and S. Yang. Curriculum development for digital libraries. In *Proceedings of the 6th ACM/IEEE-CS Joint Conference on Digital Libraries*, pages 175–184. ACM, New York, 2006. DOI: 10.1145/1141753.1141787 Cited on page(s) 18

[187] H. J. Porck and R. Teygeler. *Preservation Science Survey: An Overview of Recent Developments in Research on the Conservation of Selected Analog Library and Archival Materials*. CLIR, Washington, D.C., 2000. http://www.clir.org/pubs/abstract/pub95abst.html [last visited July 4, 2012]. Cited on page(s) 17

[188] R. Prince, J. Su, H. Tang, and Y. Zhao. The design of an interactive online help desk in the Alexandria Digital Library. In *Proc. of the Int. Joint Conf. on Work Activities and Collaboration: WACC '99*, pages 217–226, San Francisco, CA, 1999. DOI: 10.1145/295665.295692 Cited on page(s) 29

[189] N. Ramakrishnan. PIPE: Web Personalization By Partial Evaluation. *IEEE Internet Computing*, 4(6):21–31, 2000. DOI: 10.1109/4236.895012 Cited on page(s) 71

[190] S. R. Ranganathan. *A Descriptive Account of Colon Classification*. Bangalore: Sarada Ranganathan Endowment for Library Science, 1965. Cited on page(s) 35

[191] A. Rauber. DELOS and the Future of Digital Libraries. *D-Lib Magazine*, 10(10). http://www.dlib.org/dlib/october04/10inbrief.html#RAUBER[last visited July 4, 2012], October 2004. Cited on page(s) 11

[192] U. Ravindranathan. Prototyping Digital Libraries Handling Heterogeneous Data Sources – An ETANA-DL Case Study. Master's thesis, Virginia Tech CS Department, April 2004. http://scholar.lib.vt.edu/theses/available/etd-04262004-153555/ [last visited July 4, 2012]. Cited on page(s) 23, 44, 77, 84

[193] U. Ravindranathan, R. Shen, M. A. Gonçalves, W. Fan, E. A. Fox, and F. Flanagan. Prototyping Digital Libraries Handling Heterogeneous Data Sources - the ETANA-DL Case Study. In *Proc. 8th European Conf. Research and Advanced Technology for Digital Libraries, ECDL*, number 3232 in LNCS, pages 186–197, Bath, UK, Sept. 2004. Springer-Verlag. DOI: 10.1007/978-3-540-30230-8_18 Cited on page(s) 84

[194] U. Ravindranathan, R. Shen, M. A. Gonçalves, W. Fan, E. A. Fox, and J. W. Flanagan. ETANA-DL: managing complex information applications – an archaeology digital library. In *JCDL '04: Proceedings of the 4th ACM/IEEE-CS Joint Conference on Digital Libraries*, pages 414–414, New York, NY, USA, 2004. ACM Press. DOI: 10.1145/996350.996481 Cited on page(s) 23, 77, 84

[195] R. Reddy and I. Wladawsky-Berger. Digital Libraries: Universal Access to Human Knowledge - A Report to the President. President's Information Technology Advisory Committee (PITAC), Panel on Digital Libraries. http://www.itrd.gov/pubs/pitac/pitac-dl-9feb01.pdf, 2001. Cited on page(s) 33

[196] S. E. Robertson. The probability ranking principle in IR. *J. Documentation*, 33:294–304, 1977. DOI: 10.1108/eb026647 Cited on page(s) 28

[197] P. Rödig, U. M. Borghoff, J. Scheffczyk, and L. Schmitz. Preservation of digital publications: an OAIS extension and implementation. In *Proceedings of the 1st ACM Symposium on Document Engineering*, pages 131–139, Grenoble, France, 2003. http://doi.acm.org/10.1145/958220.958245 [last visited July 4, 2012]. DOI: 10.1145/958220.958245 Cited on page(s) 17

[198] S. Ross and M. Hedstrom. Preservation research and sustainable digital libraries. *Int. J. on Digital Libraries*, 5(4):317–324, 2005. DOI: 10.1007/s00799-004-0099-3 Cited on page(s) 21

[199] M. B. Rosson. Integrating development of task and object models. *Communications of the ACM*, 42(1):49–56, 1999. DOI: 10.1145/291469.293168 Cited on page(s) 65

[200] M. B. Rosson and J. M. Carroll. Object-oriented design from user scenarios. In *Proc. of ACM CHI 96 Conf. on Human Factors in Computing Systems*, pages 342–343, 1996. DOI: 10.1145/257089.257359 Cited on page(s) 65

[201] J. Rothenberg. *Avoiding Technological Quicksand: Finding a Viable Technical Foundation for Digital Preservation*. CLIR, Washington, D.C., 1999. Cited on page(s) 17

[202] G. Salton. *Automatic Text Processing: The Transformation, Analysis and Retrieval of Information by Computer*. Addison-Wesley, Boston, Massachusetts, USA, 1989. Cited on page(s) 79

[203] G. Salton, E. A. Fox, and H. Wu. Extended Boolean information retrieval. *Communications of the ACM*, 26(11):1022–1036, November 1983. DOI: 10.1145/182.358466 Cited on page(s) 80

[204] G. Salton and M. E. Lesk. The SMART Automatic Document Retrieval System - An Illustration. *Communications of the ACM*, 8(6):391–398, 1965. DOI: 10.1145/364955.364990 Cited on page(s) 28

[205] G. Salton, A. Wong, and C. S. Yang. A vector space model for automatic indexing. *Communications of the ACM*, 18(11):613–620, 1975. DOI: 10.1145/361219.361220 Cited on page(s) 63

[206] T. Saracevic. Relevance: a review and a framework for thinking on the notion in information science. *Journal of the American Society for Information Science*, 26:321–343, 1975. DOI: 10.1002/asi.4630260604 Cited on page(s) 40

[207] H.-J. Schek and H. Schuldt. DelosDLMS - Infrastructure for the Next Generation of Digital ManagementSystems. *ERCIM News, Special Issue on the European Digital Library*, 66:22–24, July 2006. Cited on page(s) 22

[208] M. F. Schwartz and D. C. M. Wood. Discovering shared interests using graph analysis. *Communications of the ACM*, 36(8):78–89, Aug. 1993. DOI: 10.1145/163381.163402 Cited on page(s) 39

[209] E. Sciascio, F. Donini, and M. Mongiello. Spatial layout representation for query-by-sketch content-based image retrieval. *Pattern Recognition*, 23(13):1599–1612, 2002. DOI: 10.1016/S0167-8655(02)00124-1 Cited on page(s) 89

[210] D. E. Shackelford, J. B. Smith, and F. D. Smith. The architecture and implementation of a distributed hypermedia storage system. In *Proc. of the 5th Conf. on Hypertext*, pages 1–13, Seattle, Washington, Nov. 1993. DOI: 10.1145/168750.168753 Cited on page(s) 71

[211] C. E. Shannon. A mathematical theory of communication. *Bell System Technical Journal*, 27:379–423, 623–656, July, Oct. 1948. DOI: 10.1145/584091.584093 Cited on page(s) 24

[212] R. Shen. *Applying the 5S Framework to Integrating Digital Libraries*. Ph.D. dissertation, Virginia Tech CS Department, Blacksburg, Virginia, 2006. `http://scholar.lib.vt.edu/theses/available/etd-04212006-135018/` [last visited July 4, 2012]. Cited on page(s) xx, 40, 47, 48, 49, 50, 51, 52, 53, 54, 55, 56, 77, 79, 80, 81, 82, 85, 88, 89, 90, 91, 92, 93, 94, 95, 96, 97, 98, 99, 100, 102

[213] R. Shen, M. A. Gonçalves, W. Fan, and E. A. Fox. Requirements Gathering and Modeling of Domain-Specific Digital Libraries with the 5S Framework: An Archaeological Case Study with ETANA. In *Proc. European Conference on Digital Libraries, ECDL 2005, Vienna, Sept. 18-23*, pages 1–12. Springer, 2005. `http://dl.acm.org/citation.cfm?id=2142714` [last visited July 4, 2012]. DOI: 10.1007/11551362_1 Cited on page(s) 23, 44, 88

[214] R. Shen, N. S. Vemuri, W. Fan, R. da S. Torres, and E. A. Fox. Exploring digital libraries: integrating browsing, searching, and visualization. In *JCDL '06: Proceedings of the 6th ACM/IEEE-CS joint conference on Digital libraries*, pages 1–10, New York, NY, USA, 2006. ACM. DOI: 10.1145/1141753.1141755 Cited on page(s) 40, 47, 48, 49, 50, 51, 52, 53, 54, 55, 56, 91, 92, 93, 94, 96, 98, 99, 100

[215] R. Shen, N. S. Vemuri, W. Fan, and E. A. Fox. Integration of complex archeology digital libraries: An ETANA-DL experience. *Information Systems*, 33(7-8):699–723, 2008. `http://dx.doi.org/10.1016/j.is.2008.02.006` [last visited July 4, 2012]. DOI: 10.1016/j.is.2008.02.006 Cited on page(s) 23

[216] R. Shen, N. S. Vemuri, V. Vijayaraghavan, W. Fan, and E. A. Fox. EtanaViz: A Visual User Interface to Archaeological Digital Libraries. Technical Report TR-05-14, Computer Science, Virginia Tech, October 2005. `http://eprints.cs.vt.edu/archive/00000725/` [last visited July 4, 2012]. Cited on page(s) 85

[217] M. Singhal and N. Shivaratri. *Advanced Concepts in Operating Systems: Distributed, Database, and Multiprocessor Operating Systems*. McGraw-Hill, New York, 1994. Cited on page(s) 65

[218] T. Staples and R. Wayland. Virginia Dons FEDORA: A Prototype for a Digital Object Repository. *D-Lib Magazine*, 6(7/8), 2000. July/August. DOI: 10.1045/july2000-staples Cited on page(s) 21

[219] T. Staples, R. Wayland, and S. Payette. The Fedora Project: An Open-source Digital Object Repository Management System. *D-Lib Magazine*, 9(4), Apr. 2003. `http://www.dlib.org/dlib/april03/staples/04staples.html` [last visited July 4, 2012]. Cited on page(s) 21, 68

[220] H. Suleman. *Open Digital Libraries*. PhD thesis, Virginia Tech CS Department, Blacksburg, Virginia, 2002. `http://scholar.lib.vt.edu/theses/available/etd-11222002-155624/` [last visited July 4, 2012]. Cited on page(s) 23

[221] H. Suleman and E. A. Fox. A Framework for Building Open Digital Libraries. *D-Lib Magazine*, 7(12), 2001. DOI: 10.1045/december2001-suleman Cited on page(s) 23

[222] H. Suleman and E. A. Fox. Designing protocols in support of digital library componentization. In *Proceedings of the 6th European Conference on Research and Advanced Technology for Digital Libraries (ECDL2002), LNCS 2458*, pages 75–84. Springer, Rome, Italy, 2002. DOI: 10.1007/3-540-45747-X_43 Cited on page(s) 23

[223] A. Sutcliffe. A technique combination approach to requirements engineering. In *Proc. of the 3rd Int. Symp. on Requirements Engineering*, pages 65–77, Annapolis, 1997. IEEE. DOI: 10.1109/ISRE.1997.566843 Cited on page(s) 30

[224] A. G. Sutcliffe, N. A. M. Maiden, S. Minocha, and D. Manuel. Supporting scenario-based requirements engineering. *IEEE Trans. on Soft. Engineering*, 24(12):1072–1088, 1998. DOI: 10.1109/32.738340 Cited on page(s) 30

[225] R. Tansley, M. Bass, M. Branschofsky, G. Carpenter, G. McClellan, and D. Stuve. DSpace System Documentation: An Introduction, 2005. https://wiki.duraspace.org/download/attachments/19006155/DSpaceSysDoc1.2.1-2.pdf [last visited July 4, 2012]. Cited on page(s) 11, 22

[226] R. Tansley, M. Bass, D. Stuve, M. Branschofsky, D. Chudnov, G. McClellan, and M. Smith. DSpace: An Institutional Digital Repository System. In *Proc. of the 3rd Joint Conference on Digital Libraries*, pages 87–97, Houston, Texas, 2003. DOI: 10.1109/JCDL.2003.1204846 Cited on page(s) 11, 22

[227] R. Tansley, M. Bass, D. Stuve, M. Branschofsky, D. Chudnov, G. McClellan, and M. Smith. The DSpace institutional digital repository system: current functionality. In *JCDL '03: Proceedings of the 3rd ACM/IEEE-CS joint conference on Digital libraries*, pages 87–97, Washington, DC, USA, 2003. IEEE Computer Society. DOI: 10.1109/JCDL.2003.1204846 Cited on page(s) 11, 21, 22

[228] R. Tansley and S. Harnad. Eprints.org software for creating institutional and individual open archives. *D-Lib Magazine*, 6(10), October 2000. Cited on page(s) 23

[229] M. Taube and et al. Storage and retrieval of information by means of the association of ideas. *American Documentation*, 6(1):1–18, 1955. DOI: 10.1002/asi.5090060103 Cited on page(s) 10

[230] H. R. Tibbo. Archival perspectives on the emerging digital library. *CACM*, 44(5), 2001. DOI: 10.1145/374308.374345 Cited on page(s) 21

[231] S. Urs and E. A. Fox. Indo-US Workshop on Open Digital Libraries and Interoperability, 23-25 June 2003, Arlington, USA, June 2003. http://www.indousstf.org/details.aspx?

`mostprvmytitle=Past%20Programs&prevmytitle=Bilateral%20Workshops/` `%20Symposia/%20Roundtables&id=200&name=Indo-US%20Workshop%20on%200pen` `%20Digital%20Libraries%20and%20Interoperability` [last visited July 4, 2012]. Cited on page(s) 16

[232] U.S. National Archives and Records Administration. National Archives homepage. `http://` `www.archives.gov/` [last visited July 4, 2012]. Cited on page(s) 21

[233] B. C. Vickery. Faceted classification schemes. In *Rutgers Series for the Intellectual Organization of Information – Volume 5*. Rutgers University Press, New Brunswick, NJ, USA, 1965. Cited on page(s) 35

[234] W3C. *Resource Description Framework (RDF) Model and Syntax Specification: W3C Proposed Recommendation 05 January*, 1999. `http://www.w3.org/TR/1999/PR-rdf-syntax-` `19990105/` [last visited July 4, 2012]. Cited on page(s) 66

[235] W. Wang and R. Rada. Structured hypertext with domain semantics. *ACM Transactions on Information Systems*, 16(4):372–412, October 1998. DOI: 10.1145/291128.291132 Cited on page(s) 70

[236] S. Warner. Exposing and Harvesting Metadata Using the OAI Metadata Harvesting Protocol: A Tutorial. *High Energy Physics (HEP) Libraries Webzine*, 2001(4), June 2001. `http://library.web.cern.ch/library/Webzine/4/papers/3/` [last visited July 4, 2012]. Cited on page(s) 22

[237] D. Waters and J. Garrett. *Preserving Digital Information: Report of the Task Force on Archiving of Digital Information*. CLIR, Washington, D.C., 1996. Cited on page(s) 17

[238] D. J. Waters. What Are Digital Libraries? *CLIR Issues*, 1998(4), July/August 1998. `http://` `www.clir.org/pubs/issues/issues04.html` [last visited July 4, 2012]. DOI: 10.1300/J105v22n03_09 Cited on page(s) 4

[239] Webimage. Several Societies graphic obtained online, 2012. `http://kusu.cq.uk/` [last visited July 4, 2012]. Cited on page(s) 32

[240] S. Weibel. The State of the Dublin Core Metadata Initiative: April 1999. *D-Lib Magazine*, 5(4), 1999. DOI: 10.1045/april99-weibel Cited on page(s) 21

[241] S. L. Weibel and T. Koch. The Dublin Core Metadata Initiative: Mission, Current Activities, and Future Directions, available at http://www.dlib.org/dlib/december00/weibel/12weibel.html. *D-Lib Magazine*, 6(12), December 2000. DOI: 10.1045/december2000-weibel Cited on page(s) 21

[242] J. Weise. Brief survey of digital library software systems, 2010. `http://mblog.lib.umich.edu/blt/archives/2010/07/brief%5Fsurvey%5Fof.html` [last visited July 4, 2012]. Cited on page(s) 22

[243] H. G. Wells. World Brain: The Idea of a Permanent World Encyclopaedia. In *Encyclopédie Française*. Anatole de Monzie and Lucien Febvre, 1937. `http://sherlock.berkeley.edu/wells/world_brain.html` [last visited July 4, 2012]. Cited on page(s) 13

[244] D. West, M. Finnegan, R. Lane, and D. Kysar. *Analysis of Faunal Remains Recovered from Tell Nimrin, Dead Sea Valley, Jordan, final report*. Case Western Reserve University, 1996. Cited on page(s) 52, 53

[245] G. Wiederhold. Digital libraries, value, and productivity. *Communications of the ACM*, 38(4):85–96, 1995. DOI: 10.1145/205323.205347 Cited on page(s) 31

[246] R. Wilkison and M. Fuller. Integration of information retrieval and hypertext via structure. In *Information Retrieval and Hypertext*, pages 257–271. Kluwer Academic Publishers, 1996. Cited on page(s) 31

[247] M. Williams. What makes RABBIT run? *International Journal of Man-Machine Studies*, 21(4):333–352, 1984. DOI: 10.1016/S0020-7373(84)80052-8 Cited on page(s) 45

[248] G. Winskel. *The Formal Semantics of Programming Languages: An Introduction*. Foundations of Computing series. MIT Press, Cambridge, MA, USA, Feb. 1993. Cited on page(s) 32, 65

[249] I. Witten, D. Bainbridge, and S. J. Boddie. Greenstone Open-Source Digital Library Software. *D-Lib Magazine*, 7(10), 2000. Cited on page(s) 22

[250] I. H. Witten and D. Bainbridge. *How to Build a Digital Library*. Morgan Kaufmann Publishers, San Francisco (CA), USA, 2003. Cited on page(s) 4, 22

[251] I. H. Witten and D. Bainbridge. A retrospective look at Greenstone: Lessons from the first decade, Research Commons at The University of Waikato. In *Proceedings of the 7th ACM/IEEE-CS joint conference on Digital libraries, Vancouver, BC, Canada June 18 - 23, 2007*, pages 147–156. ACM, 2007. DOI: 10.1145/1255175.1255204 Cited on page(s) 22

[252] I. H. Witten, D. Bainbridge, and S. Boddie. Greenstone: Open-source DL software. *Communications of the ACM*, 44(5):47, 2001. DOI: 10.1145/374308.374338 Cited on page(s) 22

[253] I. H. Witten, D. Bainbridge, and D. M. Nichols. *How to Build a Digital Library, 2nd ed.* Morgan Kaufmann Publishers, San Francisco (CA), USA, 2009. Cited on page(s) 1, 12

[254] I. H. Witten, D. Bainbridge, G. Paynter, and S. Boddie. The Greenstone plugin architecture. In *JCDL '02: Proceedings of the 2nd ACM/IEEE-CS joint conference on Digital libraries*, pages 285–286, New York, NY, USA, 2002. ACM. DOI: 10.1145/544220.544285 Cited on page(s) 22

[255] I. H. Witten, D. Bainbridge, R. Tansley, C. Huang, and K. Don. StoneD: A bridge between Greenstone and DSpace. *D-Lib Magazine*, 11(9), September 2005. DOI: 10.1045/september2005-witten Cited on page(s) 22

[256] I. H. Witten, R. J. McNab, S. J. Boddie, and D. Bainbridge. Greenstone: A comprehensive open-source digital library software system. In *Proc. of the 5th ACM Int. Conf. on Digital Libraries*, pages 113–121, San Antonio, TX, June 2-7, 2000. DOI: 10.1145/336597.336650 Cited on page(s) 22

[257] I. H. Witten, A. Moffat, and T. C. Bell. *Managing Gigabytes: Compressing and Indexing Documents and Images*. Morgan Kaufmann Publishers, 2nd edition, 1999. Cited on page(s) 22

[258] K. Wittenburg and E. Sigman. Integration of browsing, searching, and filtering in an applet for web information access. In *Proceedings of CHI*, pages 293–294, 1997. DOI: 10.1145/1120212.1120400 Cited on page(s) 45

[259] WordNet. WordNet interactive site, 2012. http://wordnetweb.princeton.edu/perl/webwn [last visited July 4, 2012]. Cited on page(s) 26, 28, 30, 31, 33

[260] J. Zhao. Making Digital Libraries Flexible, Scalable, and Reliable: Reengineering the MARIAN System in JAVA. Master of science thesis, Virginia Tech Department of Computer Science, 1999. http://scholar.lib.vt.edu/theses/available/etd-070499-204531/ [last visited July 4, 2012]. Cited on page(s) 23

[261] Q. Zhu. 5SGraph: A Modeling Tool for Digital Libraries. Masters thesis, Virginia Tech Dept. of Computer Science, 2002. http://scholar.lib.vt.edu/theses/available/etd-11272002-210531/ [last visited July 4, 2012]. Cited on page(s) 100

[262] Q. Zhu, M. A. Gonçalves, R. Shen, L. Cassel, and E. A. Fox. Visual semantic modeling of digital libraries. In *Proc. 7th European Conference on Digital Libraries (ECDL 2003), 17-22 August, Trondheim, Norway, Springer LNCS 2769*, pages 325–337. Springer, 2004. DOI: 10.1007/b11967 Cited on page(s) 100

[263] N. Ziviani, E. S. de Moura, G. Navarro, and R. Baeza-Yates. Compression: A key for next-generation text retrieval systems. *IEEE Computer*, 33(11):37–44, Nov. 2000. DOI: 10.1109/2.881693 Cited on page(s) 29

Authors' Biographies

EDWARD A. FOX

Edward A. Fox grew up on Long Island, New York. He attended the Massachusetts Institute of Technology (MIT), receiving a B.S. in 1972 in Electrical Engineering, through the Computer Science option. His undergraduate adviser was J.C.R. Licklider. His thesis adviser was Michael Kessler. At MIT he founded the ACM Student Chapter and the Student Information Processing Board, receiving the William Stewart Award.

From 1971–1972 he worked as Data Processing Instructor at the Florence Darlington Technical College. From 1972–1978 he was Data Processing Manager at Vulcraft, a Division of NUCOR Corporation, also in Florence, SC. In the fall of 1978 he began his graduate studies at Cornell University in Ithaca, NY. His adviser was Gerard Salton. He received an M.S. in Computer Science in 1981 and a Ph.D. in 1983. From the summer of 1982 through the spring of 1983 he served as Manager of Information Systems at the International Institute of Tropical Agriculture, Ibadan, Nigeria. From the fall of 1983 through the present he has been on the faculty of the Department of Computer Science at Virginia Tech (also called VPI&SU or Virginia Polytechnic Institute and State University). In 1988 he was given tenure and promoted to the rank of Associate Professor. In 1995 he was promoted to Professor.

Dr. Fox has been a member of ACM since 1968. He was vice chairman of ACM SIGIR 1987–1991. Then he was chair 1991–1995. During that period, he helped launch the new ACM SIG on Multimedia. He served as a member of the ACM Publications Board 1988-1992 and as Editor-in-chief of ACM Press Database and Electronic Products 1988–1991, during which time he helped conceive and launch the ACM Digital Library. He served 2000–2006 as a founder and Co-editor-in-chief of the ACM Journal of Education Resources In Computing (JERIC), which led to the ACM Transactions on Education. Over the period 2004–2008 he served as Chairman of the IEEE-CS Technical Committee on Digital Libraries, and continues to serve on its Executive Committee. Dr. Fox served 1995–2008 as Editor of the Morgan Kaufmann Publishers, Inc. Series on Multimedia Information and Systems. He has been a member of Sigma Xi since the 1970s and a member of Upsilon Pi Epsilon since 1998.

In 1987 Dr. Fox began to explore the idea of all students shifting to electronic theses and dissertations (ETDs), and has worked in this area ever since. He led the establishment of the Networked Digital Library of Theses and Dissertations (operating informally starting in 1995, incorporated in May 2003). He serves as founder and Executive Director of NDLTD. He won its 1st Annual NDLTD Leadership Award in May 2004.

Dr. Fox has been involved in a wide variety of professional service activities. He has chaired scores of conferences or workshops, and served on hundreds of program or conference committees. At present he serves on more than ten editorial boards, and is a member of the board of directors of the Computing Research Association (CRA; he is co-chair of its membership committee, as well as a member of CRA-E, its education committee). He also chairs the steering committee of the ACM/IEEE-CS Joint Conference on Digital Libraries.

Dr. Fox has been (co)PI on over 110 research and development projects. In addition to his courses at Virginia Tech, Dr. Fox has taught over 77 tutorials in more than 28 countries. His publications and presentations include: 15 books, 104 journal/magazine articles, 48 book chapters, 180 refereed (+40 other) conference/workshop papers, 59 posters, 66 keynote/banquet/international invited/distinguished speaker presentations, 38 demonstrations, and over 300 additional presentations. His research and teaching has been on digital libraries, information storage and retrieval, hypertext/hypermedia/multimedia, computing education, computational linguistics, and sub-areas of artificial intelligence.

MARCOS ANDRÉ GONÇALVES

Marcos André Gonçalves is an Associate Professor at the Computer Science Department of the Universidade Federal de Minas Gerais (UFMG), Brazil. He holds a Ph.D. in Computer Science (CS) from Virginia Tech (2004), an M.S. in CS from State University of Campinas, Brazil (Unicamp, 1997), and a B.S., also in Computer Science, from the Federal University of Ceará, Brazil (UFC, 1995). Professor Gonçalves has served as referee on different journals (TOIS, TKDE, IP&M, Information Retrieval, Information Systems, etc.) and at several conferences (SIGIR, CIKM, JCDL, TPDL, etc.). His research interests include information retrieval, digital libraries, text classification and text mining in general, having published more than 150 refereed journal articles and conference papers in these areas. Marcos is currently an affiliate member of the Brazilian Academy of Sciences.

RAO SHEN

Rao Shen received her Ph.D. in Computer Science from Virginia Tech in 2006. Her advisor was Edward A. Fox. Her research interests include digital library, information retrieval, information visualization, and machine learning. She joined the web search relevance team at Yahoo! in May 2006. She is working on problems related to federated search in Yahoo! Labs.

Index

5S, viii, xiii–xvi, xx, 1, 2, 7–9, 13, 23, 24, 28, 35, 40, 41, 43, 44, 46, 57, 63, 64, 66, 77, 100–103

5SGen, 23, 100–103

5SGraph, 100–103

5SL, 101, 103

5SQual, 103

5SSuite, xiv, 100, 103

access, xv, 1, 3–5, 10, 13–17, 21–23, 33, 36, 38, 40, 46, 49, 57, 66, 68, 78, 87, 92, 103, 104, 106, 107, 110, 112, 114, 116, 121, 122

algorithm, 27, 29, 71, 103, 120

analysis, 18, 20, 28, 35, 41, 46, 50, 100, 101, 103, 108, 111, 112, 114, 118, 122

analyst, 65, 103

anchor, 70, 103, 112, 119

animation, 87, 103, 113, 122

annotation, viii, xiv, 36, 37, 39–41, 45, 85, 104, 119

API, 45, 97, 104

archive, xvi, 1, 4, 5, 9, 10, 17, 21, 23, 38, 41, 104, 106, 110, 113

audio, 4, 7, 10, 24, 37, 66, 68–70, 104, 110, 113, 119, 122

authentication, 38, 39, 104

authorization, 38, 39, 104

base document, 104, 119, 122

browse, 23, 36, 39, 40, 43, 45–47, 49, 51, 53–55, 57, 64, 71, 72, 76–78, 85, 94–98, 101, 102, 104, 108, 119, 122

catalog, xiv, 2, 7, 8, 17, 21, 22, 36, 37, 39, 40, 64, 66, 72, 75, 77, 78, 83–85, 101, 102, 105, 107

CBIR, viii, xv, 105, 106

classify, viii, 34, 36, 37, 39, 40, 105, 108, 115, 117, 120, 123

CLIR, 105, 106

cluster, 20, 28, 35, 36, 40, 43, 44, 50, 51, 57, 78–80, 85, 87, 90–94, 99, 105

CMS, xiii, 105, 106

collaboration, 36, 40, 105

collection, 3–8, 10, 17, 20–23, 28, 33, 36, 37, 39, 40, 46, 60–62, 64, 66, 68–70, 72, 75, 77–82, 87, 94, 100, 101, 105, 106

community, 3, 4, 18, 22, 32, 34, 39, 40, 73, 105

completeness, 105

complex object, viii, xiv, 3, 105

composite object, 105

compound object, 105

compress, 29, 106

conceptual representation, 20, 29, 35, 40, 41, 64, 68, 75, 78, 88–91, 109, 113, 116–118, 120, 122

consistency, 72, 84, 106

Content Management System (CMS), xiii, 105, 106

content-based image retrieval (CBIR), viii, xv, 105, 106

copyright, 38, 84, 106

course, viii, xiii, xv, xvi, xx, 13, 19, 37, 41, 104, 106, 107, 112

coverage, xv, xvi, 3, 10, 18, 48, 106, 108

crawl, 20, 36, 40, 106

cross language information retrieval (CLIR), 105, 106

curation, 36, 107, 113

curriculum, viii, 2, 18, 19, 107, 113

data confidentiality, 107

data integrity, 4, 106, 107

database, xiii, 2, 3, 20, 26, 27, 37, 38, 45, 71, 85, 107, 110

DELOS Reference Model, 11, 22, 32, 34, 40, 41

Denial of Service (DoS), 107

descriptor, 38, 64, 107, 120

designer, 36, 101, 103, 119

digital library, viii, ix, xiii–xvii, xx, 1–6, 9–26, 28–43, 57, 58, 63, 66, 72, 77, 78, 84, 103, 105–109, 111–113, 115–122

digital library administrator, 36, 107

digital object, viii, xiv, 4, 7–9, 20, 21, 23, 39, 40, 47, 64–66, 68–72, 74, 75, 77–80, 82, 84, 87, 92, 94, 98–100, 107

digital rights management, 17, 33, 38, 84, 104, 107, 108, 111, 115

digitize, 6, 9, 16, 17, 36, 40, 107

dimension, 5, 6, 20, 29, 46–49, 51, 57, 63, 68, 78, 95, 100, 107

dimensionality reduction, 108, 112

dissemination, 68, 108, 109

DoS, 107

DRM, 17, 33, 38, 84, 104, 107, 108, 111, 115

DSpace, xiii, 11, 21–23

Dublin Core, 21, 67, 108

e-science, viii, xv, 3, 17

economics, 4, 13, 16–18, 32, 33, 38, 39

education, viii, xiii, xv, xx, 4, 13, 16–18, 20, 21, 38, 104, 106–108, 112, 113, 119, 120, 149, 150

educational institution, xix, xx, 4, 16, 17, 108, 112, 149

entity, 4, 6, 9, 32, 34, 103–105, 107–110, 113–118, 120, 121

Envision, 13

EPrints, 21, 23

evaluation, viii, xiv, 5, 20, 36, 40, 43, 44, 54, 55, 57, 108

event, 8, 31, 32, 57, 63–65, 73, 75, 76, 82, 90–95, 99, 100, 114, 115

experiment, viii, xv, 17, 54–57, 63, 108, 114, 118, 119

explore, viii, 30, 31, 40, 43–46, 48–51, 54–57, 66, 78, 82, 87, 90–94, 97, 98, 100, 104, 108, 117

facet, 4, 35, 39, 43, 57, 108, 117

feature, 28, 35, 41, 45, 57, 64, 68, 75, 105, 109, 121, 122

feature extraction, 109

federation, 11, 22, 36, 40, 103, 111, 151

feedback, 46, 108, 109, 115

filter, 1, 36, 40, 45, 46, 69, 109

Functional Requirements for Bibliographic Records (FRBR), 9

functionality, 4, 6, 22, 109, 115, 118

gazetteer, 37, 64, 109

generation, xvii, 23, 33, 39, 45, 50, 100, 101, 103, 109, 111, 112, 119

geo-coding, 109

geo-parsing, 109

geographic, 10, 50, 109, 110, 112, 117

grammar, 24, 59, 60, 65, 109, 110, 113, 116

graph, 59, 60, 64–66, 69–72, 74, 76–78, 81, 83, 87–89, 110

Greenstone, xiii, 22

handle, 37, 69, 71, 74, 75, 78, 83, 116, 121
harvest, 36, 40, 78, 85, 102, 110
hierarchy, 39, 45–50, 57, 67, 71, 97, 110, 121
hybrid, 9, 21
hyperbase, 37, 106, 110, 112, 113, 119
hyperlink, 37, 45, 70, 103, 110, 112
hypermedia, viii, xiv, 2, 3, 10, 18, 31, 37, 71, 110, 150
hypertext, viii, xiv, xv, 2, 3, 10, 18, 25, 37, 38, 64, 70, 71, 75–77, 81, 87, 88, 92, 93, 110, 150

IDF, 111, 122
image, viii, xiv, xv, 3, 4, 7–10, 20, 24, 28, 29, 32, 37, 47, 66, 68–71, 88–90, 105, 106, 111
index, 1, 8, 63, 64, 66, 68, 69, 72, 75, 77, 111
indexing, 3, 14, 20, 23, 29, 36, 40, 64, 66, 68–70, 72, 75, 77, 92, 111
information life cycle, xiv, 1, 2, 4, 9, 41
institutional repository, xiii, 15, 21, 22
integration, viii, xiv, xvi, 3, 4, 13, 15, 17, 23, 43, 45, 46, 48–50, 57, 58, 84, 100–102
intellectual property rights (IPR), 17, 38, 111
interoperate, 23, 38, 111
inverse document frequency (IDF), 111, 122
IPR, 17, 38, 111

Kessler, xix, 149
knowledge base, 37, 110, 111

Latent Dirichlet Allocation (LDA), 111, 112
latent semantic analysis (LSA), 112, 114
LDA, 111, 112
learner, 18, 32, 36, 104, 112
lecture, 28, 112, 113
lexicon, 112, 120
Licklider, xix, 10–12, 28, 149

link, 4, 8, 36, 39, 40, 45, 55, 70–72, 76, 79, 81, 84, 93, 94, 112
location, 22, 23, 29, 32, 33, 48, 65, 69, 89, 109, 110, 112, 115, 121
LSA, 112, 114
LSI, 112

mapping, 46, 67, 69, 78, 83, 85, 95, 99–102, 112
mark, 51, 78, 79, 87, 100, 112
Memex, 10
metadata, viii, xiii–xv, 2, 4, 7–10, 20, 21, 23, 37, 39–41, 64–70, 72–75, 78, 83, 84, 89, 101, 112
metadata extraction, 112
MIT OpenCourseWare, 112
modeling, 2, 20, 24, 36, 39, 65, 100, 109, 113, 116
module, 4, 18–20, 37, 41, 106, 113
multi-modal search, 113
multimedia, viii, xv, 2, 3, 16, 18, 21, 24, 29, 37, 38, 66, 68, 113, 149, 150
museum, 1, 4, 17, 26, 38, 50

National Science Digital Library (NSDL), 6, 7, 16, 17, 113
navigate, 36, 43, 45, 47–50, 52, 54–56, 88–90, 93–99, 113, 114
non-repudiation, 113
NSDL, 6, 7, 16, 17, 113
NSF, xx, 11, 12, 113

OAI, 10, 11, 17, 21, 41, 113
OAI-ORE, 113
OAI-PMH, 113
ontology, xiv, 37, 39, 108, 113
Open Archives Initiative (OAI), 10, 11, 17, 21, 41, 113
Open Archives Initiative Object Reuse and Exchange (OAI-ORE), 113

Open Archives Initiative Protocol for
    Metadata Harvesting (OAI-PMH),
    113
OpenCourseWare, 112

parse, 113
PDF, 112, 114
PDF/A, 114
personalization, viii, xiii, xv, 1, 6, 17, 20, 36,
    38–40, 71, 109, 114
PLSA, 111, 112, 114
PLSI, 111, 112, 114
policy, 21, 38, 114
precision, 59, 114
presentation specification, 114
preservation, xvi, 5, 17, 20, 21, 33, 84
preserve, xiii, 1, 4, 16, 21, 114
Principal Component Analysis (PCA), 108
privacy, 17, 33, 38, 114
probability, 8, 29, 61, 63, 72, 114
profile, 37, 39, 114, 115
provenance, 115

quality, xiv, xv, 4, 5, 13, 14, 17, 39, 40, 42, 100,
    101, 115
query, 2, 27, 36, 39, 40, 45, 46, 48–50, 52, 63,
    69, 75, 80, 88–100, 105, 106, 110,
    113, 115, 117, 120–123
query expansion, 36, 39, 40, 45, 46, 49, 98, 115

ranking, 22, 46, 115
rating, 36, 40, 115
RDF, 66, 67, 115, 116, 118
recall, 115
recommend, 20, 36, 40, 85, 115
record, 37, 104, 105, 107, 111–113, 115, 119
reducing, 17, 20, 34, 54, 56, 106, 108, 112, 116,
    119
regular expression, 116, 120, 123

relationship, xiv, 4, 7–9, 21, 25, 28, 32, 37, 39,
    46, 50, 66, 72, 73, 89, 91, 92, 110, 116
relevance, 20, 63, 109, 115, 116, 151
repository, xiii, 2, 7, 8, 11, 15, 21, 22, 37, 40, 64,
    66, 68, 72, 75, 78, 82, 84, 85, 116
representation, xiv, xvi, 4, 9, 18, 20, 24, 29, 35,
    40, 41, 64, 66, 68, 69, 75, 78, 88–91,
    100, 105, 106, 108, 109, 111,
    113–120, 122
Resource Description Framework (RDF), 66,
    67, 115, 116, 118
result, xv, 10, 17, 39, 45, 46, 49, 52, 56, 57,
    79–81, 84, 86, 91–100, 106, 109–111,
    113–118, 122
retrieval, viii, xiii–xv, xix, 1–4, 9, 18, 20–22, 25,
    28, 33, 37, 38, 43, 45, 46, 51, 63, 69,
    84, 88, 89, 91, 93, 94, 100, 105, 116,
    150, 151
robustness, 117

Salton, xix, 28, 149
scenario, viii, xiii, xv, xvi, 1, 7, 8, 29, 31, 40, 47,
    51, 64, 65, 69, 72, 73, 75–77, 82, 91,
    94, 100–103, 117
schema, 26, 37, 47, 83, 100–102, 117, 119
score, 83, 117, 122
search, xiv, xv, 1, 3, 9, 10, 20, 22, 23, 36, 40,
    43–51, 54–58, 64, 66, 72, 75, 77, 78,
    85, 88, 90–94, 97–102, 106, 117, 151
search engine, 117
security, viii, xiv, xv, 3, 17, 33, 38, 117
security policies, 117
semantic network, 37, 72, 118, 120
Semantic Web, xiv, 66, 116, 118
sequence, xv, 24, 31, 32, 47, 52, 59–61, 69,
    72–74, 77, 82, 87, 90, 91, 93, 94, 96,
    113, 117–120
service, xiii, xiv, xvi, 1, 3, 5–9, 13, 15, 17, 20–22,
    29, 31, 32, 35, 38–41, 43, 44, 46–49,

54, 55, 57, 64–66, 68–73, 75–77, 85, 88, 90–94, 97–102, 118, 122

similarity, 34, 64, 79, 80, 105, 112, 117, 118, 120, 122

simulation, viii, xv, 17, 103, 113, 118, 119

singular value decomposition (SVD), 111, 118, 119

smoothing, 118

social network, viii, xiii, xv, xvi, 18, 39, 118

society, viii, xiii, xv, xvi, 1, 7, 8, 32–34, 39, 40, 64, 65, 72, 73, 77, 78, 83–86, 101, 103, 118

space, viii, xiii, xv, 1, 4, 7, 8, 10, 27, 29, 30, 39, 40, 44, 47, 49, 61, 63, 64, 68, 72, 77, 78, 89, 94, 97, 98, 101, 103, 105, 107, 109, 118

span, 68, 112, 119

SQL, 107

stem, 69, 111, 113, 119, 120, 122

stream, viii, xiii, xv, 1, 7, 8, 24–26, 28, 30, 39, 40, 64, 65, 68–75, 77, 78, 87–89, 101, 103, 119

structure, viii, xiii–xv, 1, 6–8, 26, 28, 31, 39, 40, 45–48, 57, 64, 66, 68–75, 77, 78, 87–89, 93, 95, 101, 103, 119

subdocument, xiv, 104, 119, 122

superimposed document, xiv, 119

SVD, 111, 118, 119

tag cloud, 119

tagging, 36, 40, 105, 106, 119, 122, 123

taxonomy, 1, 34–38, 40, 41, 120

teacher, xix, 32, 36, 39, 101, 120

term, 1, 3, 6, 21, 26, 32, 35–41, 59, 63, 64, 67–69, 107–109, 111, 112, 115, 117, 120, 122

term extraction, 120

text, xiv, 1, 3, 4, 8, 10, 24, 27, 43, 45, 63, 66, 69, 71, 79, 88, 120, 150

TF, 120

thesaurus, 37, 39, 64, 120, 122

threshold, 79, 80, 120

token, 69, 120

topic, xvi, 10, 16–20, 107, 111, 112, 114, 120–122

topic spotting, 121

transaction, 2, 107, 115, 121

tree, 45, 50, 52, 57, 60, 67, 71, 120, 121

trust, xv, 17, 38, 121

Twitter, xvi, 121

Uniform Resource Identifier (URI), 121

Uniform Resource Locator (URL), 121

Uniform Resource Name (URN), 121

union, 59, 61, 67, 73, 78, 82–84, 86, 102

URI, 37, 121

URL, 37, 121

URN, 37, 121

usability, xx, 20, 38, 54, 108, 121

user interface, 15, 37, 39, 79, 103, 113, 121

Vannevar Bush, 10

vector, 8, 78, 100, 121

vector space, xv, 28, 29, 61, 63, 68, 72, 78, 87, 109, 111, 122

vector space model, 63, 80, 114, 122

video, 4, 7, 8, 10, 21, 24, 37, 66, 68, 100, 122

view-in-context, 122

visualize, xiv, xv, 23, 29, 31, 36, 40, 43, 44, 46, 47, 49, 50, 54, 57, 78, 85, 90–92, 100, 122, 151

W3C, 3, 116, 122

Web (WWW), viii, xv, 3, 5, 17, 37, 43, 45, 46, 49, 50, 70, 71, 81, 87, 92, 106, 109, 110, 112, 113, 116, 117, 121, 122

weight, 63, 64, 109, 111, 115, 117, 122

wild card, 123

WordNet, 24, 25, 27, 29, 32, 123

workflow, 14, 15, 17, 29, 32, 65

World Wide Web Consortium (W3C), 3, 116, 122

WWW, viii, xv, 1, 3, 5, 10, 17, 22, 37, 43, 45, 46, 49, 50, 70, 71, 81, 87, 92, 106, 109, 110, 112, 113, 116, 117, 121, 122

XML, xiii, 20, 25, 45, 103, 117, 122, 123